The INSTANT
CHEF

A COMPLETE GUIDE TO SURVIVING
THE KITCHEN JUNGLE!

by

Gail Hurst and Judy L. Smith

1st Printing January, 1990
New Revised Edition 1995

Library of Congress Catalog Card Number 95-92214
ISBN 0-9623169-1-1

Trade names have been used only
when necessary for the success of the recipe.

Printed in the USA by

WIMMER
The Wimmer Companies, Inc.
Memphis • Dallas

THE INSTANT CHEF
A Complete Guide to Surviving the Kitchen Jungle

Take a danger-free safari through the Kitchen Jungle!

Simply use THE CHEF'S recommended:

Indestructable Ingredients,

Easy Directions,

Streamlined Methods,

Ten Commandments, Hints, and Planning Guides,

and you will soon discover that you have become

a chef yourself while enjoying scrumptious meals

and party fun.

TO
FRANCIS GWALTNEY CHENAULT
who believed in us, encouraged us
and whose gallant struggle
against unbeatable adds
inspired us,

we dedicate this little book.

ACKNOWLEDGMENTS

Our thanks to our husbands, children, and friends (and their long-suffering taste buds) whom we neglected, over-fed, under-fed, and whose patience we pushed to the breaking point.

A special word of appreciation to Darlene Steadman, our typist; Dianna Holsomback, our friend and mutual housekeeper; and to Lecia Maurer, our enthusiastic and creative artist. Without their loyalty and willingness to go the extra mile with us, this book would never have become a reality; to Gobble-Fite Lumber Co., Inc., for the use of their office equipment; and last of all, to Keefer, the Hurst family German Shepherd, who waggingly disposed of all the failures.

COVER CONCEPT:
Paler and Associates
Cover Art: Robert Haydon

ORIGINAL ART:
Lecia Maurer

TABLE OF CONTENTS

BARE ESSENTIALS

If your new kitchen is as bare as a Playboy centerfold, there's an easy way to cover that situation. Simply start with these basics and add items as your cooking and bank balance improve. The first list looks absurd, but the equipment should last for years unless you cook with all the grace and ease of Hagar the Horrible.

POTS AND PANS AND THINGS

Pots and Pans	Size or Type	Amount
Baking Dish or Pan	9" x 13" x 2"	1
Broiler (Roasting) Pan with rack		1
Cake Pans (round or square)	8" or 9"	2
Casseroles, with lids	1, 1½, 2 quart	3
Coffee Pot	stove top or electric	1
Cookie sheet (or baking pan)		1
Mixing bowls	small, medium, large	3
Saucepans (with lids)	1, 2, 3 quart (1 with double-boiler)	3
Skillet (with lid)	stove-top or electric	1 or 2

Gadgets	Type	Amount
Bottle opener	with corkscrew and punch	1
Can opener	electric or manual	1
Colander	metal or plastic	1
Cutting Board (chopping block)	wooden or acrylic	1 or more
Fork	long handled	1
Grater	stainless steel	1
Hot pads (pot holders)	thick, padded	2
Knives	paring, slicing, carving	1 each
Measuring cups (for liquids)	1 or 4-cup size	1
Measuring cups (for solids)	1/4, 1/3, 1/2 and 1 cup	1 set
Measuring spoons	plastic or metal	1 set
Mixer	electric or rotary	1
Spatula		1 or more
Spoon	long handled	1
Vegetable peeler	metal	1
Wire Whisk	medium or large	1 or more

Table Toppers	
Basket	For breads, crackers, fruits, or chips
Dishes	Plates, cups, saucers, soup/salad/cereal bowls, serving bowls, platter, butter dish, salt and pepper shakers, sugar bowl, cream pitcher
Flatware	Knives, forks, spoons, 2 large serving spoons (one slotted), sugar spoon, large meat fork, butter knife
Glasses	Three sizes for juice, water and tea
Linens	Placemats or tablecloths and either cloth or paper napkins
Pitchers	One or two
Trivet	One or two for hot dishes
Dirty Dish Duty	
Dish Cloths	2 (for washing)
Dish Detergent	1 for dish washer (if you have one) 1 for hand washing (even if you have a dishwasher!)
Dish Drainer	1
Dish Towels	2 (for drying)
Pot Scrubbies	cloth or nylon mesh
Health Department Hang-Ups	**Wrappers and Wipers**
Broom and dust pan Cleaners (all purpose and powdered) Kitchen garbage can and liner Mop Outside garbage can with lid Soap (hand) - liquid in a pump bottle is quickest	Foil Paper towels and holder Paper napkins Plastic wrap Waxed paper

Eventual Add Ons

Pots and Pans	Size or Type	Amount
Double Boiler		1
Dutch oven	Heavy metal with lid	1
Griddle		1
Loaf pan	9" x 5" x 3"	1
Muffin Tin	6 or 12 muffin size	1
Tea Kettle	A 'whistler' won't let you forget it!	1
Turkey Roaster	dark enamel (with lid)	1
Gadgets	**Size or Type**	**Amount**
Biscuit Cutter	2"	1
Cannister set	extra-large (flour) large (sugar) medium (coffee) small (tea bags)	1 (4-piece set)
Fire Extinguisher	Halon	1
Jar Opener	rubber disk or metal	1
Ladle	metal or plastic	1
Masking tape and water-proof pen	for labeling freezer foods	1 each
Meat Thermometer		1
Pastry Brush	small	1
Pie Server		1
Potato Masher		1
Rolling Pin	wooden or marble	1
Scissors	kitchen	1
Strainer	medium	1
Timer	A "must" if your oven lacks one!	1
Electric Creature Comforts	**Size or Type**	**Amount**
Blender	at least 3 speeds	1
Deep-fat fryer	with basket	1
Can opener		1
Knife		1
Toaster	2 or 4 slots	1
Waffle Iron	2 or 4 sections	1

CARTONS, CANS AND JARS

Keep your cabinet **fully stocked!** It may seem extravagant to have a bulging pantry, but the convenience of always having the needed ingredients on hand for that last minute or impromptu meal saves time, money, and much hassle in the long run. The following is a basic list of the things needed for many of The Chef's recipes. You'll soon have your favorites, and keeping these ingredients handy is a must!

STAPLES	CANNED GOODS	
Baking powder	**Meats:**	**Fruits:**
Baking soda (for fires)	Chicken	Cocktail or mixed
Biscuit Mix	Clams	Maraschino cherries
Boullion cubes	Ham or Luncheon	Peaches
(beef, chicken)	Oysters	Pears
Cornmeal mix	Tuna	Pineapple
Flour (self-rising)	Salmon	
Jelly	Shrimp	**Juices:** (your favorite)
Pasta (spaghetti, macaroni)		Apple, Grape,
Peanut butter	**Soups:**	Grapefruit, Orange,
Rice (long grain or	Beef broth or boullion	Vegetable
converted)	Chicken broth	
Sugar (white, granulated)	Cheese	**Veggies:**
Syrup or Honey	Cream of chicken, celery,	Asparagus
Vegetable oil	mushroom, shrimp	Beans (green and/or lima)
Vegetable spray	French onion	Corn
Vegetable shortening (solid)		Mushrooms
Yeast	**CONDIMENTS**	Peas (green and/or blackeye)
SPICES	Dressing for salads	Potatoes (whole and sliced)
	Lemon juice (bottled)	Spinach
Instant:	Mayonnaise	Squash
Bell pepper	Mustard	
Celery flakes	Sherry (cooking)	
Onions (chopped, minced)	Soy sauce	**PERISHABLES**
Parsley	Tabasco	Bread
	Worcestershire	Butter
Ground:		Cheese (shredded
Chili powder		Cheddar, mozzarella,
Cinnamon		Parmesan)
Curry powder		Eggs
Garlic powder		Milk
Mustard (ground dry)		Sour cream
Nutmeg		
Oregano		
Paprika		
Pepper (black and cayenne)		
Poultry seasoning		
Salt		
Flavorings:		
Vanilla		

THE MECHANICS

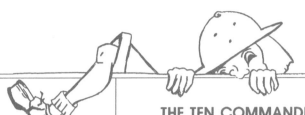

SOME LIKE IT HOT!
THE INSTANT CHEF has tried to hit a happy medium with the amount of seasonings used, but these can be adjusted to suit your own tastes.

CAUTION:
High Heat:
For stove-top cooking, high heat is used only briefly. . . rarely for long periods of time.

THE TEN COMMANDMENTS
Warning!! Read and Heed!!

Until now, the ground rules of cooking have been the best kept secret since the A-Bomb. (You were supposed to have learned these through osmosis from your ninety-three year old grandmother.)

1. **BAKING:** Before baking, pre-heat the oven at least five to ten minutes or until the "ready" light goes off. When a recipe specifies a certain oven temperature, the oven must be set on BAKE (not broil) with the rack in the CENTER position of the oven. All baking is done UNCOVERED unless other directions are given.

2. **BROILING:** All broiling is done with the oven set on BROIL, and the oven rack five to seven inches from the broiling element (that's the coil in the top of an electric oven or the jets in a gas oven.) In an electric oven, the door must be left open five to six inches to keep the thermostat from cutting off automatically when it reaches 500°.

3. **CORRECT MEASUREMENTS:** All measurements are level unless the recipe says "heaping" or "rounded."

11

LID LIFTING
You can painfully alter your facial features by incorrectly taking the lid off a hot pot. NEVER lift the lid straight up! Always tilt the back of the lid up first at an angle away from your face, holding it between you and the scalding steam. This allows the condensation to drip back in the pot rather than on the stove.

The times and temps in all recipes may vary with different equipment. Gas stoves cook faster than electric; light weight cookware will burn foods faster than heavy; glassware designed for stove-top cooking also causes variations depending on the brand. Some are faster, retain heat longer and can cause over-cooking.

Mayo: When using low-cal mayonnaise in making salad dressings or casseroles, it may be necessary to reduce or increase the amount or other liquids to maintain the correct texture.

4. **BUTTER VS. MARGARINE:** Either may be used unless the recipe says "no substitutions," but **Never** use "whipped" or "diet" types in cooking because the added water or air can drastically change the finished product.

5. **CANNED SOUPS:** Do not dilute soups and consommés unless the recipe states differently.

6. **GREASING:** When a recipe says "grease", use either vegetable spray, solid shortening, or vegetable oil unless the recipe is specific.

7. **DRAINING:** All liquids are drained in a colander. All grease or oil is drained on absorbent paper. . .either paper grocery bags or paper towels.

8. **PAN SIZES: Always** use the pan or casserole size called for in the recipe to avoid possible disaster. If you are not positive how many cups a container holds, simply measure the number of cups of water needed to fill it.

9. **GLASS:** Glass casseroles on the top of the stove will explode unless they are specifically designed for stove-top use. When baking cakes or breads in glass pans (except freezer-to-oven types), the oven temperature must be reduced by 25°.

10. **WHEN A RECIPE CALLS FOR:**
    EGGS - use large, not small or medium
    FLOUR - use plain white, not self-rising
    MAYONNAISE - use "real", not salad dressing
    MUSTARD - use plain bottled, not spiced, dry, or ground
    SPICES - use ground, not whole unless indicated
    SUGAR - use white, not brown or powdered

THE MAGIC WORDS
The Most Common Stumbling Blocks in Cookbooks!

Au jus - thin, clear pan gravy.
Baste - to spoon or pour liquid over food to keep it moist while cooking.
Boiling Point - large groups of air bubbles break the surface (212°F).
Bread - to coat by dipping in flour, then in beaten egg or other liquid, and finally in cornmeal, bread, or cracker crumbs.
Coat (dredge) - to cover thinly.
Condensed milk - sweetened evaporated milk.
Cream - to make smooth by blending with the back of a spoon or in a mixer; to cook with milk or in a sauce made from butter, flour, and milk.
Croquette - a small ball of finely chopped meat, vegetables, or rice.
Evaporated milk - unsweetened whole milk that has 60% of the water removed.
Julienne - to cut into thin strips about the size of fat match sticks.
Marinate - to improve food flavor and/or tenderness by soaking in seasoned liquid.
Mince - to chop or cut very finely.
Parboil - to partially or completely cook food in a boiling liquid.
Roux (rhymes with boo) - to brown an equal mixture of flour and oil until extremely dark, but not burned; used as thickening or seasoning for gravies or Creole foods.
Saute (pan fry) - to cook or brown in a small amount of butter or oil.
Sear - to quickly brown the outside of food on HIGH without burning.
Score - to cut shallow gashes in the outer layer of food.
Steep - to let stand in hot liquid below the boiing point until flavor and color is extracted.
Stock - the liquid left from cooking meats, vegetables, poultry, or seafoods.

ARCHAIC COOKING TERMS
found in some old or regional cookbooks:
Cube - ¼ lb stick of butter
Oleo - margarine
Scant - (cup, tablespoon, etc.) - not quite full
Sweet milk - whole milk

HOW TO MEASURE

If you have not read **The Ten Commandments,** shame on you! Go back and check number three.

1. All liquid measurements are read at eye level with a measuring cup on a flat surface. (Bend over if your're taller than a three-foot countertop.)

2. All dry and solid measurements are leveled off with the back of a knife unless indicated as "rounded" or "heaping."

3. **Stir** flour or powdered sugar and gently spoon into a measuring cup. **No sifting is needed.**

4. **Firmly** pack brown sugar, butter, or shortening.

5. **Lightly** pack bread crumbs, dried fruit, or nuts.

6. Before measuring honey or syrup, grease the measuring cup for easy removal.

7. A **ruler** for measuring pan sizes and a **spaghetti gauge** are on the inside back cover.

WHAT TO USE	
TO MEASURE:	**USE:**
Less than ¼ cup dry, solid or liquid	Measuring Spoons
More than ¼ cup dry or solid	Graduated Measuring Cups
More than ¼ cup liqud	Standard Measuring Cup

HOW TO HALVE UNEVEN MEASUREMENTS	
PROBLEM MEASUREMENTS:	**SOLUTION:**
¾ cup	¼ cup + 2 Tablespoons
⅓ cup	2 Tablespoons + 2 teaspoons
1 Tablespoon	1½ teaspoons
1½ Tablespoons	2¼ teaspoons
1 egg	Combine white and yolk and discard half or use whole egg and decrease the liquid in the recipe by 1 Tablespoon

MEASUREMENT EQUIVALENTS
Equations will follow you everywhere ... even into the kitchen.

STANDARD	
AMOUNT	**EQUIVALENT**
Dash	$\frac{1}{16}$ teaspoon (6 liquid drops)
Pinch	$\frac{1}{8}$ teaspoon
3 teaspoons	1 Tablespoon
1 Tablespoon	$\frac{1}{16}$ cup
2 Tablespoons	$\frac{1}{8}$ cup (1 liquid ounce)
4 Tablespoons	$\frac{1}{4}$ cup (2 liquid ounces)
5$\frac{1}{3}$ Tablespoons	$\frac{1}{3}$ cup
8 Tablespoons	$\frac{1}{2}$ cup (4 liquid ounces)
12 Tablespoons	$\frac{3}{4}$ cup (6 liquid ounces)
16 Tablespoons	1 cup (8 liquid ounces)
1 cup	$\frac{1}{2}$ pint (8 liquid ounces)
2 cups	1 pint (16 liquid ounces or 1 pound)
4 cups	1 quart (32 liquid ounces or 2 pounds)
2 quarts	$\frac{1}{2}$ gallon (64 liquid ounces or 4 pounds or 8 cups)
4 quarts	1 gallon (128 liquid ounces or 8 pounds or 16 cups)

METRIC			
LIQUID		DRY	
AMOUNT	**EQUIVALENT**	**AMOUNT**	**EQUIVALENT**
1 liter	33.8 ounces	1 Gram	.035 ounce
3.8 liters	1 gallon	28$\frac{1}{3}$ Grams	1 ounce
		453 Grams	1 pound

EQUIVALENTS AND SUBSTITUTIONS

ITEM	AMOUNT	EQUIVALENT	SUBSTITUTION
Allspice	1 teaspoon		½ teaspoon cinnamon ⅛ teaspoon cloves ¼ teaspoon nutmeg
Baking Powder	1 teaspoon		¼ teaspoon baking soda ½ teaspoon cream of tartar
Beans (dried)	½ cup uncooked	1½ cups cooked	
Bell Pepper	FRESH: (chopped) 2 Tablespoons ½ cup 1 cup 1 small 1 medium 1 large	 ¼ cup (fresh) ⅓ cup (fresh) ½ cup (fresh)	INSTANT FLAKES: 1 Tablespoon ¼ cup (4 Tablespoons) ½ cup (8 Tablespoons)
Broth (Beef or Chicken)	1 cup 10¼ oz. can (undiluted) 14½ oz. can (undiluted)		1 cup boiling water and 1 bouillon cube 1⅓ cup boiling water and 1⅓ bouillon cubes 1¾ cups boiling water and 1¾ bouillon cubes
Butter or Margarine	¼ stick ½ stick 1 stick 4 sticks	⅛ cup (2 Tablespoons) ¼ cup (4 Tablespoons) ½ cup (8 Tablespoons) 2 cups (1 pound)	
Buttermilk (For cooking only)	1 cup		A. 1 cup whole milk, 1 Tablespoon lemon juice or vinegar (let stand 5 minutes before using) B. ¼ cup buttermilk powder and 1 cup water C. 1 cup unflavored yogurt
Catsup	⅔ cup		½ cup tomato sauce, 2 Tablespoons sugar, 1 Tablespoon vinegar
Celery	FRESH: ½ cup 2 Tablespoons 1 fresh rib	 ½ cup chopped	INSTANT FLAKES: ¼ cup 1 Tablespoon
Cheese	4 oz. (¼ pound)	1 cup, shredded	
Chicken	5 oz. can	1 cooked chicken breast half, skinned & boned	

ITEM	AMOUNT	EQUIVALENT	SUBSTITUTION
Chicken (con't)	1 pound fresh chicken (with skin and bones)	1 cup cooked, diced meat	
Chocolate	1 oz. square		4 Tablespoons cocoa ½ Tablespoon butter
Crab	1 cup fresh 1 pound fresh 6 hard shell (cooked)	3 cups 1 cup	1 (6½ oz.) can
Crumbs	Bread: 1 slice 1 cup	½ to ¾ cup (soft) ¼ cup (toasted)	A. ¾ cup cracker crumbs B. 1⅓ cup uncooked oats
	Cracker:	1 cup	A. 15 ginger snaps B. 14 graham cracker squares C. 22 Ritz crackers D. 28 saltine crackers E. 22 vanilla wafers
Eggs	2 large	3 small	
Flour	1 pound	4 cups	
Flour (Self-Rising)	1 cup		1 cup plain flour 1½ teaspoons baking powder ¼ teaspoon salt
Foil	1 piece heavy duty		2 pieces regular weight
Garlic	1 fresh clove (minced)		⅛ teaspoon garlic powder
Herbs	1 Tablespoon fresh		1 teaspoon dried
Lemon or Lime	1 medium fresh		2 Tablespoons bottled juice
Lobster	1 pound (in shell) 1 cup meat	⅔ cup cooked, diced	6 oz. frozen
Marshmallows	1 large 16 large 10 mini 1 cup mini	¼ oz. 4 oz. 1 large 2 oz. (8 large)	
Mayonnaise	1 cup		A. ½ cup mayo and ½ cup yogurt B. 1 cup sour cream C. 1 cup cottage cheese (process in blender until smooth)

Equivalents and Substitutions

ITEM	AMOUNT	EQUIVALENT	SUBSTITUTION
Milk (for cooking only) Whole or Skim	1 cup		A. ½ cup evaporated milk ½ cup water B. ⅓ cup non-fat powdered milk ⅞ cup water (add 1 Tablespoon melted butter to make whole milk)
Sweetened, Condensed	1 cup		1 cup non-fat powdered milk ½ cup boiling water ⅔ cup sugar 3 Tablespoons melted butter (process in blender until thick and smooth)
Mushrooms	½ pound fresh		4 o 6 oz. canned
Mustard	1 Tablespoon prepared		1 teaspoon dry
Nuts (Shelled)	1 cup almonds peanuts pecans pistachio walnuts	4½ oz. 5⅓ oz. 4 oz. 4 oz. 5½ oz.	
Onion	1 small fresh 1 medium fresh 1 large fresh	FRESH, chopped: ¼ cup ½ cup ¾ cup 1 cup	INSTANT MINCED ONIONS: 1 teaspoon 2 teaspoons 1 Tablespoon 1 Tablespoon + 1 teaspoon
Onion Soup Mix	2 Tablespoons dry mix		1 Tablespoon instant minced onion 1 beef bouillon cube
Orange	1 medium fresh		6 to 8 Tablespoons juice
Oysters	12 medium	1 pint	
Pasta: Macaroni Noodles Spaghetti Lasagna Manicotti	UNCOOKED 2 oz. (½ cup) 1 lb. (4 cups) 2 oz. 1 lb. 2 oz. 1 lb. 1 oz. 1¾ oz.	COOKED SERVES 1 - 1¼ cup 1 8 - 9 cups 8 1 cup 1 8 cups 8 1 cup 1 8 cups 8 1 noodle 1 noodle	
Popcorn	¼ cup unpopped kernels	6 to 8 cups popped corn	

ITEM	AMOUNT	EQUIVALENT	SUBSTITUTION
Potatoes	1 lb. (3 to 4 medium)	3 cups sliced, 2½ cups diced, 2 to 2½ cups cooked (mashed)	
Poultry Seasoning	1⅓ teaspoons		¾ teaspoon sage ¼ teaspoon thyme ⅛ teaspoon cloves ¼ teaspoon pepper
Rice	UNCOOKED ⅓ cup converted ¼ cup reguar ½ cup instant ¼ cup brown ¼ to ⅓ cup wild	COOKED: 1 cup 1 cup 1 cup 1 cup 1 cup	
Scallops	1 pound	1 pint	
Shrimp	1 pound unshelled (raw) 1 cup fresh (cooked and shelled)	½ pound shelled (cooked)	1 (5 oz.) can
Sour Cream (For cooking only)	1 cup		A. ⅞ cup buttermilk or plain yogurt 3 Tablespoons butter B. 1 cup evaported milk 1 Tablespoon vinegar C. 8 oz. cottage cheese 1 Tablespoon lemon juice ¼ cup water or milk ⅛ teaspoon salt (process in blender on HIGH 30 seconds)
Sugar Granulated Powdered Low Calorie	 1 cup 1¾ cups 1 (.035 oz.) package 6 packages	 2 teaspoons ¼ cup	(For sweetening only - not baking) A. 1 cup honey B. 2 cups corn syrup C. 1½ cups powdered sugar 1 cup granulated (process on HIGH in a blender until almost double in bulk)
Thickening Agent (For 1 cup of liquid to medium thickness)	2 Tablespoons flour		1 Tablespoon cornstarch

Equivalents and Substitutions

ITEM	AMOUNT	EQUIVALENT	SUBSTITUTION
Tomatoes	1 cup canned		A. 1⅓ cups chopped fresh (simmer 10 minutes)
	1 (8 oz.) can		A. 8 oz. stewed (blend on HIGH until smooth) B. 1½ to 2 medium fresh (blend on HIGH until smooth) C. ½ cup pureé and ½ cup water. D. 3 oz. tomato paste and 4½ oz. water
Whipping Cream (Unwhipped)	1 cup (½ pint)	2 cups whipped	
(Whipped and Sweetened for cooking only)	1 pint		A. 1 pint sour cream 1 teaspoon vanilla 1 Tablespoon powdered sugar (Mix well but do not whip) B. 1 pint frozen whipped topping
Whipped Topping	4 oz. carton 8 oz. 12 oz.	1¾ cups 3½ cups 5¼ cups	
White Sauce	1 cup		10¾ oz. can *cream-style* soup undiluted (mushroom, chicken, celery, onion)
Wine (Cooking)	1 cup		A. 1 cup wine ¼ teaspoon salt B. 1 cup apple juice or cider

INTERCHANGEABLE PAN SIZES

IF YOU DON'T HAVE A:	YOU MAY USE:	IT WILL HOLD:
1 Quart Casserole	10" pie plate 8" cake pan 7⅜" x 3⅝" x 2¼" loaf pan	4 cups
1½ Quart Casserole	8" or 9" x 11½" layer cake pan 9" x 5" x 3" loaf pan	6 cups
2 Quart Casserole	8" x 8" x 2" square pan 11" x 7" x 1½" baking pan	8 cups
2½ Quart Casserole	9" x 13" x 2" baking pan 9" x 9" x 2" square pan	10 cups
3 Quart Casserole	14" x 10½" x 2½" roasting pan Bundt cake pan	12 cups

PIE PLATE VS. CAKE PAN:

They are not interchangeable. The sides of a pie plate slant while those of a cake pan are straight. Do not try to bake a cake in a pie plate...it will not rise!

Measure pie plates from the outside edges of the rim.

CASSEROLE VS. BAKING DISH:

A casserole is round or oval and deep. A baking dish is flat and shallow.

TEMPERATURES

DEEP FAT TEMPERATURES	
(To Cook a 1" Bread Cube Golden Brown)	
Temperature	**Time**
345º - 355º	65 seconds
355º - 365º	60 seconds
365º - 375º	50 seconds
375º - 385º	40 seconds
385º - 395º	20 seconds

OVEN TEMPERATURES	
Very slow	250º F
Slow	300º F
Medium Slow	325º F
Medium	350º F
Medium Hot	375º F
Hot	400º F
Very Hot	450º - 500º F

HOW TO CONVERT TEMPERATURES
On the outside chance you move your villa to the Riviera:
FAHRENHEIT TO CELSIUS
Subtract 32, Multiply by 5, and Divide by 9.
CELSIUS TO FAHRENHEIT
Multiply by 9, Divide by 5, and Add 32

SANITATION ENGINEERING
How to Avoid Ptomaine, Botulism, Salmonella or Helly-Belly

Medical authorities estimate as high as 80% of all cases of "The 24 Hour Bug" are actually mild forms of food poisoning.

The **Staphylococcus** (Staff) is the most common cause of food poisoning, and will grow in most foods that are inadequately cooked or refrigerated. **Ptomaine** alters the taste, texture, and smell of food, and is the only one of these "bug-causing" organisms that can be detected before human consumption. Ptomaine poisoning is rare — even your four-legged friends won't eat rotten food! **Salmonella** bacteria is present in 1/3 of all raw poultry, but is easily killed by adequate cooking. If you like rare poultry, you are gambling with high stakes. **Botulism** is the tasteless killer that lurks in canned or preserved foods which have not been properly processed or that have damaged containers. Heating food **above the boiling point** for two minutes will put Botulism away for life!

The secret is in the storage, cooking, and cleanliness, and not keeping fresh foods until they turn green and grow hair. These few foolproof facts will foil the fungus:

1. The temperature of the refrigerator is inversely proportional to the number of times the door is opened per day and how much stuff is crammed into it. The ideal temperature is 34° to 40°. If you open it fifty times a day and keep it full, lower the thermostat to accomodate.

2. The more food surface that is exposed to air, the shorter the life span! This is why ground meat spoils faster than a whole roast.

3. Sponsor a Seek and Destroy Mission within the refrigerator every week. Your life may depend on it!

4. Throw away leaking or bulging cans or any unopened jars that do not "pop" when first opened.

5. The cutting blade of the can opener can be a villian also — KEEP IT CLEAN!

6. Anything that has been at an unsafe temperature (over 40° or below 140°) for an *accumulated* total of four hours may be lethal.

7. Thaw all meats in the refrigerator. . .NOT on the countertop!

LEFTOVERS:

1. Leftovers keep the same length of time or less than the uncooked version. The longer it has been stored before cooking, the less time it will keep after cooking.

2. Beware of **any** leftovers using mayonnaise. Tuna and potato salad are the big losers in the germ warfare department.

3. Never reheat anything more than three times. Reheat only the portions to be served.

4. Never return anything to the refrigerator after it has been on a picnic!

FREEZER STORAGE

1. Do not freeze raw eggs, cheese (it gets rubbery), or sandwiches with mayonnaise (See Lunchbox Lifesavers, LUNCH).

2. Everything should be **sealed airtight, labeled, and dated.** Once frost has formed on the package you will never recognize the contents.

3. **Nothing** should be left in the freezer over one year.

4. Freeze raw fish, shrimp, wild dove or quail covered in cold water. Clean, cardboard milk cartons are terrific.

5. The ideal freezer temperature should be 0° or below.

BREAKFAST

BREAKFAST-IN-THE-BLENDER

Makes: 1 (10 oz. serving)
Groundwork: 2 minutes
Blend: 30 seconds
Need: blender

COFFEE NOG
1 cup milk
3 to 4 ice cubes
½ teaspoon ground cinnamon
2 teaspoons instant coffee granules
2 Tablespoons honey
½ teaspoon vanilla

Makes: 1 (10 oz. serving)
Groundwork: 2 minutes
Blend: 1 minute
Need: blender

LOW-CAL NOG
6 oz. orange juice
½ medium banana
(or 5 fresh strawberries)
½ teaspoon sugar (or honey or sugar substitute)
3 to 4 ice cubes

1. Combine everything in the blender container and blend on HIGH until well mixed and foamy.

SHAKES

GREAT GRAIN A-GO-GO

Makes: 2 (8 oz.) servings
Groundwork: 1 minute
Blend: 1 minute
Need: blender

1 (8 oz.) carton flavored yogurt
1 (6½ oz.) can fruit (undrained) OR
½ cup fresh or frozen fruit
1 (1 oz.) pkg. instant oatmeal
4 to 5 ice cubes

GREAT GRAIN COMBOS:

YOGURT	FRUIT	OATMEAL
Peach	Peach	Cinnamon & Spice
Blueberry	Banana (fresh)	Plain
Plain	Apple (fresh)	Maple & Brown Sugar
Plain	Raisins	Apple & Cinnamon
Strawberry	Strawberries (fresh or frozen) OR 1 banana (fresh)	Plain

*Note: When using fresh fruit, it is sometimes necessary to add a pinch of sugar.

Some blenders resent ice cubes and won't crush many at a time. For this neurotic behavior, simply add one cube at a time.

THE CLOCK-WATCHER SHAKE

8 oz. milk
1 egg
1 teaspoon sugar
¼ teaspoon vanilla

CLOCKWATCHER OPTIONS:
Add any one of the following:

Makes: 1 (10 oz.) serving
Groundwork: 2 minutes
Blend: 1 minute
Need: blender

A. **1 Tablespoon chocolate syrup**
B. **1 banana OR 5 fresh strawberries**
C. **1 Tablespoon peanut butter**
D. **½ cup any canned fruit (drained)**
E. **1½ teaspoons instant coffee granules**

1. Combine everything in the blender container and blend on HIGH until well mixed and foamy.

BREAKFAST-IN-A-BAR

Makes: 54 bars
Groundwork: 2 minutes
Cook: 7 minutes - LOW
Need: large saucepan
9" square cake
pan

Pop a plastic
sandwich bag on your
hands for greasing
pans or handling
sticky stuff.

3 cups marshmallows
½ cup butter
½ cup peanut butter
4 cups any unsweetened cereal (Rice Krispies, Cheerios, Rice Chex, etc.)
½ cup cocoa
1 cup raisins
½ cup instant non-fat dry milk

1. Lightly grease the bottom and sides of 9-inch square cake pan.

2. Combine the marshmallows and butter in a large saucepan on LOW, and stir constantly until the marshmallows have melted.

3. Add the peanut butter, and stir until well blended.

4. Add the cocoa, dry milk, and raisins, and stir until well blended.

5. Add the cereal and stir gently until it is completely coated.

6. Gently press the warm mixture into the cake pan and cool completely.

7. Cut into 1 x 1½-inch bars.

8. Cover with foil and store at room temperature.

QUICK GLAZED DONUTS

Makes: 10
Groundwork: 3 minutes
Cook: 3 to 4 min. -
        MED HIGH
Need: deep fat fryer
        OR large
        saucepan
        1" screw-on
        soda-bottle cap
        small paper bag

**1 (5 count) pkg. flakey refrigerator
    biscuits**
Oil for frying
½ cup powdered sugar or a glaze

1. Preheat at least 4 inches of oil in a deep fat fryer or large saucepan on MEDIUM HIGH.

2. Separate the biscuits and divide each sideways to make 2 thin rounds from each one (making a total of 10 rounds).

3. Cut a 1 inch circle from the center of each biscuit using either a sharp knife tip or a screw-on soda-bottle cap as a cutter.

The oil is ready when a 1 inch bread cube will brown in 60 seconds.

4. Carefully drop a few donuts and holes into the hot oil. Don't crowd them!

5. Cook until brown on one side, turn only once, and brown the other side.

6. Drain, and drop them into the bag of powdered sugar, or glaze with one of the following:

Glaze

Mix together in a small bowl:

A. ½ cup powdered sugar
   2 to 3 teaspoons milk, maple syrup, or orange juice

Make your own powdered sugar by putting granulated sugar in the blender on HIGH until it almost doubles in amount (½ cup granulated sugar makes ⅞ cup powdered).

B. ½ cup powdered sugar
   1 teaspoon cocoa
   2 to 3 teaspoons milk

Option:

A. Instant FRENCH DONUTS

   1. Cut each biscuit into 4 pieces, fry according to the directions for glazed donuts, and drop into the bag of powdered sugar.

TOPSY TURVIES

Makes: 5 biscuits
Groundwork: 3 minutes
Bake: 12 minutes
Oven Temp: 400°
Need: muffin tin

1 (5 count) pkg. refrigerator biscuits
1 choice of glaze (listed below)

1. Preheat oven to 400°.

2. Heavily grease 5 muffin cups.

3. Place the glaze ingredients in the order listed in the bottom of **each** of the 5 muffin cups.

4. Top the glaze with the biscuits.

5. Bake 12 minutes until the biscuits are golden brown.

6. Invert the pan over a platter for 2 to 4 minutes before removing the biscuits.

GLAZES: (place the amount listed in **each** *muffin cup in the order given).*

A. Pineapple-Cherry
    1 teaspoon butter
    1 teaspoon brown sugar
    1 maraschino cherry
    2 teaspoons crushed pineapple
     (drained)

B. Nut and Honey:
    1 teaspoon butter
    $1\frac{1}{2}$ teaspoons chopped pecans
    1 teaspoon honey or maple
     syrup
    pinch of allspice or cinnamon

C. Fruit and Oats:
    1 teaspoon butter
    $1\frac{1}{2}$ teaspoons oatmeal
    $1\frac{1}{2}$ teaspoons jelly (any flavor)

PANCAKES AND WAFFLES

Pancakes are just one of many creations of the Middle Ages that has passed the test of time. Waffles, rumor has it, also date back to the infamous knight in shining armor who accidently sat upon his "hearth cake" leaving behind the imprint of his ornate suit. Being a bit miffed with his wife, he gave it to her out of spite. But she had the last laugh on him. Her butter and honey stayed on the top and not in the plate and the knight had a new nightly duty — sitting on supper!

GRANDMA'S PANCAKES

Makes: 6 (4") pancakes
Groundwork: 5 minutes
Cook: 5 minutes -
  MEDIUM
Need: griddle or large
heavy skillet
medium mixing bowl

1 cup self-rising flour
1 egg
1 Tablespoon vegetable oil
1 Tablespoon sugar
¾ cup milk or club soda
vegetable spray or oil for greasing the griddle

1. Lightly grease a heavy skillet or griddle and preheat it on MEDIUM. (The pan is ready when a drop of water beads up and dances on the surface.)

2. While the pan is heating, combine all the ingredients in a medium mixing bowl with a wire whisk until the batter is smooth.

3. Pour ¼ cup of batter 2 inches apart on the griddle and cook (without turning) until the pancakes are full of tiny bubbles and the edges begin to dry.

4. Gently turn the cakes over with a spatula and brown the other side. (Turn only once, or they'll be tough as nails!)

Serve hot with one of the TERRIFIC TOPPERS (Waffles, page 34).

Options:

A. Replace the flour with 1 (7 oz.) pkg. muffin mix (plain, blueberry, strawberry or banana) and omit the oil and sugar.

Bake: 12 to 15 minutes
Oven Temp: 425°
Need: 9" cake or pie
pan

Add a small amount
of sugar to the batter
for a rich, even
browning.

Makes: 4 (7") waffles
Groundwork: 4 minutes
Cook: 5 minutes
Need: waffle iron
medium mixing bowl

Waffle irons are
famous for being
cranky and making
waffles stick. To keep
this from happening,
never wash the grids
with detergent. If
particles stick, clean
them off with a brush
and wipe the grids
clean with a paper
towel.

Serve hot with one of
the TERRIFIC TOPPERS
(Waffles, page 34).

B. **Oven Pancakes:**
1. Follow the directions for Grandma's Pancakes, EXCEPT:
2. Preheat the oven to 425°.
3. Grease a 9 inch cake or pie pan, pour the batter evenly in the bottom and bake 12 to 15 minutes until it is golden brown.
4. Slice into triangle-shaped pancakes.

C. Add one of the INTERESTING BATTER ADD-ONS (Waffles, page 32).

GRANDMA'S WAFFLES

1 cup self-rising flour
⅔ cup milk or club soda
1 egg
2 Tablespoons vegetable oil
vegetable spray or oil (not butter) for greasing iron

1. Lightly grease the waffle iron and preheat until a drop of water sizzles on it or until the "ready" light comes on if your waffle iron has one.

2. While the waffle iron is heating, mix all the ingredients in a medium mixing bowl with a wire whisk until the batter is smooth.

3. When the waffle iron is hot, pour on just enough batter to evenly cover the bottom grid.

4. Quickly close the top, and bake until the steaming stops and the waffle is brown (If you are cooking more than one waffle, allow a few minutes between "cookings" for the waffle iron to reheat to the proper temperature.

Options: Add one of the BATTER ADD-ONS, page 32.

INTERESTING BATTER ADD-ONS

Add ¼ cup of your choice to the batter before cooking (finely diced or grated): fresh, frozen or canned fruit, Parmesan or cheddar cheese, cooked bacon, ham or deviled ham; chopped pecans or walnuts; chopped dates; raisins; ripe mashed bananas; finely diced apple plus 1 teaspoon of sugar and ¼ teaspoon cinnamon.

FRENCH TOAST

Makes: 1 serving
Groundwork: 3 minutes
Cook: 4 to 5 minutes —
　　MEDIUM HIGH
Need: medium mixing
　　bowl
　　medium skillet

To keep the bread from getting too soggy and tearing apart in the egg mixture, either pop it in the toaster for 10 seconds, or let it air-dry while the skillet heats.

To avoid Monday morning madness, dip several extra pieces of French Toast and freeze them, (uncooked and uncovered) on a cookie sheet. Package the frozen slices in plastic bags. Then, just pop them (straight from the freezer) onto a greased cookie sheet and bake at 500° for 6 to 7 minutes.

1 egg
2 slices bread
1 Tablespoon butter OR heavy coating
**　of vegetable spray**
2 teaspoons milk
dash of salt

1. Melt the butter in (or spray heavily) a skillet or griddle on MEDIUM HIGH until a drop of water sizzles on it.

2. While the skillet is heating, blend everything but the bread with a wire whisk in a medium mixing bowl. (Make sure the bowl is large enough for a piece of bread to fit flat on the bottom.)

3. Dip the bread quickly into the egg mixture and coat each side completely.

4. Cook until golden brown on each side, turning once.

Serve hot with butter and one of the Terrific Toppers.

FRENCH TOAST IN THE OVEN

Bake: 5 minutes
Oven Temp: 500°
Need: cookie sheet

1. Preheat the oven to 500°.

2. Follow the directions for French Toast EXCEPT:

3. Grease a cookie sheet.

4. Place the prepared slices on the cookie sheet and bake for 5 minutes until the toast is brown.

FRENCH TOAST WAFFLES

Need: waffle iron

1. Preheat the waffle iron until a drop of water sizzles on it or until the ready light comes on.

2. Follow the directions for French Toast EXCEPT:

3. Place the prepared slices on the waffle iron and bake until the toast is brown.

Keep Um Hot:
Preheat the oven to 200° and stack the pancakes or waffles on a cookie sheet between paper towels to keep them hot until serving time (but no more than 30 to 45 minutes).

FRENCH TOAST OPTIONS

A. Add ¼ teaspoon cinnamon and ½ teaspoon sugar to the egg mixture.

B. Use raisin, rye, pumpernickle, 1-inch thick slices of French or Italian bread.

C. Double-Deckers:
   1. Dip one slice of bread in the egg mixture and top with one of the following: cooked sliced ham, crumbled crisp bacon, soft cream cheese and jam, or banana slices.

   2. Dip a second slice of bread in the egg mixture and place it on top of the filling before cooking.

D. Fingers:
   1. Cut the bread slice into 4 fingers before dipping in the egg mixture.

Warm any syrup by putting the bottle in a pan of hot water while the pancakes or waffles are cooking.

Try these two wonderful butters on hot biscuits, muffins, rolls, croissants, or toast.

EMERGENCY SYRUP:
1 cup brown sugar
¼ cup water
1 Tablespoon butter
⅛ teaspoon vanilla

1. Combine the sugar and water in a medium saucepan on MEDIUM.

2. Add the butter and cook until the butter melts and the sugar is very hot.

3. Add the vanilla and stir to mix.

Serve hot.

TERRIFIC TOPPERS

Top hot buttered pancakes, waffles, or French toast with:

A. Syrup, honey, jam, jelly, preserves, molasses, marmalade, apple butter, pie filling, or powdered sugar.

B. **Honey Butter**
   ½ cup (1 stick) butter (room temp)
   ¼ cup honey

   1. Stir the butter in a small mixing bowl until smooth.

   2. Add the honey and stir well. (Corn oil margarine will separate, and must be stirred before each use.)

C. **Strawberry Butter**
   ½ cup (1 stick) butter (room temp)
   ¼ cup frozen sweetened strawberries (thawed)

   1. Combine the ingredients in a small mixing bowl with a mixer.

   Option:

   a. Replace the strawberries with: any fresh fruit (bananas, raspberries, peaches) and add powdered sugar to taste.

D. Cottage cheese and pineapple chunks

E. Whipped cream cheese and chives

F. Peanut butter and honey

G. Processed cheese spread

H. S.O.S. (Sandwiches - LUNCH)

THE EGG BASKET

Eggs are delicate and very sensitive to heat and (with only one or two exceptions) are always served very fresh and cooked gently on MEDIUM LOW. The following will help you achieve eggstra-special dishes every time.

BUYING:

1. **Always check the carton** for breakage or cracks. Cracks allow bacteria to enter the egg. If you crack one accidentally, use it immediately.

2. Check the **date** stamped on the carton. If there are two, the first is the packing date and the one stamped EXP (expiration) is the last date for legal sales. Always buy the freshest unless you plan to hard-cook them all.

3. Buy only the eggs that are refrigerated, not the ones in floor displays.

4. Only at Easter does the **color** of the egg matter. Regardless of the color, the contents are the same.

5. **FRESHNESS TEST:**
   A. **A very fresh egg** will sink to the bottom of a bowl of water and lie horizontally on its side.

   B. **A week old egg** will tilt the larger end upward at a 45° angle.

   C. **An older egg** will stand completely upright.

   D. **A spoiled egg** will float.

6. Eggs will keep refrigerated for 3 to 4 weeks.

SEPARATING YOLKS FROM WHITES:

1. Use cold eggs and two bowls.

2. Carefully crack the egg in the middle, holding it over one bowl.

3. Place your thumbs in the crack and break the egg in half, keeping both the yolk and white in one half.

4. Pour the egg back and forth between the halves allowing the white to drain into the bowl, being careful not to break the yolk on the sharp edge of the shell.

35

HARD AND SOFT-COOKED HINTS

1. **Never let eggs boil!** High heat causes a green sulphur ring to form around the yolk. It won't hurt you, but it looks terrible (except to Dr. Suess) and smells worse.

2. This is the exception to the "Freshness" rule: **Week old eggs are best** for hard or soft cooking because very fresh eggs are impossible to peel.

3. **To keep the yolks centered** in the egg, stir them gently several times during the cooking process.

4. **Hard-cooked or Raw?** To tell which is which, just spin the egg on a flat surface. A **hard-cooked egg will spin,** but a raw one will not.

5. **To Peel A Hard-Cooked Egg:** When the eggs are ready, pour off the hot water and fill the pan with cold water. When the eggs are cool enough to handle, crack each shell all over by hitting it lightly against the pan or sink. Start peeling at the fat end! There is an air bubble there that makes it easy to begin peeling off the shell and inside membrane together so it will peel off like a glove.

6. **ROOM TEMPERATURE:** The safest way to bring a refrigerated egg to room temperature is to cover it with hot (not boiling) water from the tap.

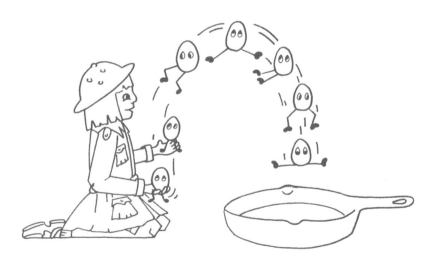

HARD AND SOFT-COOKED EGGS

Makes: 1 serving
Groundwork: 30
  seconds
Temp: HIGH/LOW
Standing Time: See
  recipe
Need: saucepan

1 egg   **water**

COLD WATER METHOD
(Produces Crack-Free Eggs)

1. Completely cover the egg in the saucepan with cold water.

2. Bring the water and egg to a boil on HIGH (uncovered).

3. **Immediately** turn off the heat, cover, and begin timing.

Soft Cooked	Hard Cooked
2 minutes - very soft	23-25 minutes
3 minutes - medium soft	
4 minutes - firm	

4. At the end of the timing, drain the water off **immediately** and run cold water over the egg for a few seconds to stop the cooking process (but not long enough to cool the egg).

BOILING WATER METHOD

1. Allow the egg to come to room temperature.

2. Fill the saucepan with 3 inches of hot tap water, cover the pan, and bring to a boil on HIGH.

3. When the water comes to a boil, carefully lower the egg into the water (use a spoon to prevent cracking the egg).

4. Reduce to LOW and simmer, uncovered, below the boiling point until the egg is ready.

Soft-Cooked	Hard-Cooked
3 minutes - very soft	18-20 minutes
4 minutes - medium soft	
5 minutes - firm	

IMPORTANT TIMING NOTE!
Add 8 to 10 minutes to the listed cooking time to allow the water to come to a boil.

For the boiling water method, start with hot tap water and cover the pan to bring the water to the boiling point faster.

NOTE: Water is boiling when **large groups** of air bubbles roll to the top, not just a few single bubbles.

For extra convenience, hard-cook enough eggs for several meals. Date each egg with a pencil or laundry marking pen. Cooked eggs will keep up to 10 days in the refrigerator.

SCRAMBLED EGGS

Makes: 1 serving
Groundwork: 2 minutes
Cook: 3 minutes -
  MEDIUM
Need: small mixing
  bowl
small skillet

ROAD RUNNER EGGS:
Spoon the hot eggs
into the pocket of a
warm pita bread,
hollowed-out roll, or in
the middle of a hot
biscuit and you can
be a gone goose!

For light, fluffy
scrambled eggs, stir
them with a **wire whisk**
during cooking.

**1 Tablespoon butter OR light coating
  of vegetable spray**
2 eggs
1 Tablespoon milk or water
¼ teaspoon salt
⅛ teaspoon pepper

1. Melt the butter in a small skillet on
    MEDIUM.

2. Combine the eggs, milk, salt, and
    pepper in a small mixing bowl, and
    blend thoroughly with a wire whisk.

3. When the butter is melted, add the
    egg mixture to the skillet, and stir
    constantly (make sure to scrape the
    entire bottom and sides) until eggs
    are fluffy and done.

FRIED EGG

Makes: 1 serving
Groundwork: 2 minutes
Cook: 3 to 4 min. -
  MEDIUM
Need: saucer
small skillet

CAUTION:
Slightly undercook
eggs — they will
continue cooking
briefly when removed
from the heat.

**1½ teaspoons butter OR light coating
  of vegetable spray**
1 egg

1. Melt the butter in a small skillet on
    MEDIUM.

2. Crack the egg into a saucer and
    slide it into the melted butter or
    crack the egg directly into the
    butter.

3. Fry until the white is no longer
    transparent (without turning) for
    Sunny-Side Up; turn once for Over
    Easy.

POACHED EGG

Makes: 1 serving
Groundwork: 2 minutes
Cook: 5 min. - HIGH
3 min. - LOW
Need: egg poacher or
skillet with a lid and
an empty tuna fish
can, custard, or
coffee cup

REMOVING SHELL FRAGMENTS:
If a small piece of
shell accidentally
drops into the eggs (or
some of the yolk falls
into the separated
whites), use a large
piece of egg shell for
easy removal.

Water
1 egg
½ teaspoon butter OR light coating of vegetable spray

With An Egg Poacher:

1. Bring 1½ inches of water to a boil on HIGH in the bottom section of a poacher.

2. While the water is heating, lightly grease the egg container section.

3. Crack the egg into the egg container, and place it on the bottom section over the boiling water.

4. When the steam starts to escape, reduce the heat to LOW, cover, and continue cooking approximately 3 minutes until the white is firm.

Without An Egg Poacher:

A simple but terrific egg poacher can be made with custard or coffee cups or clean 6½ oz. tuna cans and a skillet with a lid!

1. Bring ½ inch of water to a boil in the skillet on HIGH.

2. While the water is heating, grease the sides and bottom of the cups or cans.

3. Crack the egg into the cup or can and place it in the skillet.

4. Reduce the heat to LOW, cover, and cook for approximately 3 minutes until the white is firm.

BAKED EGGS

Makes: 1 serving
Groundwork: 3 minutes
Bake: 15 to 20 minutes
Oven Temp: 350°
Need: small, shallow
baking dish or
custard cup

If you are cooking
several, place the
dishes on a cookie
sheet for easy handling
while baking.

For a festive touch,
garnish these with a
sprig of parsley.

1 egg
1 teaspoon butter
1 Tablespoon milk or sour cream
salt and pepper to taste
dash paprika (optional)

1. Preheat the oven to 350°.

2. Thoroughly grease the bottom and
   sides of the baking dish with ¾ teaspoon butter.

3. Add the milk or sour cream.

4. Break the egg into the greased dish,
   top with the remaining ¼ teaspoon
   of butter, and sprinkle with salt,
   pepper, and paprika.

5. Bake 15 minutes or until the whites
   are firm (the yolks should remain
   soft).

EGG IN A HOLE

Makes: 1 serving
Groundwork: 1 minute
Cook: 3 to 4 min. -
   MEDIUM
Need: small skillet
biscuit cutter

EASIER CLEAN UP:
Rinse **raw egg or milk**
from dishes and
utensils in cold water
and **cooked** egg in
hot water immediately
after using.

1 Tablespoon butter
1 slice of bread
1 egg

1. Melt the butter in a small skillet on
   MEDIUM.

2. While the butter is melting, cut out a
   2-inch round hole in center of the
   bread using a small biscuit cutter or
   small juice glass.

3. Put the bread and cut-out round in
   the skillet.

4. Gently crack the egg into the hole
   and cook until the bread is lightly
   browned.

5. Turn with a spatula, and cook until
   the bread is brown and the egg is
   ready.

EGG-ON-A-MUFFIN

Makes: 1 serving
Groundwork: 3 minutes
Cook: 4 min. - MEDIUM
　　LOW
Need: large skillet

1 Tablespoon butter
1 egg
1 English Muffin
1 slice of American cheese (or 1 Tablespoon shredded Cheddar cheese)
1 slice ham, turkey, or Canadian bacon
salt and pepper to taste

1. Melt the butter in a large skillet on MEDIUM LOW.

2. Place the ham on one side of the pan and crack the egg onto the other side.

3. Add the salt and pepper.

4. Break the egg yolk with a spatula to allow the yolk to spread over the egg white (optional).

5. Cook until the ham is lightly browned and the egg is firm, turning each once.

6. While the ham and egg are cooking, split the muffin, spread with butter, and lightly toast both halves.

7. About 30 seconds before removing the ham, put the cheese on the ham slice to melt.

8. Remove the egg and place it on one half of the muffin.

9. Top with the cheese-coated ham and the other half of the muffin.

BREAKFAST MEATS

BACON

Makes: 1 slice
Groundwork: 1 minute
Fried 5 to 7 min. -
    MEDIUM
Broiled 5 to 7 min. -
    BROIL
Baked 20 to 25 minutes
Oven Temp:
    300° (regular slice)
    350° (thick slice)
Need: skillet, griddle,
    or broiler pan

QUICKIE: To separate individual slices of bacon easily, remove the bacon from the paper carton, tightly roll the slab of bacon lengthwise into a tube, unroll, and peel them off.

To prevent curling and slightly reduce shrinkage, sprinkle the bacon **lightly** with flour **before** cooking.

FLAVOR SAVER: Save cooled bacon drippings in a glass jar with a lid. Refrigerated, it keeps indefinitely and can be used to season other dishes. Dispose of other meat drippings in disposable jars or cans — not down the drain! That's a quick way to become a real plumber's friend.

PAN FRIED

1. Place the individual slices side-by-side in a **cold** skillet (if the skillet is hot, the bacon will stick!).

2. Fry on MEDIUM until lightly browned.

3. Turn and continue cooking to the desired crispness.

4. Drain.

BROILED

1. Adjust the oven rack 5 to 7 inches from the broiling element.

2. Turn the oven to BROIL.

3. Place individual slices on a broiler pan or a rack with a pan underneath to catch the drippings.

4. Broil 2½ to 3½ minutes.

5. Turn and continue broiling 2½ to 3½ additional minutes to the desired crispness.

5. Drain.

BAKED

1. Preheat the oven to 300° for regular slices, 350° for thick slices.

2. Place the individual slices side-by-side on a broiler pan or a rack with a pan underneath to catch the drippings.

3. Bake 20 to 25 minutes.

4. Drain.

This method takes longer but has the advantage of not having to be watched carefully or turned over — maybe time for a quick shower!

SAUSAGE

GROUND

Makes: 1 serving
Groundwork: 3 minutes
Cook:
Pan Fried 12 to 15 min.
Baked 20 - 30 min.
Oven Temp: 400° -
    bake
Need: small skillet

Tube: Slice through the plastic or cloth tube making ⅓ inch thick patties and remove the wrapping. (It slices more easily if it is very cold).

Bulk: Scoop out 2 Tablespoons (about the size of a golf ball), and flatten on waxed paper until the patty is ⅓ inch thick.

PAN FRIED

Sausage patties can be frozen very easily. Just stack the patties with 2 pieces of waxed paper between each one. They can be cooked without thawing — just increase the cooking time.

1. Put the sausage patties in a cold skillet on MEDIUM. **Do Not** preheat the skillet or the patties will stick.

2. Fry until brown on both sides, turning only once. Spoon out the excess drippings as they accumulate.

BAKED

1. Preheat the oven to 400°.

2. Arrange the patties in a heavy skillet.

3. Bake 20 to 30 minutes, turning once.

LINK

Groundwork: 1 minute
Cook: 10 min. - MEDIUM
5 min. - LOW
Need: small skillet with
    lid

PAN FRIED

1. Lightly grease a medium skillet.

2. Brown the desired number of links on MEDIUM. Turn often, being careful not to puncture them.

3. Reduce to LOW, cover, and steam 4 to 5 minutes until tender.

BAKED

1. Follow the directions for GROUND, EXCEPT reduce the baking time to 15 minutes. Bake, covered, for more moist links.

COUNTRY HAM WITH RED-EYE GRAVY

Makes: 1 serving
Groundwork: 1 minute
Cook: 6 min. - MEDIUM
3 to 5 min. -
MED LOW
5 min. - LOW
Need: medium skillet
with lid

In the deep South, red-eye gravy is traditionally served by making a depression in a mound of hot grits and filling it with gravy - hense the name.

1 (¼ inch thick) slice country ham
½ cup strong black coffee OR
1 teaspoon instant coffee granules
and ½ cup water

1. Trim off the hard, outer rind and discard it.

2. Scrape both sides of the ham with a knife to remove the excess salt and marrow.

3. Trim off the fat and fry it in a medium skillet on MEDIUM until partially cooked.

4. Add the ham and continue frying for 3 to 5 minutes until the fat and ham begin to brown, turning several times.

5. Reduce the heat to MEDIUM LOW, cover, and cook an additional 3 to 5 minutes.

6. Remove the ham and drain.

7. Reduce to LOW, add the coffee, stir, and simmer 5 minutes, stirring frequently until the gravy is a rich, reddish-brown color.

BRUNCH
FOR THE LEISURE MORNING BUNCH

Great brunch additions, (found in ACCOMPANIMENTS) include:

Baked Apples   Cheese Grits Casserole
Curried Fruit   Glazed Grapefruit
Winter Fruit Bowls

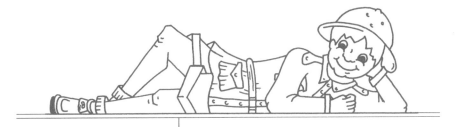

LUMBER JACK

Makes: 2 servings
Groundwork: 3 minutes
Bake: 18 to 20 minutes
Oven Temp: 325°
Need: 1 quart
    casserole with lid

1 (12 oz.) can corned beef hash
2 eggs
⅛ teaspoon salt
⅛ teaspoon pepper

1. Preheat the oven to 325°.

2. Lightly grease the casserole.

3. Spread the corned beef hash evenly in the baking dish (don't pack it down).

4. With the back of a large spoon (or bottom of a small glass), make 2 depressions in the hash large enough to hold one egg each.

5. Gently crack the eggs into the depressions.

6. Cover, and bake 18 to 20 minutes until the hash is hot and the eggs are firm.

SAUSAGE SCRAMBLE

Makes: 2 servings
Groundwork: 1 minute
Cook: 18 min. - MEDIUM
Need: small mixing
      bowl
      large skillet

**FOR A SPECTACULAR
CHANGE:**
Serve sausage
scramble (or plain
scrambled eggs) in
hot baked puff pastry,
tart shell, inside a
large broiled mush-
room cap, or scooped-
out baked tomato.

**½ pound sausage
4 eggs
3 Tablespoons milk
¼ teaspoon salt
¼ teaspoon pepper
dash cayenne pepper (optional)
½ cup (½ of 4 oz. pkg.) shredded
   Cheddar cheese**

1. Crumble the sausage into a large
   skillet and fry on MEDIUM 15 minutes
   or until the sausage is brown.

2. Beat the eggs, milk, and spices in a
   small mixing bowl until well mixed.

3. Drain the sausage, add the egg
   mixture, and cook on MEDIUM 3 to 4
   minutes, stirring constantly until the
   eggs begin to set.

4. Just before the eggs are completely
   cooked, add the cheese and
   continue cooking, stirring constantly
   until the cheese melts and the eggs
   are firm.

OPTIONS:

A. Add the following vegetables
   when the sausage has cooked
   enough to produce some
   drippings and sauté them with
   the sausage:
   ¼ cup chopped onions
   ¼ cup chopped bell pepper
   ½ cup chopped mushrooms OR
   1 (4 oz.) can sliced mushrooms
   (drained)

EGGS BENEDICT

Makes: 2 small or 1
    medium sized
    serving
Groundwork: 5 minutes
Cook: 15 min. -
    MEDIUM HIGH
Need: medium skillet
    egg poacher
    small saucepan
    small baking
    sheet

If time permits, try one
of the Hollandaises in
SAUCES AND GRAVIES.

---

1 Tablespoon butter or heavy coating
  of vegetable spray
2 thin slices ham or Canadian bacon
2 poached eggs
1 (1¼ oz.) pkg. Hollandaise sauce mix
¾ cup milk
1 English muffin (split)

1. Melt the butter in (or spray with vegetable spray) a medium skillet on MEDIUM HIGH.

2. Add the Canadian bacon or ham and cook until the slices are lightly brown.

3. Poach the eggs. (The Egg Basket in BREAKFAST will help.)

4. While the meat and eggs are cooking, combine the milk and Hollandaise sauce mix in a small saucepan and prepare according to the directions on the package.

5. Split the English muffin, spread with ½ teaspoon butter, and toast very lightly.

6. Place a slice of Canadian bacon on each muffin half, top with a poached egg and Hollandaise sauce.

Serve immediately.

OPTIONS:

  A. Replace the ham with crab meat.

  B. Replace the muffins with split and toasted bagels.

  C. Layer the Canadian bacon or ham with hot asparagus tips or spears.

  D. Replace the poached egg with scrambled eggs.

CHEESE STRATA

Makes: 2 servings
Groundwork: 5 minutes
Bake: 45 minutes
Oven Temp: 350°
Need: 1 quart
  casserole
small mixing bowl

All stratas will become lighter if refrigerated for ½ hour to overnight before cooking.

---

2 eggs
1 cup milk
½ teaspoon salt
¼ teaspoon pepper
2 slices bread
1 cup (4 oz. pkg.) shredded Cheddar cheese

1. Preheat the oven to 350°.

2. Grease the sides and bottom of a 1 quart casserole.

3. Mix the eggs, milk, salt, and pepper in a small mixing bowl until well blended.

4. Cut or tear 1 slice of bread into small pieces and fit it into the baking dish, sprinkle ½ of the cheese over the bread, and pour ½ of the egg mixture over the cheese.

5. Repeat the layers with the remaining ingredients.

6. Bake for 45 minutes until the strata is puffy and brown.

OPTIONS:

A. **Sausage Strata:**
   Use only ½ cup milk; replace the Cheddar cheese with ⅓ cup Swiss cheese, and add the following to the egg mixture:
   ½ teaspoon Worcestershire
   ½ teaspoon prepared mustard
   ⅓ pound hot sausage (cooked, crumbled, and drained)

B. Replace the bread with 2 cups of herb-seasoned croutons.

To freeze a sausage strata, combine the cooked sausage, mustard, Worcestershire, and cheese and spread the mixture over the bread. Thaw, and add the egg mixture just before baking.

OMELET

Makes: 1 serving
Groundwork: 3 minutes
Cook: 5 min. - MED. LOW
Need: small mixing
  bowl
small skillet

1 Tablespoon butter
2 eggs
2 Tablespoons milk, sour cream, club
  soda, or water
¼ teaspoon salt
⅛ teaspoon pepper

1. Melt the butter in a small skillet on MEDIUM LOW.

2. Combine all the other ingredients in a small mixing bowl until very well blended and foamy (or 30 seconds in the blender for a lighter omelet).

3. Add the egg mixture to the melted butter and cook until the eggs begin to get firm. **Do Not Stir!.**

4. Carefully lift the edges of the omelet and tilt the pan so the uncooked mixture can run underneath. Repeat several times until the omelet is nearly firm in the center.

5. Add your choice of FANTASTIC FILLINGS (page 50-51).

6. Fold the omelet in half and continue cooking for 30 seconds; carefully slide it from the pan or remove it with 2 spatulas to prevent tearing.

OPTIONS:

A. For a gourmet touch, try topping a plain or filled omelet with a first-rate sauce (SAUCES AND GRAVIES): Warm Hollandaise, Cheese, Bernaise, Taco, Pizza or Spaghetti sauce.

B. **OVEN OMELET:**
    Preheat the oven to 325°; lightly grease a pie plate; combine the ingredients (fillings included) in a small mixing bowl and pour into the pie plate; bake 15 to 20 minutes until eggs are firm.

49

Groundwork: 2 to 8 minutes depending on your choice of filling

---

IMPORTANT:
When using **instant** onion, bell pepper, or celery flakes, in omelets, first soak them in cold water for **10** minutes and drain.

When substituting **fresh,** first sauté them in the melted butter just until tender (do not brown).

⅔ teaspoon instant minced onions = 2 teaspoons fresh

1½ teaspoons instant celery or bell pepper = 1 Tablespoon chopped fresh.

FANTASTIC FILLINGS

Before you start cooking the omelet, choose a filling and do the groundwork. When the omelet is nearly firm in the center, add your choice to one half and cook for 30 seconds. Fold the plain half over the filing and continue cooking for 30 seconds longer.

ALL AMERICAN

A. ¼ cup shredded (or 1 slice) cheese (American, Cheddar, Monterrey Jack, cottage, Velveeta, or Gruyere)

B. ¼ cup sausage or bacon (cooked, drained & crumbled)
⅔ teaspoon instant minced onions

C. ¼ cup cooked ham (diced or sliced)
¼ cup Swiss or Cheddar cheese (shredded or sliced)

D. 1 Tablespoon blue cheese (crumbled finely)
2 slices bacon (cooked and crumbled)

VEGETARIAN

A. ¼ cup cut asparagus (drained)
¼ cup American, Cheddar cheese (cubed or shredded)

B. ¼ cup canned mushrooms (drained and chopped)
¼ teaspoon minced onions
1 Tablespoon instant bell pepper flakes

C. ¼ cup jam, jelly, or preserves

IMPRESSIVE INTERNATIONALS

Argentine:
  2 slices dried beef (chipped)
  1 Tablespoon Cheddar or cream
      cheese (shredded or cubed)
  1 teaspoon instant minced onions

Italian:
  2 Tablespoons pizza sauce with
      pepperoni (or add 4 to 6 slices
      pepperoni)
  2 Tablespoons Parmesan cheese
  1/8 teaspoon oregano (optional)

Mexican: (hold onto your Sombrero!!)
  1/4 cup canned chili
  1/4 teaspoon instant minced onions
  2 Tablespoons Cheddar cheese
      (shredded or diced)
  2 drops Tabasco sauce

Scandinavian:
  1/4 cup salmon (drained and flaked
      with bones and skin removed)
  2 Tablespoons sour cream
  1/2 teaspoon dill weed

Spanish:
  2 Tablespoons fresh tomatoes
      (peeled and chopped)
  2/3 teaspoon instant minced onions
  1/4 teaspoon instant bell pepper
  1/8 teaspoon garlic powder

SPANISH OPTIONS:

A. Add: 2 black olives (sliced),
      1 teaspoon instant celery flakes,
      1 Tablespoon canned mushrooms
      (drained and chopped)

B. Pour 1/4 cup bottled (warm) spaghetti
      sauce over a plain or Spanish
      omelet.

CLASSICAL QUICHE

Quiche is easy once you understand the three basic parts: the crust, the custard, and the additions:

QUICHE CRUST

Choose one:

A. **1 (9") frozen pie crust** - Thaw and prick the sides and bottom every ½ inch with a fork.

B. **1 refrigerator pie crust** - Unfold the crust and line the pie plate according to the directions on the package.

C. **1 cup (26 to 28 crackers) saltine cracker crumbs and 5 Tablespoons melted butter —**

1. Preheat the oven to 350°.

2. Melt the butter in a pie plate while the oven preheats.

3. Crush the crackers finely, add to the melted butter, and stir to mix well.

4. Firmly press the mixture into the bottom and up the sides of the pie plate.

5. Bake 8 minutes until light brown.

QUICHE CUSTARD

1 cup (8 oz.) milk or half-and-half
2 eggs
½ teaspoon salt
¼ teaspoon pepper
⅛ teaspoon nutmeg (optional)
pinch cayenne pepper

1. Preheat the oven to 450°.

Individual quiches can be made by using frozen pastry tart shells and reducing the cooking time by 5 to 10 minutes.

CRACKER CRUST:
Crust Groundwork: 5 minutes
Bake: 8 minutes
Oven Temp: 350°
Need: 9" pie plate

You'll think this saltine crust won't hold together but it will.

Makes: 2 servings
Custard Groundwork: 4 minutes
Bake: 15 min. - 450°
20 to 25 min. - 350°
Need: 9" pie plate
medium mixing bowl
Standing Time: 5 to 10 minutes

TEST FOR DONENESS:
Quiche is done when
a knife blade inserted
in the center comes
out clean.

For color, add 1
teaspoon paprika to
the custard.

When using the classic
deep 10" quiche pan,
double both the
CUSTARD and
ADDITIONS recipes and
increase the 350°
baking time to 25 to
30 minutes.

ADDITIONS
GROUNDWORK:
3 to 10 minutes
depending on your
choice.

It is not necessary to
presoften instant
onions, celery or bell
pepper flakes for use
in quiche.

2. Mix all ingredients in a medium
   mixing bowl with a wire whisk until
   well blended.

3. Pour the custard slowly into the shell
   and bake 15 minutes at 450°.

4. Without removing the quiche from
   the oven, turn the oven temperature
   down to 350° and bake 20 to 25
   minutes more until it is firm in the
   center.

5. Remove the quiche from the oven
   and let it stand 5 to 10 minutes at
   room temperature before slicing.

QUICHE ADDITIONS

Transform classical quiche into a meal
for real men with a little imagination
and a bit of extra effort.

1. Choose and prepare your favorite
   ADDITIONS.

2. Arrange the ADDITIONS evenly in the
   crust and sprinkle any required
   cheese on top. (Add any **Parmesan**
   cheese, wine, or sherry to the
   custard mixture to keep it from
   floating on the top.)

3. Pour the custard slowly on top of the
   ADDITIONS and cheese.

4. Bake as directed for the Classical
   Quiche.

QUICHE LORRAINE

4 slices of bacon (cooked crisp and
    crumbled)
1½ teaspoons instant minced onions
1 cup (4 oz. pkg.) shredded or diced
    cheese (Swiss, Gruyere or Monterrey
    Jack)

When using canned seafood, (except tuna), rinse in cold water and pat dry with a paper towel.

SEAFOOD THERMIDOR

4 to 6 oz. cooked, shelled (canned, frozen, fresh) seafood (lobster, shrimp, and/or crab)
1½ teaspoons instant minced onions
1 Tablespoon white wine or sherry
1½ Tablespoons Parmesan cheese

PUTTING ON THE RITZ

½ (10½ oz.) can asparagus tips (drained)
½ cup shredded Cheddar cheese

BALI HIGH
1 (8 oz.) can French-cut green beans (drained)
¼ cup slivered almonds
1 teaspoon soy sauce

QUICHE-IN-A-BLENDER

Makes: 2 servings
Groundwork: 7 minutes
Bake: 35 to 40 minutes
Oven Temp: 400°
Need: 9" pie plate
blender

4 to 5 slices bacon
½ cup shredded Swiss cheese
1 cup milk
2 eggs
1½ teaspoons instant minced onions
⅓ cup biscuit mix
¼ teaspoon salt
¼ teaspoon pepper

Individual quiches can be made by using greased muffin tins and reducing the baking time by 5 to 10 minutes.

1. Preheat the oven to 400°.

2. Grease a 9" pie plate.

3. Fry the bacon in a medium skillet on MEDIUM until crisp; drain and crumble into the bottom of the pie plate.

4. Sprinkle the cheese evenly over the bacon.

5. Blend the remaining ingredients on HIGH for 1 minute and pour the egg mixture over the cheese and bacon.

6. Bake 35 to 40 minutes until light brown.

7. Cool 5 minutes before slicing.

LUNCH

LIGHT AND SIMPLE

The Salad Bar, The Soup Bowl, The Sandwich Board
And
Added Touches

THE SOUP BOWL

Nothing warms the old cockles like a hot bowl on a frosty day!

To enhance the flavor and richness of canned soups, add only ½ to ¾ can of additional liquid.

Makes: 2 servings
Groundwork: 3 minutes
Cook: 5 to 7 min. - MED.
Need: medium
saucepan

Garnish with croutons or chopped chives.

CHEESE SOUP

1 (10¾ oz.) can cream of potato soup
½ soup can milk
1 cup (4 oz. pkg.) shredded Cheddar cheese
1 Tablespoon butter
¼ teaspoon salt
¼ teaspoon Tabasco

1. Combine all ingredients in a medium saucepan on MEDIUM, stirring often.

2. Heat until the cheese is melted and the soup is very hot but not boiling.

CRAB BISQUE

CRAB BISQUE:
Makes: 4 servings
Groundwork: 3 minutes
Cook: 5 to 7 min. - MED.
Need: medium
  saucepan

1 (6½ oz.) can crab meat (drained)
1 (10¾ oz.) can cream of asparagus
  soup
1 (10¾ oz.) can cream of mushroom
  soup
1½ cups milk
1 to 2 Tablespoons sherry

CURRIED CRAB SOUP

CURRIED CRAB:
Makes: 4 servings
Groundwork: 3 minutes
Cook: 5 to 7 min. - MED.

1 (6½ oz.) can crab meat (drained)
1 (10¾ oz.) can split pea with ham
  soup
1 (10¾ oz.) can tomato soup
1 soup can milk
¼ teaspoon curry powder
1 to 2 Tablespoons sherry

Garnish with finely
grated lemon rind or
paprika.

When time permits, try
Grandma's Homemade
Vegetable Soup
(DINNER).

1. Rinse the crab meat under cold
   water, remove any shell or cartilage,
   and drain well.

2. Combine the soups, crab meat, and
   milk in a medium saucepan on
   MEDIUM, stirring often to prevent
   sticking.

3. Heat until very hot but not boiling.

4. Add the sherry and stir to combine.

CUCUMBER

Makes: 2 servings
Groundwork: 3 minutes
Refrigerate: 30 minutes
Need: blender

1 (10¾ oz.) can cream of chicken soup
1 (8 oz.) carton sour cream
¼ cup milk
2 small cucumbers

1. Combine the soup, sour cream, and
   milk in the blender.

Garnish with dill weed,
chives, or chopped
green onions.

2. Peel the cucumbers, cut into chunks,
   and add to the soup mixture.

3. Blend on HIGH 30 seconds until smooth.

4. Chill, and serve cold.

GUMBO

Makes: 2 servings
Groundwork: 3 minutes
Cook: 3 minutes - MED.
 HIGH
Need: medium
 saucepan

Serve "as is" or over ½
cup hot cooked rice
and with a slice of hot
garlic bread.

---

1 Tablespoon butter
1 Tablespoon flour
⅛ teaspoon pepper
⅛ teaspoon cayenne pepper
½ cup water
1 (10¾ oz.) can chicken gumbo soup
2 drops Tabasco
**1 (4½ oz.) can shrimp OR 1 (8 oz.) can
 oysters (drained)**

1. Melt the butter in a medium
   saucepan on MEDIUM HIGH.

2. Add the flour and peppers and **stir
   constantly,** scraping the bottom of
   the pan to prevent sticking until the
   mixture turns a dark, chocolate brown.

3. Add the water gradually and stir
   until smooth.

4. Add the soup and Tabasco.

5. Drain the shrimp or oysters and stir
   into the soup.

6. Heat to boiling point but do not boil.

FRENCH ONION

Makes: 2 servings
Groundwork: 5 minutes
Bake: 10 minutes
Oven Temp: 400°
Need: 2 oven-proof
 bowls

1 (10¾ oz.) can French onion soup
1 soup can water
1 cup croutons
**1 cup (4 oz. pkg.) shredded mozzarella
 cheese**

1. Preheat the oven to 400°.

2. Stir the soup in can and pour equal
   amounts into 2 oven-proof bowls.

3. Fill the soup can with water, pour equal
   amounts into the bowls, and stir.

4. Top each bowl with croutons and
   sprinkle the cheese evenly over them.

5. Bake 10 minutes until the soup is hot
   and the cheese is lightly browned.

57

THE SALAD BAR

Salads reign supreme...as a side dish, an entire meal, or a unique party. The secret is in the serving...your taste buds believe what your eyes tell them. With ten extra seconds and a colorful garnish, a simple salad becomes simply elegant.

THE SALAD BOWL

A really great tossed salad needs a contrast of tastes, textures, and colors. Take your choice of **at least one** from **each** group but, the more, the merrier.

THE GREENS	
All greens should be fresh and chilled!	
SELECT IT	**FIX IT**
Lettuce: Bibb, Boston, Butter, Field (maché), Iceburg, Leaf, or Red Interesting additions to combine with lettuce or use alone: Chickory Endive Swiss Chard Romaine Sorrel Spinach Kale Red or Green Cabbage Watercress Escarole	Rinse all greens thoroughly in cold water. Drain in a colander or pat dry with paper towels. Tear all greens into bite-size pieces. Don't use a metal knife! It cause most greens to bruise or "rust" and creates an unappetizing brown tinge within several hours. Cabbage is an exception...it can be cut or shredded without damage.
Hint: To remove the core from Iceburg lettuce, hit the core once firmly on the countertop and then pull it out.	

THE VEGGIES

All fresh vegetables should be **fresh** and chilled. Rinse in cold water even before peeling them. All canned ones should be chilled.

SELECT IT	FRESH OR CANNED	FIX IT
Artichoke Hearts	C	Drain;, cut into quarters.
Avocado	F	Peel; dice
Beans: Garbonzo or Kidney	C	Drain.
Bell Peppers: Red or Green	F	Remove the seeds; cut in rings or strips.
Beets: Plain or spiced	C	Drain; slice or dice.
Broccoli	F	Cut the flowerettes from the stem.
Carrots	F	Peel; slice or dice; or shave with a vegetable peeler.
Cauliflower	F	Cut the flowerettes from the stem.
Celery	F	Remove the strings; slice.
Cucumbers	F	Peel if waxed or mature; slice or dice.
Mushrooms	F	Remove $\frac{1}{16}$" slice from the stem; slice lengthwise.
Onions:		
Pearl or pickled	C	Drain.
White, Yellow, Red, Purple	F	Peel, slice and separate into rings or dice.
Green or Scallions	F	Remove the root end and any wilted top; slice.
Heart of Palm	C	Drain; chop.
Peas (Green)	C	Drain.
	F	Cook; drain.
	Frozen	Thaw, but do not cook.
Radish	F	Remove the root and stem ends; slice.
Sprouts: Bean or Alfalfa	F	Rinse, pat dry.
Squash: Yellow, Summer	F	Remove the stem ends; slice.
Tomatoes: Large*	F	Peel (optional); cube;
Patio or Cherry	F	Cut in half.
Water Chestnuts	C	Drain, slice if whole
Zucchini	F	Peel (optional); slice thinly

*Very ripe tomatoes are fragile. Save these for toppings, or toss in at the last minute.

The Salad Bowl

THE MEAL-MAKERS

Meats, cheeses, or eggs turn a salad into a meal, either tossed with greens and veggies or arranged on the top.

SELECT IT	FRESH OR CANNED	FIX IT
Beef	F	Cook; chill; dice or slice into strips
	C	Drain; chill; flake
Cheese:		
Cheddar, Swiss, Colby, Jack		Cut into cubes or strips
Parmesan		Grate finely
Chicken	F	Cook; chill; dice or slice into strips
	C	Drain; chill, flake
Crab	F	Cook, chill; shred
	C	Chill; drain; rinse in cold water; pat dry.
Eggs	F ·	Hard-cook; peel; grate; cut into slices, halves or quarters
Ham	F	Cook; chill; dice or slice into strips
	C	Drain; chill; flake
Salmon	C	Chill; drain; remove skin and bones; flake
Sardines	C	Drain; chop
Shrimp	F	Boil, peel, chill
	C	Chill; drain, rinse in cold water; pat dry
Tuna	C	Chill; drain; flake
Turkey	F	Cook; chill; dice or slice into strips
	C	Drain; chill; flake

Hint: Canned meats are easier to work with if drained before chilling.

	THE TOPPINGS	
SELECT IT	**FRESH OR CANNED**	**FIX IT**
Bacon	F	Cook crisp; crumble
Imitation Bacon Chips	C	
Banana Chips	C	
Capers	C	Drain
Cashew Nuts	C	
Cheese: Cheddar, Swiss, Colby, Jack, Parmesan	F	Shred
Chow Mein Noodles	C	
Coconut	F/C	Grate
Croutons	F/C	See THE BREAD BASKET
Eggs	F	Hardcook, peel, chop
Grapes: Seedless Green/Red	F	Wash; remove stems
Olives: Stuffed Green, Black or ripe	C	Use whole or slice
Onions, French Fried	C	
Oats	C	Toast
Peanuts	C	
Pecans	F	Break into pieces
	C	Break into pieces
Peppers: Jalapeño, Banana, Cherry, Chili, or Greek	C	Drain; whole or slice
Pimientos	C	Drain; cut into strips or dice
Raisins	C	
Sesame Seeds	C	Plain or toasted
Sunflower seeds	C	

THE GARNISHES		
SELECT IT	**FRESH OR CANNED**	**FIX IT**
Anchovies	C	
Carrot Curls*	F	
Celery Curls & Pinwheels*	F	
Cucumber Slices Scored	F	
Green Onion Curls*	F	
Herbs: Chives, Parsley, Basil, Marjoram, Oregano, Rosemary, Thyme, Tarragon	C F	Chop finely (add to dressing or sprinkle on salad)
Lemon or lime slices	F	Cover with parsley
Pimiento	C	Cut into strips or dice
Peppers: Jalepeño, Banana, Cherry, Chili, Greek	C	
Radish Roses*	F	

*Directions for these fancy garnishes are in ADDED TOUCHES.

THE DRESSINGS

Use your choice of bottled dressings or make your own. Never add **either** until the last minute to avoid a soggy salad.

Ways to serve your salads:	
Family Style:	Serve one or more dressings in attractive bowls or cruet bottles for individual choices.
Fast Food Style:	Toss your salad, pour the dressing on top, add the toppings and garnishes.
Gourmet Style:	Toss your salad with the dressing before adding the toppings and garnishes. This takes a moment longer but assures an even coating on all ingredients (and avoids the top's being all dressing and no salad and the reverse on the bottom.

VEGETABLE SALADS
For Color and Variety

THE CLASSICS

The following are classics to toss together for rave reviews. The proportions are entirely your choice.

FRESH SPINACH SALAD

Groundwork: 5 minutes

Just wash the spinach in cold water, drain well, remove the large stems, and tear the leaves into bite-size pieces. Add any of your choices:

GARNISH SPINACH SALAD WITH:
Bacon (cooked crisply & crumbled)
Mandarin orange slices
Raisins
Chopped nuts (pecans, peanuts, or pinenuts)

Purple or white onions (sliced thinly; separated into rings)
Sliced fresh mushrooms
Bean sprouts
Sliced green onions
Sliced water chestnuts
Diced apple
Avocado slices
Black olives
Sliced celery
Cooked, peeled shrimp
Green peas (canned or frozen, thawed but uncooked)
Hard-cooked eggs (sliced or grated)

SPINACH SALAD DRESSINGS:
Any of the following are good selections:
Russian
Italian
Ranch (try adding some dill weed for a change)
Oil and Vinegar
Caeser
Greek
Dijon Vinaigrette

CAESAR SALAD

Groundwork: 5 minutes

Iceburg lettuce
Endive
Romaine
Sliced mushrooms
Croutons
Caeser salad dressing

GREEK SALAD

Iceburg lettuce
Cherry tomatoes (whole, halved, or
    diced)
Feta cheese (cubed)
Cucumber slices
White or purple onions (sliced thinly;
    separted into rings)

Top with:

Whole anchovies
Capers
Greek peppers
Black olives

Dressing:

Drizzle with Greek dressing

OPTIONS:

A. Add your choice of one or more of
    the following:

Beet slices (cooked or canned)
Carrot slices or curls
Celery
Radishes
Salami slices

Garnish Greek Salad
with whole anchovies.

ASPARAGUS SALAD

Makes: 2 servings
Groundwork: 2 minutes
REFRIGERATE

2 lettuce leaves
1 (10½ oz.) can asparagus (chilled &
    drained)
2 Tablespoons mayonnaise
1 pimiento-stuffed olive

1. Wash the lettuce leaves and place
    them on 2 small salad plates.

2. Drain the asparagus, place ½ on
    each lettuce leaf, top each with a
    Tablespoon of mayonnaise, and
    garnish with ½ the olive.

Keep an unopened
can of asparagus in
the refrigerator for a
quick, attractive salad.

MAKE AHEAD SALAD

Groundwork: 10 minutes
Need: large mixing
bowl or salad bowl

Start with a bed of lettuce and add any or all of the following vegetables (in amounts according to the number of hungry people you are feeding).

Lettuce
Radishes
Celery
Cauliflower
Green onions
Cucumbers
Broccoli
Bell Pepper
Frozen green peas (thawed but not cooked)
Shredded Cheddar cheese
Dry salad dressing mix (ranch, creamy Italian)
Mayonnaise

QUICK THAW:
Place frozen peas in a colander under cold running water for 2 or 3 minutes.

1. Wash, drain, and cut or tear the fresh vegetables into bite-size pieces and thaw the peas.

2. Begin with the lettuce and place the other veggies on top in layers.

3. Sprinkle the dry salad dressing mix evenly over the top layer.

4. Top with the shredded cheese.

5. Spread a **thin** layer of mayonnaise over the top so that it entirely **seals** the salad.

6. Cover it tightly and refrigerate until ready to use.

7. Toss just before serving.

OPTIONS:

A. Top individual portions with crisp, crumbled bacon just before serving.

ASPARAGUS & PEAS VINAIGRETTE

Makes: 2 servings
Groundwork: 2 minutes
Refrigerate: 1 hour or
  overnight
Need: 8" flat baking
  dish

Garnish with pimiento
strips.

**1 (8.5 oz.) can small green peas
(drained)
1 (15 oz.) can asparagus spears
(drained)
½ (8 oz.) bottle Dijon Vinaigrette
dressing
lettuce leaves**

1. Drain the peas and asparagus and arrange them in a baking dish.

2. Top with the dressing.

3. Cover and refrigerate at least one hour.

4. Serve on lettuce leaves.

COLESLAW

Makes: 4 cups
Groundwork: 5 minutes
Need: medium mixing
  bowl
  grater

One pound of green
or red cabbage
makes six cups
shredded.

Old King Cole is not
responsible for this
creation. "Cole"
translates "cabbage"
in Olde English.

**1 small (¾ pound) head of cabbage
(shredded)
1 small carrot (grated)
1 to 2 Tablespoons onions (finely
chopped)
⅓ cup mayonnaise
1 Tablespoon vinegar
1 teaspoon sugar
salt and pepper to taste**

1. Remove any damaged outer leaves, and cut the cabbage into 4 quarters from the top to the stem end.

2. Cut out the core and shred the cabbage into a medium mixing bowl.

3. Peel and grate the carrot and chop the onion.

4. Combine all the ingredients and stir until well mixed.

OPTIONS:

Add:

    A. ½ teaspoon mustard, ¼ cup diced bell pepper, 1 small diced celery rib, ½ teaspoon celery seed, and ¼ cup chopped stuffed olives.

    B. 1 (8 oz.) can crushed pineapple (drained), ¼ cup raisins, and 1 small diced red apple (unpeeled).

POLYNESIAN SALAD

Makes: 4 servings
Groundwork: 3 minutes
Refrigerate: 30 minutes
Need: medium mixing
   bowl

5 medium carrots
1 (8 oz.) can crushed pineapple (drained)
½ cup raisins
⅓ cup mayonnaise

1. Wash the carrots in cold water, peel, and grate into a medium mixing bowl.

2. Drain the pineapple and add it to the carrots.

3. Add the raisins and mayonnaise and mix well.

4. Chill before serving.

COPPER PENNIES CARROTS

Makes: 4 servings
Groundwork: 3 minutes
Marinate: over night
Need: medium mixing
   bowl

½ (10¾ oz.) can tomato soup
¼ cup vegetable oil
¼ cup vinegar
¼ cup sugar
½ teaspoon salt
½ teaspoon pepper
½ teaspoon Worcestershire
½ small onion, sliced
½ medium bell pepper (cut into rings)
2 (16 oz.) cans sliced carrots (drained)

1. Combine the soup, oil, vinegar,

Copper Pennies keep for 3 to 4 weeks refrigerated in an airtight container (and they keep getting better!).

Makes: 2 servings
Groundwork: 2 minutes
Marinate: over night
Need: small mixing
  bowl

sugar, and spices in a medium mixing bowl with a wire whisk until smooth.

2. Peel the onion, slice thinly, and separate into rings.

3. Wash the pepper under cold water, remove the seeds, and slice into rings.

4. Drain the carrots and combine with the onion and pepper rings in the tomato mixture.

5. Cover and refrigerate over night.

MARINATED GREEN BEANS

½ cup **Vinegar and Oil dressing**
⅛ **teaspoon garlic powder**
pinch of cayenne pepper
1 (16 oz.) can cut or whole green beans (drained)

1. Combine the Vinegar and Oil dressing and spices in a small mixing bowl and stir to mix well.

2. Drain the beans, add to the mixture, and stir to mix.

3. Cover tightly and refrigerate overnight.

4. Drain well and serve chilled.

OPTIONS:

A. Replace the Oil and Vinegar dressing with Italian dressing.

B. Replace the Oil and Vinegar, cayenne and garlic with Catalina dressing and top the salad with cooked, crumbled bacon.

MARINATED FRESH VEGGIES

Groundwork: 5 to 7
minutes:
Refrigerate and
Marinate: 1 hour
Need: plastic bag

Broccoli
Cauliflower
Celery
Carrots
Cherry tomatoes
Yellow crook-neck squash
Bottled Italian dressing (regular, low-cal, or creamy)

This can be done a day or two ahead. Longer marinating makes them better.

1. Wash your choice of veggies in cold water, drain in a colander, and dry with a paper towel.

2. Separate the broccoli and cauliflower into flowerettes; remove the strings from the celery and cut into 2" pieces, slicing the large end down the middle to make thin strips; peel the carrots, split the large ends into fourths, and cut these into 2" pieces; cut the stem end off the cherry tomatoes; cut the stem end off the squash and cut into $\frac{1}{8}$" rounds.

3. Place the prepared vegetables in a plastic bag, pour the dressing over them, seal the bag, shake gently to coat them all thoroughly.

4. Refrigerate the bag of veggies at least an hour, turning and shaking occasionally.

5. Drain before serving.

PEAS PARISIAN

Makes: 3 servings
Groundwork: 3 minutes
Refrigerate: 15 to 20 min.
Need: small serving
  bowl

Eliminate the refrigeration time by keeping a small can of peas in the refrigerator for emergencies.

If fresh celery and onion are a problem, replace them with 2 Tablespoons instant celery flakes and 1½ Tablespoons instant minced onion and refrigerate **30** minutes to allow them to soften.

1 (8 oz.) can green peas (drained)
1 hard-cooked egg
¼ cup celery (chopped)
¼ cup onion (chopped)
2 Tablespoons mayonnaise
2 Tablespoons pimiento (diced)
¼ teaspoon salt
⅛ teaspoon pepper

1. Drain the peas and place them in a serving bowl.
2. Chop the egg, celery, and onion and add to the peas.
3. Add the mayonnaise, pimiento, salt, and pepper and stir to mix thoroughly.
4. Chill 15 to 20 minutes and serve cold.

TOMATO BRAVO

Makes: 2 servings
Groundwork: 3 minutes
Refrigerate: 15 minutes

GARNISH: Top each salad with 1 green or ripe olive.

2 lettuce leaves
1 large tomato
1 Tablespoon olive oil
½ teaspoon basil

1. Wash the lettuce leaves and place them on 2 small salad plates.
2. Wash and slice the tomato (peel if desired).
3. Arrange the slices on the lettuce leaves.
4. Drizzle each slice with the oil and sprinkle each lightly with basil.
5. Refrigerate at least 15 minutes.

OPTION:

  A. Italian Flag Salad
      1. Add sliced avocado and strips or cubes of mozzarella cheese.

POTATO SALAD

Makes: 2 servings
Groundwork: 5 minutes
Need: medium mixing
   bowl

Garnish with paprika.

---

1 (16 oz.) can whole potatoes (drained)
1 hard-cooked egg
1 small celery rib
¼ cup mayonnaise
¼ teaspoon salt
⅛ teaspoon pepper

1. Drain the potatoes, cut into ½ inch cubes, and place in a medium mixing bowl.

2. Peel and finely chop the egg and add to the potatoes.

3. Rinse the celery in cold water, remove the strings, chop it finely, and add to the potatoes.

4. Add the mayonnaise, salt, and pepper and stir gently to mix.

INFINITE OPTIONS:

There are probably as many ways to make potato salad as there are people on the planet. These are some of the favorite additions:

Sweet or dill pickle cubes
Pickle relish
Chopped olives
Diced bell pepper
Diced pimiento
Parsley
Prepared mustard
Celery seeds
Chives
Curry powder
Crumbled crisp bacon
Chopped white, red, or green onions

PASTA SALAD

Pasta salads are perfect people pleasers as the main dish or an accompaniment. Serve them either chilled or at room temperature.

Pasta cooking tips are in The Pasta Puzzle (DINNER)

Remember! Cook pasta for salads Al dente - just barely tender.

Four ounces of uncooked pasta is enough for two average servings.

PASTA CHOICES:
Select one or more of the small or medium-sized pasta shapes and prepare it according to the directions on the package. Rinse the cooked pasta under cold water and drain well. Great choices include:

Bow ties	Shells
Corkscrew (spiral)	Vermicelli
Elbows	Wagon wheels
Fettuccine	Ziti

PASTA PARTNERS:
Create your own specialty with a combination of your favorites cut into bite-sized chunks:

* Cook Starred Items
VEGGIES: (*cooked crisp, tender)
Artichoke hearts (marinated or plain)
Asparagus*
Beans* (green or red kidney)
Bean sprouts
Broccoli flowerets*
Carrots*
Cauliflower*
Celery
Cucumbers
Grapes
Greens - Spinach or Romaine (slice thinly)
Mushrooms
Olives (black or green)
Onions (slice thinly)
Peas, green (uncooked frozen or canned)
Pimientos
Peppers (red, green, or yellow bell or cherry)
Pickle cubes (sweet or dill)
Radish slices
Snow Pea Pods* (fresh or frozen)

72

Garnish pasta salads with your choice of:

Apple slices
Bacon (cooked & crumbled)
Basil
Bell pepper rings
Capers
Celery seeds
Chives
Green onions
Hard-cooked egg (wedges or grated)
Lemon slices
Olive slices
Oregano
Parmesan cheese
Parsley
Pimiento strips
Raisins
Romano cheese

Squash* (yellow crookneck)
Tomatoes
Zucchini*

MEATS: (*Cook Starred Items)
Anchovies (whole or halved)
Bologna (diced)
Chicken or turkey* (diced)
Corned beef* (diced or flaked)
Crab* (drained)
Ham (diced)
Pepperoni (sliced)
Pork* (diced)
Salami (diced)
Salmon, smoked (flaked)
Sausages* Knockwurst, Bratwurst, Franks, or Polish (sliced)
Scallops*
Shrimp*
Tuna (flaked)

DAIRY:
Cheese cubes (Cheddar, Feta, Monterey Jack, Mozzarella, Provolone, Swiss)
Hard-cooked eggs

HERBS AND SPICES:
Garlic powder   Sage
Poppy seeds   Tarragon
Rosemary   Thyme

PASTA DRESSINGS:
Use the dressing suggested with each salad or replace it with a compatible prepared dressing:

Ranch   Vinegar & Oil
Italian   Russian
Blue cheese   French
Dijon Vinaigrette   Caesar
Any sour cream dip
Soft cream cheese with chives (add milk to thin)

PASTA BEDDINGS:
Serve the salad on a bed of any crisp green leaves:

Lettuce   Romaine
Spinach   Endive

ANTIPASTO PASTA SALAD

Makes: 2 servings
Groundwork: salad - 3
   minutes
Cook: pasta 10-15
   minutes
Refrigerate: 30
   minutes
Need: medium sauce
   pan, medium mixing
   bowl

4 oz. pasta (cooked, drained)
15 pepperoni slices (cut in half)
¼ cup black olive slices (drained)
6 cherry tomatoes (quartered)
Dressing

1. Cook the pasta according to directions on package, or see THE PASTA PUZZLE, page 210.

2. While the pasta is cooking, cut the pepperoni slices in half, drain the olive slices, rinse the tomatoes under cold water, and cut into fourths.

3. Combine all the ingredients in a medium mixing bowl, add the dressing, and toss gently to combine.

Groundwork: 2 minutes
Need: small mixing
   bowl, wire whisk

4. Cover and chill 30 minutes.

DRESSING

¼ cup mayonnaise
1½ teaspoons lemon juice
⅛ teaspoon garlic powder
½ teaspoon Dijon mustard

Italian dressing also
makes an amazing
antipasto salad.

1. Combine all ingredients in a small mixing bowl and stir with a wire whisk until smooth.

ADDED SALAD ATTRACTIONS:
(Take your choice of one or more):

Marinated artichoke hearts (drained
   and quartered)
Canned whole or sliced mushrooms
   (drained)
Red kidney beans (drained)

SEAFOOD PASTA SALAD

Makes: 2 servings
Groundwork: salad 2
  minutes
Cook: pasta 10 to 15
  minutes
Need: medium sauce
  pan, medium mixing
  bowl
Refrigerate: 30 minutes

Small seashell pasta
makes pretty seafood
salad.

---

1 (6½ oz.) can shrimp (drained)
1 (6½ oz.) can crab meat (drained)
**½ (10 oz. pkg.) frozen green peas
(thawed)**
4 oz. pasta (cooked, drained)

1. Cook pasta according to directions
   on package or see THE PASTA
   PUZZLE, (page 210).

2. While the pasta is cooking, drain the
   shrimp and crab, rinse under cold
   water, and drain thoroughly.

3. Combine the shrimp, crab and
   peas in a medium mixing bowl.

4. Add the pasta and dressing and
   toss gently to combine.

5. Cover and chill 30 minutes.

DRESSING:

1 Tablespoon oil
2 Tablespoons sour cream
½ teaspoon salt
⅛ teaspoon pepper
⅛ teaspoon garlic powder
⅛ teaspoon dill weed

Groundwork: 2 minutes
Need: small mixing
  bowl
  wire whisk

Thousand Island
dressing can also be
used.

---

1. Combine all the ingredients in a
   small mixing bowl and stir with a
   wire whisk until well mixed.

OPTIONS:

A. Replace the dill weed with basil,
   thyme, or oregano.

FRUIT SALADS

Add a light, bright touch

BANANA SPLIT SALAD

Makes: 2 servings
Groundwork: 2 minutes

Lettuce leaves
1 large ripe banana
1 Tablespoon mayonnaise
2 Tablespoons peanut butter
**1 Tablespoon chopped peanuts
(optional)**

1. Cut the banana in half and cut each half lengthwise into two slices.

2. Arrange the slices (cut-side up) on the lettuce leaves, spread each slice evenly with mayonnaise, and then peanut butter.

3. Top with chopped peanuts.

Fresh fruits and melon balls make light, refreshing salads. Top with the Fruit Salad Dressing or toss the fruit with purchased strawberry pie glaze.

FRUIT COOLER

Makes: 4 to 6 servings
Groundwork: 3 minutes
Refrigerate: 30 minutes
Need: medium mixing
  bowl

1 (17 oz.) can fruit cocktail (drained)
**1 (8 oz.) can crushed pineapple
(drained)**
1 (12 oz.) carton cottage cheese
1 cup whipped topping (thawed)
1 (4-serving size) fruit-flavored gelatin

1. Drain the fruit and combine with the cottage cheese and whipped topping in a medium mixing bowl.

2. Sprinkle the gelatin on top and stir to mix well.

3. Cover and refrigerate 30 minutes.

OPTION:

A. Add ⅓ cup chopped walnuts or pecans.

This salad will thicken slightly but cannot be molded like most gelatin salads.

EASY PEAR SALAD

Makes: 2 servings
Groundwork: 2 minutes

2 lettuce leaves
1 (8 oz.) can pear halves (chilled and drained)
4 heaping Tablespoons shredded Cheddar cheese
2 teaspoons mayonnaise
2 maraschino cherries

Usually six large pear halves are in a 16 oz. can and 4 small ones in an 8 oz. can. A 20 oz. can of pineapple slices contains 10 rings. The 8 oz. can contains 4 rings.

1. Drain the pears and place them (cut-side up) on the lettuce leaves.

2. Top with cheese and mayonnaise and garnish with the cherries.

OPTIONS:

    A. Replace the Cheddar with either cottage, cream, or blue cheese and omit the mayonnaise.

FANCY FILLINGS:
Fill the center of 2 pear halves with cream cheese, press the two together, stand them upright and garnish the top with a sprig of fresh parsley to make a stem.

    B. Add to or replace the pears with pineapple rings, peach, or apricot halves.

    C. Replace the mayonnaise with whipped topping for the peach or apricot salad.

FRUIT COCKTAIL SALAD

Makes: 2 servings
Groundwork: 2 minutes
Need: small mixing
  bowl

1 (17 oz.) can fruit cocktail (chilled and drained)
1 cup cottage cheese
¼ cup mayonnaise

1. Drain the fruit cocktail and combine all the ingredients in a small mixing bowl.

Remember to keep a couple cans of fruit in the refrigerator for quick salads.

OPTION:

    A. Add ¼ cup chopped pecans or walnuts.

WALDORF SALAD

Makes: 2 servings
Groundwork: 5 minutes
Need: medium mixing
 bowl

1 medium red apple (unpeeled)
1 rib celery
1 small carrot
¼ cup raisins
¼ cup walnuts or pecans (chopped)
¼ cup mayonnaise

1. Rinse the apple, celery, and carrot in cold water.

2. Cut the apple into quarters, remove the core and dice into bite-size pieces.

3. Remove the strings from the celery and dice into bite-size pieces.

4. Peel the carrot and either grate or dice it into bite-size pieces.

5. Combine all the ingredients in a medium mixing bowl and stir to mix well.

OPTION:

A. Add ¼ cup chopped dates or pineapple tidbits.

CONGEALED SALADS
A Kaleidoscope of Scrumptious Sculptures!

An amazing metamorphosis occurs when a congealed or fruit salad is served on a bed of crisp green lettuce and topped with a dollop of dressing and a colorful tidbit (cherry, strawberry, olive, mint sprig, capers).

Use empty cans for frozen or gelatin molds. To remove the salad, either cut the bottom of the can with a can opener and push it through, forcing the salad out, or dip the can in warm water, make a small hole in the bottom and the salad should slide out.

To turn any gelatin salad into a flavorful fantasy, simply unmold and frost the entire surface with either:
A. Sour cream dressing
B. Softened cream cheese
C. Whipped topping
D. Mixture of half whipped topping and half mayonnaise.

THE MOLDS

Here's where the fun begins! If it'll hold water, you can use it. Just make sure the opening is large enough to remove the salad once it's congealed and then let your imagination take over. A few old stand-bys are:
1. Square, oblong, or round cake or baking pans.
2. Mixing bowls or casseroles.
3. Small paper or plastic cups.
4. Small plastic butter tubs.

THE METHODS

1. The most common error is incorrectly dissolving the gelatin. For fruit flavored, sweetened gelatin (such as Jello), the **water must be boiling** and the mixture stirred until it is no longer grainy. But plain, unflavored gelatin **must be dissolved in cold water.**

2. Salads will unmold easier if the mold is lightly **greased** with oil, vegetable spray, or mayonnaise before pouring in the salad mixture.

3. To unmold, fill the sink with warm (not hot) water just below the top edge of the mold. Run the tip of a sharp knife around the edge and leave the mold in the water for a minute or two until the salad is loosened. Then, invert a plate on top of the mold, turn them over together, and remove the mold. If you are serving the congealed salad on lettuce, arrange the leaves on a separate plate, use a plate moistened with water to unmold the salad, and slide it onto the lettuce.

79

ASPIC

Makes: 4 servings
Groundwork: 8 minutes
Cook: 2 to 3 min. -
  MED HIGH
Refrigerate: 1½ hours
Need: small saucepan
  2 quart square
  baking dish

Serve on a lettuce leaf
and top with a dollop
of mayonnaise or
Horseradish Sauce
(SAUCES AND GRAVIES).

Garnish with fresh
parsley, olives, or
lemon slices.

---

2 cups V-8 juice, tomato juice, or
  tomato and clam juice
1 (4-serving size) pkg. lime or lemon
  gelatin
1 Tablespoon Worcestershire
6 drops Tabasco
⅛ teaspoon course-ground black
  pepper
⅛ teaspoon salt
2 ribs celery (finely chopped)
¼ cup stuffed green or pitted black
  olives (chopped)

1. Bring 1 cup of the juice to a boil in
    a small saucepan on MEDIUM HIGH.

2. Remove from the heat, add the
    gelatin, and stir to dissolve
    thoroughly.

3. Stir in the remaining juice,
    Worcestershire, Tabasco, salt and
    pepper.

4. Pour into a baking dish.

5. Refrigerate 1 hour or until the
    mixture is beginning to get firm.

6. While the aspic is chilling, wash the
    celery, remove the strings, and finely
    chop both the celery and olives.

7. When the mixture is beginning to get
    firm, gently stir in the celery and
    olives.

8. Return the aspic to the refrigerator
    for an additional ½ hour or until it is
    totally firm.

BRIDESMAID'S SALAD

Makes: 4 to 6 servings
Groundwork: 5 minutes
Refrigerate: 1 hour
Need: medium mixing
  bowl
  3 cup mold

Don't use fresh or
frozen pineapple. . .it
causes congealed
salads to break down.

**1 (3 oz.) pkg. cream cheese (room
  temperature)**
1 (4-serving size) pkg. lime gelatin
½ cup boiling water
½ cup cold water
**1 (8 oz.) can crushed pineapple
  (drained)**
½ cup chopped pecans (optional)

1. Combine the cream cheese and
   gelatin in a medium mixing bowl
   and stir until the mixture is smooth.

2. Add the boiling water and stir until
   completely mixed. Add the cold
   water and stir.

3. Drain the pineapple, add to the
   gelatin mixture, along with the
   pecans, and stir to blend.

4. Pour the mixture into the mold and
   chill 1 hour or until firm.

STRAWBERRY-BANANA SALAD

Makes: 6 servings
Groundwork: 5 minutes
Refrigerate: 1 hour
Need: small mixing
  bowl
  medium mixing bowl
  5-cup mold

Forget to thaw the
strawberries? Just add
them to the dissolved
hot gelatin and stir
until they thaw.

**1 (4-serving size) pkg. strawberry-
  banana gelatin**
1 cup boiling water
1 large ripe banana (mashed)
1 cup sour cream
**1 (10 oz.) pkg. frozen strawberries
  (thawed)**
½ cup chopped pecans (optional)

1. Combine the gelatin and boiling
   water in a medium mixing bowl and
   stir until it is completely dissolved.

2. Mash the banana well in a small
   mixing bowl.

3. Add all the other ingredients and stir
   until well blended.

4. Pour into a mold and refrigerate 1
   hour or until firm.

CHRISTMAS CRANBERRY CONSERVE

Makes: 12 servings
Groundwork: 12
  minutes
Refrigerate: 2 hrs. plus
  2 hrs.
Need: large mixing
  bowl
  2 quart mold

Garnish with dollops of
mayonnaise.

---

1 (8-serving size) raspberry gelatin
3 cups boiling water
1 (16 oz.) can whole-berry cranberry
  sauce
1 (5½ oz.) can crushed pineapple
  (drained)
1 cup celery (diced)
1 cup pecans (chopped)

1. Combine the gelatin and boiling water in a large mixing bowl and stir until the gelatin is completely dissolved.

2. Refrigerate the gelatin until it is beginning to get firm (about 2 hours). DO NOT LET THIS GET COMPLETELY FIRM!

3. Add the cranberry sauce to the gelatin, and stir until completely combined with the gelatin.

4. Wash the celery in cold water, remove the strings, and dice finely.

5. Chop the pecans, drain the pineapple, and add to the cranberry mixture, stirring until it is very well blended.

6. Pour into the mold and refrigerate until firm.

ENTREÉ SALADS
Make Magnificent Meals

CRAB LOUIS

Makes: 1 serving
Groundwork: 6 minutes
Need: 2 small mixing
　　　bowls

1 (6 oz.) can crab meat (chilled)
1½ teaspoons lemon juice
1 Tablespoon onion (finely chopped)
1 Tablespoon celery (finely chopped)
Lettuce leaves

DRESSING:

¼ cup French or Russian dressing
2 Tablespoons mayonnaise
2 teaspoons horseradish

For a real show stopper, serve these salads in incredible edibles: Tomato Petals, Avocado, Melon or Pineapple halves, citrus shells or a bed of lettuce.

TOMATO PETALS:
Simply wash the tomato, remove the stem, and cut into 8 wedges without cutting all the way through at the bottom.

1. Drain and rinse the crab meat in cold water, pat dry with a paper towel, and place it in a small mixing bowl.

2. Add the lemon juice.

3. Finely chop the celery and onions and add to the crab meat.

4. In a separate small mixing bowl, combine the dressing, mayonnaise, and horseradish and mix well.

5. Add ½ of the dressing mixture to the crab mixture and stir.

6. Place the crab mixture on the lettuce leaves and top with the remaining dressing.

OPTIONS:

A. Replace the crab with 1 (6 oz.) can shrimp or 6 to 8 oz. frozen lobster.

B. Omit the onion and celery and arrange the crab, shrimp, or lobster on a bed of bite-size pieces of lettuce, add hard-cooked egg slices, purple onion rings, 2 to 3 ripe olives, and top with the dressing.

HARVEST MOON SALAD
(For Tuna, Chicken, Turkey, Ham)

FOUNDATION RECIPE

Makes: 2 servings
Groundwork: 5 minutes
Need: medium mixing
  bowl

**1 (5 to 7 oz.) can tuna, chicken, turkey,
Spam or ham (drained) OR
1 to 2 cups cooked, diced chicken,
turkey, or ham
1 small apple (unpeeled)
1 rib celery
¼ cup mayonnaise**

1. Drain and flake the meat (or dice it if you are using left-overs or fresh cooked).

2. Wash the apple and celery and cut them into small pieces.

3. Combine all the ingredients.

4. Add one of the OPTIONS listed below.

5. Mix well and chill before serving.

OPTIONS:

Add to the Foundation Recipe:

  A. TUNA
     2 rounded Tablespoons
      chopped sweet pickles

  B. CHICKEN OR TURKEY
     1. 2 rounded Tablespoons
        chopped sweet pickles
        AND/OR ¼ cup chopped
        pecans
     2. ½ cup seedless grapes (cut
        into halves)
        ¼ cup almonds (toasted,
        sliced, or slivered)

  C. HAM:
     1. 2 Tablespoons chopped
        sweet pickles
        2 teaspoons horseradish

Tuna packed in oil can be reduced in calories and salt (sodium) by pouring it in a colander or strainer, rinsing it in cold water, and draining it thoroughly on paper towels.

Tuna, Chicken, Turkey, and Ham salads for Sandwiches are in The Sandwich Board.

SALAD SPEED UPS:
Store canned meats and seafoods in the refrigerator (except for tuna in oil) along with hard-cooked eggs for emergency meals.

SHRIMP SALAD

Makes: 2 servings
Groundwork: 10 minutes
Need: medium mixing
bowl

1 (12 oz.) pkg. frozen shrimp (pre-cooked and shelled) OR
½ pound fresh shrimp (cooked, shelled)
2 hard-cooked eggs
2 ribs fresh celery (do not use dried flakes)
½ cup mayonnaise
¼ teaspoon salt
⅛ teaspoon pepper
⅛ teaspoon paprika
⅛ teaspoon garlic powder (optional)
dash lemon juice
2 lettuce leaves

Garnish with dollop of
mayonnaise and
sprinkle with paprika
or fresh parsley.

1. Defrost the frozen shrimp according to the directions on the package, drain well, and pat dry with paper towels. Or, if using the larger, fresh shrimp, remove the shells and cut them into halves.

2. Peel the eggs and chop finely into a medium mixing bowl.

3. Wash the celery, remove the strings, and dice finely.

4. Combine all the ingredients and mix lightly.

5. Mound onto the lettuce leaves.

OPTIONS:

   A. Add 1 Tablespoon finely chopped sweet or dill pickles.

   B. **LOBSTER SALAD**
     Replace the shrimp with frozen lobster (diced)

   C. **SALMON SALAD**
     Replace the shrimp with:
     1 (6½ oz.) can salmon (drained); add
     1 Tablespoon finely chopped onions

TOSSED TACO SALAD

Makes: 2 servings
Groundwork: 5 minutes
Cook: 5 min. - MEDIUM
10-15 min. - LOW
Need: medium skillet
medium mixing bowl
1 large salad bowl

½ **pound ground beef**
½ **pkg. Taco seasoning mix**
½ **cup water**
½ **medium head lettuce**
¼ **cup ripe olives (sliced)**
½ **cup shredded sharp Cheddar
   cheese**
1 **small tomato**
1 **small onion OR 4 green onions**
1 **(8 to 11 oz.) pkg. corn or nacho chips**
½ **cup sour cream**
Bottled or canned taco sauce

For a less spicy taco
salad, omit the taco
seasoning mix or
substitute ½ pkg. dried
onion soup mix when
cooking the meat.

Layered Taco Salad
Heat 1 (9 oz.) can
bean dip in a small
saucepan while the
meat is cooking and
(rather than tossing the
salad) layer it in the
salad bowl:
chips, meat, beans,
onions, tomato,
cheese, lettuce, olives,
sauce and sour
cream.

1. Brown the meat in a medium skillet
   on MEDIUM and drain.

2. Add the taco seasoning and water
   and stir well.

3. Simmer (uncovered) 10 to 15 minutes
   or until the water is absorbed,
   stirring frequently.

4. While the meat is cooking, tear the
   lettuce into bite-size pieces, cut the
   tomato into small pieces, peel and
   slice the onions into slices (or cut the
   green onions into pieces, tops and
   all).

5. Line the salad bowl with ½ of the
   chips.

6. Toss the lettuce, olives, cheese,
   tomato, onions, and meat mixture in
   the medium mixing bowl.

7. Pour the tossed salad onto the chips
   in the salad bowl and top with the
   remaining chips.

8. Top the individual servings with the
   sour cream and taco sauce.

OPTION:

   A. Add with the other vegetables ½
      medium avocado, cubed.

SALAD DRESSINGS

BLUE CHEESE DRESSING

Makes: 2¾ cups
Groundwork: 5 minutes
Need: small mixing
  bowl OR blender

Store all dressings
refrigerated in an air-
tight container.

If you like dressing
"Chunky," mix all the
ingredients except the
cheese. Crumble it
into the mixture last,
and stir only until well
distributed through the
dressing.

¾ cup mayonnaise
1 cup sour cream
1 (4 oz.) pkg. blue cheese (crumbled)
½ teaspoon garlic powder
1 teaspoon instant minced onions
1 teaspoon celery flakes
¼ teaspoon coarse-ground black
  pepper
1 teaspoon parsley flakes
1 Tablespoon Worcestershire
1 Tablespoon lemon juice

1. Combine the ingredients either in a
    small mixing bowl or blender and
    mix until the dressing is smooth.

LIGHT BLENDER
BLUE CHEESE DRESSING

Makes: 1 cup
Groundwork: 3 minutes
Need: blender

1 cup cottage cheese
¼ cup milk
⅛ teaspoon garlic powder
⅛ teaspoon pepper
1 oz. blue cheese

1. Combine the cottage cheese, milk,
    garlic powder, and pepper in the
    blender and process on HIGH 15
    seconds until smooth.

2. Add the blue cheese and process
    on LOW for a few seconds until the
    cheese is broken into small bits.

CAESAR SALAD DRESSING

Makes: 1½ cups
Groundwork: 3 minutes
Need: 1 pint jar and
  lid

1 egg
½ cup oil
¼ cup lemon juice
1 teaspoon Worcestershire
½ cup Parmesan cheese
½ teaspoon salt
½ teaspoon pepper
⅛ teaspoon garlic powder
½ teaspoon anchovy paste (optional)

Try this one on spinach
salad as well.

1. Pour the ingredients into a jar with a
    lid and shake well to mix.

GREEK SALAD DRESSING

Groundwork: 5 minutes
Refrigerate: 2 hours
Need: 1 pint jar with
  lid

½ cup light olive oil
¾ teaspoon oregano
¼ teaspoon garlic powder
½ teaspoon sage
⅛ teaspoon onion powder
¼ teaspoon coriander
¼ cup wine vinegar
¼ teaspoon coarse-ground black
  pepper
½ teaspoon beef bouillon granules
¼ teaspoon marjoram
¼ teaspoon thyme

This dressing will keep
indefinitely in the
refrigerator when
stored in an airtight jar
or container.

1. Combine all the ingredients in a jar
    with a lid and shake until well
    blended.

CREAMY RUSSIAN DRESSING

Makes: ¾ cup
Groundwork: 2 minutes
Need: small mixing
  bowl

½ cup mayonnaise
¼ cup catsup or chili sauce

1. Combine the ingredients in a small
    mixing bowl with a wire whisk.

FRUIT DRESSING OR DIP

Makes: ½ cup
Groundwork: 3 minutes
Need: small mixing
  bowl

A light delight with bite-sized pieces of apples, bananas, berries, cherries (with stems), seedless grapes or strawberries.

The sauce for Strawberies Romanov (The Classics) also makes a superb fruit dip.

Makes: 1 cup
Groundwork: 1 minute
Need: 8 oz. jar with lid

¼ cup mayonnaise
¼ cup sour cream
1 to 1½ Tablespoons sugar

1. Combine the ingredients in a small mixing bowl with a wire whisk.

OPTIONS:

  A. Replace the sour cream with ⅓ cup milk.

  B. Add either 2 teaspoons poppy seeds OR 1 teaspoon dried orange peel.

VINEGAR AND OIL DRESSING

⅔ cup oil (vegetable or olive, or a combination of both)
⅓ cup vinegar
½ teaspoon salt
⅛ teaspoon pepper

1. Combine all ingredients in a jar with a lid and shake well.

OPTIONS:

  A. Herb - Add ⅛ teaspoon each garlic powder, parsley flakes, and dill weed or chives.

  B. Dijon - Add 1½ teaspoons Dijon mustard.

  C. Onion - Add ¼ cup finely sliced green onions or 1½ Tablespoons instant minced onions.

  D. Add 1 (6 oz.) can shrimp (drained) to this dressing (or 1 cup of bottled Vinegar and Oil Dressing) and refrigerate.

THE SANDWICH BOARD

Dagwood has the right idea! The secret to any successful sandwich is creativity. "Anything goes" if you can fit it between two slabs of bread, in the pocket of a pita, or stuff it in a bun, roll or croissant.

Lunch Box Lifesavers!

A. To avoid early morning madness, make several day's supply of sandwiches (spread with butter, not mayonnaise), and refrigerate or freeze in air-tight containers.

B. Fill several day's supply of bags with non-perishables (napkins, plastic spoons, cookies, chips).

C. Carry mayonnaise and any crisp or juicy vegetables in separate containers.

D. Freeze a foil-covered canned drink, wrap it in two layers of paper towels and use it as a cold pack for your lunch box. It will be ready to drink by lunch time.

EGG SALAD SANDWICH

Makes: 2 sandwiches
Groundwork: 3 minutes
Need: small mixing
  bowl

2 hard-cooked eggs
1 teaspoon mustard
⅛ teaspoon pepper
2 Tablespoons mayonnaise
¼ teaspoon salt
½ teaspoon parsley flakes (optional)

Do not freeze sandwiches or fillings that contain mayonnaise, egg whites, or soft cheese.

1. Peel and mash or chop the eggs in a small mixing bowl.

2. Add the other ingredients and stir to combine.

PIMIENTO CHEESE SANDWICH SPREAD

Makes: 1¼ cups
Groundwork: 5 minutes
Need: small mixing
  bowl

Add 1 Tablespoon of sweet salad pickles or diced jalapeño peppers!

1 cup (4 oz. pkg.) shredded sharp Cheddar cheese
2 Tablespoons chopped pimiento
¼ cup mayonnaise
⅛ teaspoon salt
½ teaspoon lemon juice
⅛ teaspoon Tabasco

1. Combine the ingredients in a small mixing bowl and mix well.

MEAT SALAD FOR SANDWICHES
(Tuna, Chicken, Turkey, Ham, Deviled Ham, Spam)

FOUNDATION RECIPE

Makes: 2 servings
Groundwork: 3 minutes
Need: small mixing
   bowl

**1 (6½ oz.) can tuna, or the equivalent
   size can of chicken, turkey, ham,
   deviled ham or Spam
1 hard-cooked egg
1 rib celery
¼ cup mayonnaise
⅛ teaspoon salt
⅛ teaspoon pepper**

Avoid last minute
hassles by keeping
hard-cooked eggs
(dated on the shell) on
hand in the
refrigerator.

If you don't have time
to wait for an egg to
boil, a scrambled egg
makes a good
substitution in meat
salads!

1.   Drain and flake the meat (or dice it
     if you are using leftovers).

2.   Wash the celery, remove the strings,
     and chop finely.

3.   Peel or chop or mash the egg.

4.   Combine all the ingredients in a
     small mixing bowl.

OPTIONS:

Add:

TUNA: A. 2 Tablespoons dill pickles
           (chopped)
       B. 2 teaspoons capers
       C. Omit the salt and add: 2 to 3
           anchovies (chopped)
       D. Omit the pickles and add:
           ¼ cup fresh cucumber (finely
           chopped)
           1 Tablespoon fresh onion
           (finely chopped)

HAM   A. ½ teaspoon horseradish
OR   B. ½ teaspoon Dijon mustard
SPAM   C. 2 Tablespoons black olives
           (chopped)
       D. 2 Tablespoons dill pickles
           (chopped)
       E. 1½ Tablespoons parsley
           flakes

PINEAPPLE SANDWICH SPREAD

Makes: 1¾ cups
Groundwork: 2 minutes
Need: small mixing
 bowl

2 Tablespoons mayonnaise
1 (8 oz.) pkg. cream cheese (room temp.)
1 (5½ oz.) can crushed pineapple (drained)
¼ cup finely chopped pecans or celery (optional)

1. Combine the mayonnaise and cream cheese in a small mixing bowl and stir until smooth.

2. Drain the pineapple well and combine with the cream cheese, pecans or celery.

For a party, form into a ball and roll in chopped nuts, cherries, or parsley flakes and serve with crackers or make individual sandwiches on date nut bread.

Makes: 1 sandwich
Groundwork: 4 minutes

HOAGIE

1 small Kaiser, French, or Italian roll or sub bun (split)
2 teaspoons butter
1 lettuce leaf
2 onion slices
2 bell pepper slices (optional)
1 tomato slice
1 slice Swiss cheese
1 slice salami
1 slice boiled or baked ham
salt & pepper to taste
2 Tablespoons Creamy Italian Dressing

About 20 slices are in a 1 pound loaf of bread and 34 in a sandwich loaf.

1. Split the bun and spread both of the cut-sides with butter.

2. Wash the lettuce; wash and slice the tomato, pepper, and onion.

3. Layer the cheese, meats, or vegetables on the bottom half of the bun in the order listed above.

4. Sprinkle with salt and pepper, drizzle the salad dressing evenly over the top layer, and top with the remaining half of the bun.

CLUB SANDWICH

Makes: 1 sandwich
Groundwork: 2 minutes
Cook: 5 to 7 minutes
Need: medium skillet
   4 toothpicks

3 strips of bacon
2 lettuce leaves
4 slices fresh tomato
3 pieces of bread
2 Tablespoons mayonnaise
1 slice Swiss cheese
1 slice cooked turkey
salt and pepper

Add a stuffed olive to the toothpicks for a fancy touch.

Funwiches:
Cookie cutters transform sandwiches into characters! Try a turkey, pumpkin, heart, or bunny for the holidays. Club, diamond, or spade for the bridge bunch; or spread a triple decker and cut it into animal shapes for the little ones. Some of these will even stand upright!

1. Fry the bacon until crisp and drain on a paper towel.

2. While the bacon is frying, wash the lettuce, slice the tomato, and toast the 3 slices of bread.

3. Spread mayonnaise on one side of one slice of bread.

4. Top with the bacon, cheese, and ½ of the lettuce and tomato.

5. Spread mayonnaise on **both** sides of one slice and place it on top of the cheese layer.

6. Top this slice with the turkey, lettuce, and tomato and sprinkle with the salt and pepper.

7. Spread one side of the remaining slice of bread with mayonnaise and pop it on top to make a double decker.

8. Cut the sandwich into four triangles and spear each one with a toothpick to hold it together.

OPTIONS:

   A. Add peeled avocado slices to the top deck.

   B. Chicken Club: replace the turkey with a cooked, breaded chicken patty.

HAMBURGER PATTY WAGON

The Russian Tartars began it all with seasoned, ground beef back in the Middle Ages — but they didn't bother cooking it. The Germans decided to cook it, the English plopped it between two slabs of bread, but it was the good old U.S. of A. that baked the buns that perfected the masterpiece.

The inexpensive, hardy hamburger is quick and easy to fix:

HOW TO PAT YOUR PATTY

One pound of ground meat will make four ½ inch thick (¼ pound) patties or six ¼ inch patties.

One long piece of waxed paper will save 10 minutes of clean up. Simply divide the meat into four equal parts on the waxed paper and pack each into a patty, compressing the edges firmly to retain the shap. Make the patties ½ inch thick for Rare or Medium and ¼ inch thick for Well-Done. Add any desired seasonings (salt, pepper, garlic powder, Worchestersire).

Out of buns? Reshape your patties to fit small dinner rolls and serve a platter full.

HOW TO FREEZE YOUR PATTY

Make the patties before freezing. Stack them between **two** squares of waxed paper or foil, and wrap them in an airtight package or container.

HOW NOT TO BURN YOUR BURGER

There are several ways to cook burgers. For Pan frying, Pan broiling, Broiling or Baking, see The Meat of the Matter (DINNER). For Grilling, see The Patio Chef.

When broiling or baking, top the patty with a strip of uncooked bacon for a juicy, smokey burger.

Basting sauces are in SAUCES AND GRAVIES.

HAMBURGER TIME TABLE			
(¼" Thick Patties)			
METHOD	**RARE***	**MEDIUM**	**WELL**
Broil, Pan Broil Pan Fry	2½-3 min. each side	3-4 min. each side	5-8 min. each side
Bake	20 min. total	30 min. total	45 min. total

WARNING: Undercooked ground beef can harbor bacteria.

TOPPERS FOR A BETTER BURGER

Bacon Cheeseburgers: Cooked bacon, sliced cheese (American, Colby, Cheddar, Muenster), lettuce, tomato slices (try this on English muffins).

Mushroom Swissburger: Sliced sautéed mushrooms, sliced Swiss cheese (pita bread is a perfect partner).

California Burger: Cooked bacon, guacamole or avocado slices, sliced Colby or Brick cheese, sliced red onions (omit the bun and serve on spinach leaves).

Viking Burger: Sliced Swiss cheese, sliced cucumbers, dill weed, sliced red onion (serve on dark rye or pumpernickle bread).

Pizzaburger: Warm pizza sauce, shredded mozzarella cheese, chopped green or black olives, chopped onions (serve on a toasted bun).

Taco Burger: Taco sauce, shredded Cheddar cheese, sour cream, chopped tomato, shredded lettuce, sliced black olives, (serve on a warm tortilla).

Left Bankburger: Crumbled blue cheese, sliced sautéed mushrooms, (great on French bread slices).

PHABULOUS PHRANKPHURTERS

A hot dog by any other name — frankfurter, weiner or sausage — is still an all American favorite.

Born at the 1904 World's Fair in St. Louis, Missouri, the lowly hot dog fast became an American tradition. It's easy on the wallet, easy to embellish, and easy to fix:

HOW TO PHIX YOUR PHRANKS

There are several ways to cook hotdogs. For Simmering, Broiling, Pan frying and Steaming (using beer instead of water, see the Meat of the Matter (DINNER). For Grilling, see The Patio Chef.

HOW TO EMBELLISH YOUR BUNS

The buns can be served at room temperature, toasted, or heated (THE BREAD BASKET).

Add the hot dogs to the bun and top with your choice:

A. **Stadium Dog:** Mustard, catsup, chopped onion, sauerkraut.

B. **Chili Dog:** Mayonnaise, and/or mustard, chili, chopped onions, shredded Cheddar cheese and/or finely diced tossed salad.

C. **Coney Island:** Mustard, hot dog relish, dill pickle slices, chopped onions, chopped tomatoes, 1 hot pepper per dog.

HOT DOG CHILI

Makes: 4 servings
Groundwork: 5 minutes
Cook: 15 to 20 minutes
 - LOW
Need: small sauce
 pan

ROVERS: For a hot lunch at work, simply place a hot dog in a thermos, fill it with boiling water, and seal the lid. Carry the bun and embellishments in plastic bags. The dog will cook right in the thermos.

½ pound ground beef
1 Tablespoon water
1½ Tablespoons catsup
¼ teaspoon salt
1 Tablespoon chili powder

1. Crumble the beef into a small saucepan on MEDIUM.

2. Add the water and stir occasionally until the meat is finely crumbled and no pink remains.

3. Add the catsup, chili powder, salt and stir well.

4. Cover, reduce the heat to LOW, and cook 15 to 20 minutes.

BACON CHEESE WRAPS

Makes: 1
Groundwork: 2 minutes
Broil: 2 to 3 minutes
Oven Temp: BROIL
Need: 2 toothpicks
broiler pan

1 hot dog
1 slice cheese (American, Cheddar,
   Velveeta, Monterey Jack)
1 slice bacon
2 toothpicks

1. Preheat the oven to BROIL.

2. Make a deep lengthwise slit in the hot dog almost to each end.

3. Cut the cheese into strips and insert them in the slit.

4. Wrap the bacon strip around the hot dog and fasten both ends with toothpicks.

5. Place the dog on the broiler pan, cheese-side down, and broil 2 to 3 minutes until the bacon is brown.

6. Turn the dogs cheese side-up, repeat.

PIGS IN A POKE

Makes: 6 pigs
Groundwork: 3 minutes
Bake: 8 to 10 minutes
Oven Temp: 350°
Need: cookie sheet

If your can has 6 instead of 5 sausages, just canabilize a bit of dough from each biscuit and press together to make an extra biscuit..

These can be served as-is or with one or more dipping sauces: plain or hot and spicy mustard
catsup
barbecue sauce

1 (5 count) pkg. refrigerator biscuits
½ teaspoon mustard
1 (5½ oz.) can Vienna sausage

1. Preheat the oven to 350°.

2. Lightly grease a cookie sheet.

3. Separate the biscuits and stretch each one slightly to make a rectangle.

4. Spread each with mustard and top with a sausage.

5. Wrap the biscuit around each sausage and pinch the dough together to seal it.

6. Place each one (seam-side down) on the cookie sheet.

7. Bake 8 to 10 minutes until the biscuits are crisp and brown.

HOT CHICKEN AND ASPARAGUS

Makes: 2 servings
Groundwork: 5 minutes
Cook: 5 min. - MEDIUM
Need: medium
  saucepan
  small saucepan

1 (5 oz.) can boned chicken (drained)
1 (10¾ oz.) can cream of chicken soup
⅓ cup milk
1 cup (4 oz.) pkg. shredded Cheddar cheese
⅛ teaspoon salt
⅛ teaspoon cayenne pepper
1 (14½ oz.) can asparagus spears (drained)
4 slices bread (toasted)

1. Drain the chicken and combine with the soup, milk, cheese, salt, and pepper in a medium saucepan on MEDIUM. Stir frequently until the cheese has melted and the mixture is very hot but not boiling.

2. Heat the asparagus in a small saucepan on MEDIUM until thoroughly heated and drain well.

3. Toast the bread and top each slice with equal amounts of asparagus and sauce.

REUBEN SANDWICH

Makes: 1 sandwich
Groundwork: 3 minutes
Cook: 3 to 5 minutes -
  MED.
Need: medium skillet

2 slices rye bread
1 Tablespoon Thousand Island dressing or spicy mustard
3 oz. thinly sliced deli corned beef
1 slice Swiss cheese
¼ cup sauerkraut (drained)
1 Tablespoon butter

1. Spread one side of each piece of bread with the dressing.

2. Layer the corned beef, cheese, and sauerkraut on one slice, and top with the other slice.

3. Spread the outside of both sides with butter.

4. Grill both sides in a medium skillet on MEDIUM until light brown and the cheese is melted.

CRAB OR TUNA MELT

Makes: 2
Groundwork: 2 minutes
Bake: 10 minutes
Oven Temp: Broil &
 350°
Need: small mixing
 bowl
cookie sheet

**1 (5 oz.) can crab or (6½ oz.) tuna
 (drained)**
¼ cup mayonnaise
2 Tablespoons celery (finely diced)
1 Tablespoon instant minced onions
1 teaspoon lemon juice
**2 slices Cheddar or Monterey Jack
 cheese**
1 English muffin (split and toasted)

1. Preheat the oven to BROIL.

2. Split and toast the muffin and then
   preheat the oven to 350°.

3. Drain the crab (or tuna) and
   combine with the mayonnaise,
   celery, and onion in a small mixing
   bowl; stir well.

4. Divide the crab mixture between the
   muffins and bake 5 minutes.

5. Top each muffin with one slice of
   cheese and bake 5 additional
   minutes until the cheese has melted
   and is light brown.

Tuna Cheeseburgers:
Dice the cheese,
combine the
ingredients and
spread evenly on 3
buttered hamburger
buns. Wrap tightly in
foil and bake (350°) for
15 minutes.

GRILLED CHEESE

Makes: 1
Groundwork: 2 minutes
Cook: 5 min. MEDIUM
Need: skillet or griddle

2 slices bread
1 Tablespoon mayonnaise
1 slice cheese
1 Tablespoon butter
salt & pepper (optional)

1. Heat a skillet or griddle on MEDIUM
   until a drop of water dances on the
   surface.

2. Spread mayonnaise on 1 side of
   both pieces of bread.

3. Arrange the cheese on the bread so
   it does not hang over the edges;
   sprinkle with salt and pepper and
   top with the remaining bread slice.

For Variety try topping the cheese before grilling with any one or combination of the following:

Cooked crisp bacon
Cooked, sliced ham, turkey, chicken, Canadian bacon
Ham, turkey, or chicken salad
Dill pickle slices
Sliced salami or pepperoni
Sliced, fresh tomatoes
Sliced onion or bell pepper rings
Alfalfa sprouts
Herbs (basil, oregano, dill weed)

Makes: 2 servings
Groundwork: 3 minutes
Cook: 5 min. - MED. HIGH
Need: small skillet

The creamed beef can also be served over hot baked potatoes, cooked rice, biscuits, toast cups, waffles or broiled tomato slices.

---

4. Spread ½ of the butter on top of the bread, and place it buttered-side down in the skillet.

5. Spread the remaining butter on top of the bread and cook until the bottom slice is brown.

6. Turn with a spatula and continue cooking until the second side is brown and the cheese is melted.

Recommended Cheeses: American, Cheddar, Swiss, Velveeta, Cheese Whiz, Mozzarella, Gouda, Edam, Muenster, Monterey Jack, Provolone.

Not Recommended: Any blue-veined cheese (such as Roquefort), Parmesan, Feta, or any very soft cheese (such as Brie).

S.O.S. (Creamed Dried Beef)

2 Tablespoons butter
1 (2½ oz.) jar dried beef)
2 Tablespoons flour
1 cup milk
4 slices bread (toasted)

1. Melt the butter in small skillet on MEDIUM HIGH.

2. Shred the dried beef into bite-size pieces, add to the melted butter and cook until it is a rich brown.

3. Add the flour and stir until it is completely absorbed into the butter.

4. Add the milk and stir well.

5. Continue cooking until the sauce is hot and thickened.

6. Toast the bread and spoon the beef and sauce equally over the toast.

HERCULES

Makes: 2 sandwiches
Groundwork: 5 minutes
Broil: 3 to 5 minutes
Need: medium mixing
  bowl
cookie sheet

1 (6¾ oz.) can chunky ham
¼ cup mayonnaise
¼ cup sour cream
2 Tablespoons instant minced onions
2 Tablespoons parsley flakes
¼ teaspoon garlic powder
¼ teaspoon pepper
2 small Kaiser, French, or Italian rolls or sub buns (split)
3 oz. Swiss or Cheddar cheese (shredded)
4 bell pepper slices
4 ripe olives

1. Flake the ham into a medium bowl and add the mayonnaise, sour cream, onion, parsley and spices.

2. Stir to mix well.

3. Split the buns and cover all four split sides with the ham mixture.

4. Divide the cheese evenly over the four halves and top each with a bell pepper slice and olive.

5. Broil on a cookie sheet 3 to 5 minutes until the cheese is melted and begins to bubble.

6. Serve as a hot open-faced sandwich.

SUPER SUB

Makes: 1 sandwich
Groundwork: 3 minutes
Bake: 5 to 10 minutes
Oven Temp: 350°
Need: Cookie sheet

**1 small Kaiser, French, or Italian roll or
  sub bun (split)**
1 Tablespoon mayonnaise
**1 teaspoon mustard (hot, brown, spicy
  or regular)**
1 slice of American cheese
1 slice Swiss or Provolone cheese
salt & pepper to taste
**1 slice each (or choice of several) of
  the following:**

Cotto salami	**Hard salami**
Bologna	**Luncheon loaf**
Boiled ham	**Olive pimiento loaf**
Salami for beer	**Honey loaf**
Liverwurst	**Summer sausage**
Knockwurst	

This transports well
when wrapped in
aluminum foil to keep
warm and makes a
man-sized work-day or
before-the-game
lunch.

For a crowd of four or
more, use a large loaf
of French or Italian
bread, increase all the
ingredients propor-
tionately, and slice
into individual
servings.

1. Preheat the oven to 350°.

2. Split the bun lengthwise and spread
   with mayonnaise and mustard.

3. Cut the meats and cheeses to fit the
   shape of your roll if necessary.

4. Layer the meats on the bottom half
   of the roll and top the layers with
   one slice of cheese.

5. Place the other slice of cheese on
   the cut-side of the top half of the
   roll.

6. Sprinkle with salt and pepper.

7. Place both halves (open face) on a
   cookie sheet and bake at 350° for 5
   to 10 minutes until the meats are
   warmed and the cheese melts and
   becomes bubbly.

8. Put the two sides together and serve
   hot.

THE ADDED TOUCHES

To add Pizzaz to your soup, salad, or
sandwich lunch!

STUFFED CELERY

Groundwork: 5 minutes
Need: small mixing
  bowl

A "rib" of celery is one
individual piece — the
whole "bunch" is
called a "stalk."

Unstuffed celery can
be stored for several
days by covering it
with cold water and
refrigerating.

GARNISHES: Top with
one of the following:

Caviar
Chives
Olive slices (stuffed or
black)
Paprika
Pimiento strips

Celery
Stuffing

1. Rinse the celery ribs individually in
cold water.

2. Remove the leaves and trim off the
stem end. Remove all strings with a
vegetable peeler or sharp knife.

3. Cut the ribs into desired lengths.

4. Combine the stuffing ingredients in a
small mixing bowl and fill the center
of each rib with your choice of
stuffing:

QUICKIE CHEESE (no bowl needed)

**1 (5 oz.) jar cheese spread (Old
English, Bacon, Olive-Pimiento)**

CREAM CHEESE

**1 (3 oz.) pkg. cream cheese (room
temp.)**
⅛ teaspoon garlic powder
½ teaspoon instant minced onions
½ teaspoon salt

OPTIONS:

A. Add 2 mashed anchovies and 1
teaspoon anchovy oil to cream
cheese stuffing and omit the salt.

PIMIENTO CHEESE

**1 (8 oz.) carton pimiento cheese
spread**
1 Tablespoon lemon juice
½ teaspoon salt
⅛ teaspoon Tabasco

103

DEVILED EGGS

Makes: 4 halves
Groundwork: 5 minutes
Need: small mixing
bowl

2 hard-cooked eggs
2 teaspoons mayonnaise
½ teaspoon mustard
¼ teaspoon salt
⅛ teaspoon pepper

1. Peel the eggs and cut them in half lengthwise.

2. Carefully remove the yolks and mash with a fork until smooth.

3. Add the mayonnaise, mustard, salt, (and selected option, if desired) and mix well.

4. Mound equal amounts of the mixture into the egg whites.

REMEMBER:
Very fresh eggs are almost impossible to peel when hard-cooked! Week-old eggs work well.

Deviled eggs can be served or transported easily by placing each one in a mufffin paper.

Deviled eggs look more attractive and are easier to work with if the yolk is in the exact center of the white. To make this happen, simply stir the eggs frequently during the cooking process.

Garnish With:
Paprika, parsley flakes, pimiento strips, cooked asparagus tips, caviar.

OPTIONS:

A. Select one or more:
    1 teaspoon finely diced sweet or dill pickles
    4 drops Tabasco or lemon juice
    ⅛ teaspoon celery or caraway seeds
    1 tablespoon finely chopped celery

CROWD PLEASER EGGS:

1. For 6 hard-cooked eggs, replace the ingredients for Deviled Eggs with your choice:

A. **Double Deviled:**
    1 (2¼ oz.) can deviled ham
    1½ teaspoons sour cream
    ½ teaspoon mustard
    1 teaspoon instant minced onions
    2 Tablespoons pickle relish, sweet or dill pickle cubes

B. **Simple Seafoods:**
    1 (5 to 6 oz.) can tuna, boneless salmon, or chicken (drained)
    ⅓ cup mayonnaise
    1 Tablespoon mustard

FANCY SHAPES FOR VEGGIES

SCORED CUCUMBER SLICES

1. Wash a cucumber in cold water and peel if it is waxed.

2. Press the prongs of a fork into one end and pull the fork down to the other end, making long grooves. Repeat until the entire cucumber is grooved all the way.

3. Slice into thin rounds.

RADISH ROSES

Refrigerate: At least 1 hour
Need: deep mixing bowl

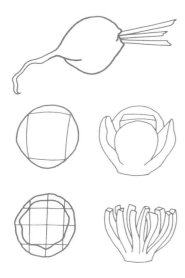

1. Wash the radish in cold water and remove the root and stem end.

2. Make rose petals by EITHER:

   A. Cutting a THIN slice of peeling on four sides from the top of the radish down almost to the stem end.

   B. Cutting THIN, parallel slices the entire width of the radish almost down to the stem end.

   C. Following method "B", turn the radish to a right angle and repeat the cuts.

3. In a mixing bowl, cover the roses with cold water, add a few ice cubes, and refrigerate one hour until they blossom.

CARROT CURLS

Refrigerate: At least 1
  hour
Need: deep mixing
  bowl

The fancy veggies
shapes may also be
refrigerated in the
cold water over night.

1. Wash a carrot in cold water, remove the stem, and peel.

2. Shave long, thin strips from the entire length of the carrot with a vegetable peeler.

3. Roll up the strips and thread a toothpick through them to prevent uncurling (several curls can be skewered on one pick).

4. In a deep mixing bowl or jar, cover the skewered curls with cold water, add a few ice cubes, and refrigerate one hour or until they are crisp and will not unroll when removed from the picks.

CELERY CURLS

Refrigerate: at least 2
  hr.
Need: deep mixing
  bowl

1. Wash the celery in cold water, cut off the leaf and root ends.

2. Remove the strings and cut into 3 inch pieces.

3. Starting 1 inch from each end, make $\frac{1}{8}$ inch wide cuts to the opposite end, leaving a small, uncut section in the center.

4. In a deep mixing bowl, cover the celery with cold water, add a few ice cubes, and refrigerate one hour.

5. Drain well before serving.

OPTION:
    A. Replace the celery pieces with whole GREEN ONIONS (cutting the green end only).

SUPPER

EASY-DOES-IT-IN-ONE-DISH

PLUS
THE SUPER SPUD
AND
UNCANNY VEGETABLES

To save as much time as possible, all recipes in this section are made with instant and canned ingredients. If time permits each can be replaced with fresh ingredients prepared as follows:

INSTANT	FRESH	DIRECTIONS FOR FRESH
Minced onion: ¼ teaspoon	1 Tablespoon	Peel, chop, and cook in melted butter until transparent but not brown.
2 teaspoons	1 small onion	
Garlic powder: ⅛ teaspoon	1 clove	Peel, crush, or dice very finely.
Bell Pepper: Celery Flakes:	Use twice as much as instant	Chop and cook in melted butter until tender but not brown.
1 (5 oz.) can boneless chicken	1 chicken breast half OR 1 cup diced, leftover chicken	Cook in boiling, salted water 20 to 25 minutes until tender; cool, remove the skin and bones, and cut into bite-size pieces.
1 (4¼ oz.) can shrimp	1 cup peeled OR ¾ lb. uncooked in shell OR 7 oz. frozen, peeled	Cook according to the directions (Seafood, DINNER).

CASSEROLE TOPPERS:

Most toppers are interchangeable and add an interesting texture to the finished product. Try a different one each time just for the heck of it:

1. **PLAIN OR ITALIAN BREAD CRUMBS** dotted with butter.

2. **CRUSHED RITZ, SALTINES, OR CHEESE CRACKERS** dotted with butter and sprinkled with sesame seeds.

3. **HERB-SEASONED STUFFING MIX** dotted with butter.

4. **CANNED FRENCH FRIED ONION RINGS OR CRUSHED PLAIN OR SEASONED POTATO CHIPS** (add only during the last 5 to 10 minutes of baking).

107

PIZZA

1 (12" crust)
½ to 1 cup pizza sauce (any flavor)
cheese filling
toppers

Makes: 1 (12") pizza
2 servings
Groundwork: 10
minutes
Bake: 20 minutes
Oven Temp: 425°
Need: small mixing
bowl
12" pizza pan OR
cookie sheet

Serve with side bowl of
Parmesan cheese and
crushed red peppers
for extra umph!

Makes: 1 cup
Groundwork: 3 minutes
Need: small mixing
bowl

1. Preheat the oven to 425°.

CRUST:

2. Prepare the crust. (PRESTO PIZZA
    CRUST or commercial crust mix.)

3. While the dough is rising, prepare
    the sauce, cheeses, and toppers.

SAUCE:

½ to 1 cup any flavor bottled pizza
  sauce OR
1 (8 oz.) can tomato sauce
½ teaspoon oregano
1 teaspoon Italian seasoning
2 teaspoons instant minced onions
⅛ teaspoon garlic powder
⅛ teaspoon pepper

4. Combine all the ingredients in a small
    mixing bowl and stir to mix well.

5. Spread the sauce evenly over the crust.

CHEESE FILLING:

1 cup (4 oz. pkg.) shredded mozzarella
  or Provolone cheese
1 cup (4 oz. pkg.) shredded Cheddar
  cheese
2 Tablespoons grated Parmesan
  cheese
¼ teaspoon oregano
⅛ teaspoon crushed red peppers
  (optional)

CALZONE:
Place the sauce and
toppers on half the
pizza dough, fold the
other half over, press
the edges closed, and
make a small steam
hole in the top. Bake
as you do a regular
pizza or until the top is
puffy and brown.

6. Spread the cheeses evenly over the
    sauce.

7. Sprinkle with oregano and red
    peppers. Top with one or more
    toppers, if desired.

Make ahead:
Make the pizza as directed but do not cook. Cover it tightly with plastic wrap or foil and freeze (a week to 10 days). Cook without thawing.

PERSONAL PIZZA CRUSTS:
Use **split** English muffins, bagels; small sub, Kaiser, French or Italian loaves.

Makes: 1 (12") pizza
Groundwork: 10 minutes
Need: medium mixing bowl
12" pizza pan OR cookie sheet

Uncooked pizza dough can be frozen for later use. Let it thaw for several hours in the refrigerator before trying to shape it.

To prepare ahead, (up to 4 hours), simply spread the dough on the pan, (do not cook or add the sauce), cover with foil or plastic wrap and refrigerate.

For a crispy crust, bake pizza on the lower rack of the oven.

TOPPERS:

1¼ oz. pkg. pepperoni (sliced)
½ cup ground beef (cooked and crumbled)
½ cup sausage (cooked and crumbled)
½ cup Canadian bacon (sliced)
½ cup fresh or canned mushrooms (sliced)
¼ cup black or green olives (sliced)
6 to 8 fresh bell pepper rings
1 (2 oz.) can anchovies (drained)
12 large shrimp (cooked and cut in half)
6 to 8 fresh or canned pineapple rings

8. Bake 20 minutes at 425°.

PRESTO PIZZA CRUST (12" pizza)

1 (¼ oz.) pkg. yeast
½ cup warm water
1 Tablespoon vegetable oil
1½ cups flour
pinch salt
vegetable spray or shortening
2 Tablespoons extra flour

1. Combine the yeast, water, oil, salt, and 1½ cups flour in a small mixing bowl and stir to mix well.

2. Cover and let the mixture stand for 5 minutes.

3. After the dough has risen, coat your hands with the extra flour and lightly dust the dough ball. Knead it several times, adding more flour if needed, until the dough is no longer sticky.

4. Grease the pizza pan or cookie sheet and your hands with the vegetable spray, and spread the dough into a 12 inch round crust, turning the edges up to make a rim. (Be sure to cover the pan completely leaving no holes before adding the sauce and toppers.)

CHILI

Makes: 2 servings
Groundwork: 10
  minutes
Cook: 30 minutes -
  LOW
Need: Dutch oven with
  lid

1 lb. ground beef
½ (8 oz.) can tomato sauce
1 cup water
2 Tablespoons instant minced onions
1 Tablespoon chili powder
½ teaspoon garlic salt
⅛ teaspoon pepper
¼ teaspoon cayenne pepper
1 teaspoon oregano
1½ teaspoons paprika
½ teaspoon cumin (optional)
THICKENING AGENT:
*1 Tablespoon corn meal
water to make paste

*Thickening Agent:
Stone ground corn
meal (mesa flour) is
the traditional
thickening agent, but
all-purpose corn meal
or cornstarch makes a
fair substitute.

The browning time for
ground beef is always
included in the
groundwork time. It
takes approximately 8
minutes to brown 1
pound of ground beef
in a medium skillet on
MEDIUM HIGH.

Chili Change: Try chili
over hot spaghetti
noodles, corn tortillas
or chips, or in a hot
baked potato and
add some toppers!

1. Crumble the meat into a Dutch oven
   and brown on MEDIUM HIGH, stirring
   frequently to separate.

2. Add all the other ingredients except
   the thickener and stir to mix well.

3. Reduce the heat to LOW, cover, and
   simmer 30 minutes, (longer is even
   better!), stirring occasionally.

4. For thicker, extra flavorful chili,
   combine the corn meal with enough
   water to make a paste and slowly
   stir it into the chili.

OPTIONS:

A. Replace the water with 8 oz.
   beer for an exciting flavor.

B. Add 1 (16 oz.) can kidney, pinto,
   or hot chili beans (drained).

C. Replace the water with 1 (16 oz.)
   can stewed or chopped
   tomatoes (do not drain).

TERRIFIC TOPPERS

Chopped onions
Shredded Cheddar cheese
Crushed red peppers or sliced
Jalapeño pepper

CHILI MAC

Makes: 2 servings
Groundwork: 9 minutes
Bake: 45 minutes
Oven Temp: 350°
Need: medium skillet
1 quart casserole with
   lid

Forget to thaw the
ground meat for
tonight's casserole? No
sweat! Just use a
coarse grater and
grate it right into the
skillet.

**TIME AND MONEY
SAVER:**
Large packages of
ground beef are
usually less expensive
but (unless you
happen to be the old
lady in the shoe) it is
hard to use it all while
it's still fresh. Next time
brown it **all** at one
time, package it in
one pound portions,
and freeze. You'll have
super simple suppers
in a snap. No need to
even thaw before
using — just hit the
package on the
counter edge to
separate.

½ **pound ground beef**
1 **cup water**
½ **cup elbow macaroni (uncooked)**
1 **(8 oz.) can tomato sauce**
1 **(4 oz.) can mushroom stems & pieces
   (drained)**
2 **Tablespoons instant minced onions**
3 **Tablespoons instant bell pepper**
1½ **teaspoons Worcestershire**
1 **Tablespoon chili powder**
¼ **teaspoon salt**
¼ **teaspoon pepper**
½ **cup shredded Cheddar cheese
   (optional)**

1. Preheat the oven to 350°.

2. Crumble the meat into the skillet
   and brown on MEDIUM HIGH, stirring
   frequently to separate.

3. While the meat is cooking, combine
   all the other ingredients in the
   casserole.

4. Drain the meat and add to the
   casserole, stirring to mix thoroughly.

5. Cover and bake 30 minutes;
   uncover and bake 15 additional
   minutes until the macaroni is
   cooked, casserole is bubbly, and
   the liquid is absorbed.

OPTIONS:

A. Add 4 drops of Tabasco for a
   spicier version.

B. Before baking, top with (or stir into
   the casserole) ½ cup (½ of 4 oz.
   pkg.) shredded Cheddar cheese.

C. Replace the elbow macaroni
   with any medium-sized noodles:
   (egg noodles, rotelle, rigatoni, or
   small seashells.)

FAT CAT SPECIAL (LASAGNA)

Makes: 4 servings
Groundwork: 8 minutes
Cook: 15 minutes -
 LOW
Bake: 50 to 55 minutes
Oven Temp: 375°
Need: large skillet with
 lid
8" x 8" baking dish

Italian seasoning sub-
situte (1 Tablespoon):
 1 teaspoon basil
 2 teaspoons oregano

The amount of any of
the cheese can be
changed to suit your
taste.

For Emergencies:
Double this one and
freeze either just the
sauce, or the entire
extra casserole (before
or after cooking).

1 pound ground beef
½ teaspoon salt
1 teaspoon garlic powder
½ teaspoon pepper
1 (15 oz.) can tomato sauce
¼ cup water
1 Tablespoon Italian seasoning
2 Tablespoons instant minced onions
1 Tablespoon parsley flakes
1 cup (4 oz. pkg.) shredded mozarella
 cheese
1 (12 oz.) carton cottage or Ricotta
 cheese
¼ cup Parmesan cheese
6 uncooked lasagna noodles

1. Preheat the oven to 375°.

2. Crumble the meat into a large
    skillet, season with the salt, garlic
    powder, and pepper and brown on
    MEDIUM, stirring frequently to
    separate. Drain the meat.

3. Stir in the tomato sauce, water,
    Italian seasoning, onion, and parsley.

4. Reduce the heat, cover, and simmer
    on LOW 15 minutes.

5. Grease the bottom and sides of the
    baking dish and line the bottom with
    3 of the noodles, breaking them if
    necessary to fit the dish.

6. Layer with ½ of the cottage cheese,
    mozzarella, meat sauce, and
    Parmesan.

7. Add the other 3 noodles and repeat.

8. Cover tightly and bake 45 minutes
    until the noodles are done and the
    casserole is bubbly (uncover, and
    bake an additional 5 to 10 minutes
    if it is still too liquid.

9. Allow to stand 5 minutes to continue
    firming.

Makes: 4 to 6 servings
Cook: LOW - 20 to 25
  min.
Need: large saucepan
  with lid

OPTIONS:

A. **Laid Back Skillet Lasagna:**

1. Replace the lasagna noodles with 6 oz. uncooked egg noodles.

2. Stir the noodles into the meat and tomato sauce in the skillet and heat to boiling.

3. Reduce the heat to LOW, cover, and simmer 15 minutes, stirring occasionally.

4. Add the mozzarella, cottage, and Parmesan cheeses and stir to mix well.

5. Sprinkle an extra ¼ cup Parmesan cheese over the top and continue to cook, uncovered, without stirring, approximately 2 to 3 minutes until the cheeses have melted.

B. **Lazy Lasagna:** for a **really** lazy and less spicy lasagna, simply replace the tomato sauce, water, and spices with a 15½ oz. jar of spaghetti sauce for the Fat Cat Special, or a 32 oz. jar for the Laid Back Skillet Lasagna.

SPAGHETTI SAUCE

Makes: 4 servings
Groundwork: 10
  minutes
Cook: 30 min. - LOW
Need: large skillet
Dutch oven OR large
  saucepan with lid

1 pound ground beef
1 teaspoon garlic powder
½ teaspoon pepper
½ teaspoon salt
1 (15 oz.) can tomato sauce
1 (6 oz.) can tomato paste
2 Tablespoons instant minced onions
1 cup water
1 Tablespoon instant bell pepper
1 teaspoon celery flakes
1 Tablespoon Italian seasoning
8 oz. uncooked spaghetti noodles

1. Crumble the meat into a Dutch

NOTE:
This is quick and easy! Don't let the long list of ingredients scare you! Everything is in your pantry — no chopping, peeling, and cooking all day like Mama Rosa had to do.

A salad, hot garlic Italian bread, and a glass of Chianti or Frascotti and you'll think you're in old Napoli!

Double and freeze this one for later convenience.

For an Old World touch:
Form the seasoned meat into 1 inch balls (about like ping-pong balls), brown them in a medium skillet on MEDIUM HIGH, turning carefully to prevent breaking them apart. Add the meatballs to the tomato sauce, pasta, and spices and simmer 20 to 25 minutes.

oven or large saucepan, season with the garlic, salt, and pepper and brown on MEDIUM HIGH, stirring frequently to separate.

2. Drain, add the tomato sauce, paste and the remaining ingredients, stirring to mix well.

3. Reduce the heat to LOW, cover, and simmer 30 minutes, stirring occasionally. (If the sauce is too liquid, cook uncovered a few minutes — or too dry, add a little water.)

4. While the sauce is simmering, cook the noodles according to the directions on the package.

OPTIONS:

A. **Couch Potato Spaghetti**
   1. Fifteen minutes before the end of the cooking time, increase the temperature to MEDIUM HIGH, stirring constantly, until it comes to a boil. (Be careful not to burn it on the bottom.)

   2. Break the spaghetti noodles in half and add them to the sauce.

   3. Immediately reduce the temperature to LOW, cover, and simmer 15 to 20 minutes until the noodles are tender.

B. Add one or more:
   1. 1 (4 oz.) can sliced mushrooms (drained)

   2. 10 to 15 slices pepperoni

   3. ¼ lb. hot or mild Italian sausage (cut into 1 inch pieces)

   4. 1 (4 oz.) can sliced ripe olives (drained)

SAUCY MEATBALLS

Makes: 24 meatballs
Groundwork: 10
  minutes
Cook: 30 min. - LOW
Need: large skillet with
  lid
  medium mixing bowl

1 lb. ground beef
¼ cup bread crumbs
1 teaspoon garlic salt
1 teaspoon instant minced onion
1 egg
1 Tablespoon Worcestershire
½ teaspoon pepper
1 choice of sauces

1. Combine all the ingredients **except the sauce** in a medium mixing bowl and mix until thoroughly blended.

2. Form into meatballs using a heaping tablespoon of fresh meat for each.

3. Brown the meatballs well on all sides in a large skillet on MEDIUM HIGH.

4. Drain, reduce the heat to LOW, add your choice of sauce, cover, and simmer 30 minutes, stirring occasionally until the sauce has thickened slightly.

SAUCY SAUCES

A. **Swedish**
   1 (10¾ oz.) can mushroom soup
   ½ soup can of water

   1. Combine, pour over the meatballs, and scrape the brown dripping off the bottom of the pan for a dark, rich sauce.

B. **Italian**
   1 (15½ oz.) jar spaghetti sauce
   ¼ teaspoon oregano

C. **Sweet and Sour**
   1 (8 oz.) can tomato sauce (or chili sauce)
   1 (8 oz.) jar grape jelly

   1. Combine and pour over the meatballs.

Make small meatballs in sweet and sour sauce for a bountiful appetizer.

PIZZA CASSEROLE

Makes: 2 servings
Groundwork: 10
  minutes
Bake: 12 to 15 minutes
Oven Temp: 375°
Need: medium skillet
1 quart casserole

Serve with a side bowl
of extra Parmesan
cheese.

½ pound ground beef
¼ teaspoon salt
¼ teaspoon pepper
½ (14 oz.) jar Pizza sauce
1 cup (4 oz. pkg.) shredded mozzarella
  cheese
¼ teaspoon oregano
⅛ cup Parmesan cheese
1 (4 count) pkg. refrigerator crescent
  rolls

1. Preheat the oven to 375°.

2. Crumble the meat into a medium
    skillet and brown on MEDIUM HIGH,
    stirring frequently to separate.

3. Lightly grease the casserole.

4. Drain the meat well, add the salt
    and pepper and pour into the
    casserole.

5. Stir in the pizza sauce, top with the
    cheeses, and sprinkle with oregano.

6. Stretch the crescent rolls over the
    top to form a crust.

7. Bake, uncovered, 12 to 15 minutes
    until the crust is light brown and the
    casserole is bubbly.

OPTIONS:

  A. Replace the beef with sausage.

  B. Add your choice of the toppings
      (PIZZA) before putting on the crust.

  C. Add 1 teaspoon instant minced
      onions and ⅛ teaspoon crushed
      red pepper to the meat and
      sauce mixture before baking.

TACO CASSEROLE

Makes: 2 servings
Groundwork: 8 minutes
Bake: 15 to 20 minutes
Oven Temp: 350°
Need: medium skillet
1 quart casserole

½ pound ground beef
¼ (10 oz.) pkg. corn chips
⅛ teaspoon salt
¼ teaspoon pepper
⅛ teaspoon garlic powder
1 (14 to 16 oz.) jar taco sauce
1 Tablespoon instant minced onions
½ cup (½ of 4 oz. pkg.) shredded
   Cheddar cheese

For a spicier casserole,
cook the meat with ½
(1¼ oz.) pkg. taco
seasoning as directed
on the package.

Garnish with sour
cream and sliced
black olives.

1. Crumble the meat into a medium skillet and brown on MEDIUM HIGH, stirring frequently to separate.

2. While the meat is cooking, lightly grease the casserole and line the bottom with ½ the corn chips.

3. Drain the meat, add the salt, pepper, garlic powder, taco sauce, and onions and mix well.

4. Spread ½ the meat mixture over the chips and top with ½ the cheese and the remaining chips.

5. Preheat the oven to 350°. Layer with the remaining meat and cheese.

6. Bake, uncovered, 15 to 20 minutes until the casserole is bubbly and the cheese melts.

MEAT LOAF

Makes: 4 servings
Groundwork: 5 minutes
Bake: 1 hour
Oven Temp: 350°
Need: loaf pan or
   shallow baking pan
medium mixing bowl

1 pound ground beef
1 Tablespoon instant minced onions
1 egg
2 teaspoons Worcestershire
1 teaspoon salt
½ teaspoon pepper
¼ cup milk (optional)

1. Preheat the oven to 350°.

2. Lightly grease a loaf pan or a shallow baking pan.

To speed the baking time, divide the meat mixture into two small loaves and bake 45 minutes, or divide it into six equal portions and bake in a greased muffin pan for 30 minutes.

Sauced meat loaf slices are great served on hot spaghetti or egg noodles.

Place firmly crumpled foil in the baking pan under the meat loaf to hold it out of the drippings.

Any meat loaf can be topped with bacon slices for a moist and smokey loaf.

3. Combine all ingredients in a medium mixing bowl and stir until thoroughly mixed. If not well mixed, the meat loaf may crumble after baking!

4. Pack the meat mixture into the loaf pan (or form it into a loaf on the baking pan).

5. Bake 1 hour until brown.

OPTIONS:

A. **Sauced Loaf**
   Sauces: Omit the milk and add ½ cup sauce to the meat mixture and pour ½ cup over the meat loaf before baking. Take your choice of:

   1. Barbecue, chili, pizza, spaghetti, taco, or tomato sauce.

   2. 1 (10¾ oz.) can soup: cream of mushroom, onion, celery, tomato, or Cheddar cheese.

B. **Loaf Stretchers**
   Add to the meat loaf with the milk or sauce:

   1. ½ cup uncooked oats, cracker or bread crumbs.

C. **Loaf Toppers**
   Add on during the last 15 minutes of the baking time:

   1. 1 cup mashed potatoes

   2. 1 (4 oz.) pkg. shredded Cheddar cheese

ROAST BEEF HASH

Makes: 2 servings
Groundwork: 5 minutes
Cook: 11 minutes -
  MEDIUM
3 to 4 minutes - LOW
Need: large skillet

Hash may be served
"as is" or over cooked
rice, noodles, split hot
biscuits, or in a pastry
shell.

1½ cups cooked roast beef (cubed)
1 small potato (cubed)
1 small onion (diced)
¼ teaspoon salt
¼ teaspoon pepper
2 Tablespoons vegetable oil
1 cup gravy OR
1 cup boiling water and 1 bouillon
  cube

1. Cut the beef into bite-size cubes,
    peel, cube and dice the onions and
    potatoes.

2. Salt and pepper the vegetables.

3. Heat the vegetable oil in a medium
    skillet on MEDIUM.

4. Carefully add the vegetables and
    cook 5 minutes, stirring constantly.

5. Stir in the beef and continue to cook
    and stir 5 additional minutes until
    the vegetables are brown and
    tender and the beef is hot.

6. Add the gravy (or water and
    bouillon cube), stir, reduce the heat
    to LOW, and continue to cook 3 to 4
    minutes until the gravy is hot.

OPTIONS:

Add:
  A. A pinch of garlic powder, basil,
      thyme, or savory; and/or 1
      teaspoon parsley flakes.

  B. Cook with the vegetables ½ cup
      sliced mushrooms, ¼ cup diced
      bell pepper, and/or diced
      celery.

  C. Replace the gravy with 1 cup
      sour cream, tomato sauce, or
      cream of mushroom or celery
      soup.

HAMMUS ALABAMUS

Makes: 2 servings
Groundwork: 6 minutes
Cook: 15 minutes -
  MEDIUM
Bake: 25 minutes
Oven Temp: 400°
Need: cookie sheet
  aluminum foil
  small saucepan

Replace the ham with
1 (5 oz.) can boneless
chicken, tuna, or
shrimp, OR 1 cup
cooked leftover
chicken, turkey, or
ham.

Replace the puff
pastry shell with hot
cooked rice or
noodles, toast cups,
Chow Mein noodles,
or split hot biscuits.

---

4 puff pastry shells
1 cup ham (diced and cooked) OR
1 (6¾ oz.) can chunky ham or
   luncheon meat (diced)
1 (10 oz.) pkg. frozen broccoli with
   cheese sauce

1. Preheat the oven to 400°.

2. Bake the puff pastry shells for 25 minutes or as directed on the package.

3. Seal the ham in foil and heat in the oven while the shells are baking.

4. Prepare the broccoli with cheese sauce according to the directions on the package.

5. Open the package and stir before removing the broccoli.

6. Divide the ham evenly into the shells and top each with an equal amount of broccoli and sauce.

SAUSAGE AND RICE

Makes: 2 servings
Groundwork: 3 minutes
Bake: 30 minutes
Oven Temp: 350°
Need: 1 quart
  casserole

1 (16 oz.) can Spanish Rice
dash cayenne pepper
⅛ teaspoon chili powder
6 small pork, Italian, or Polish sausage
   links
4 drops Tabasco

1. Preheat the oven to 350°.

2. Combine the Spanish Rice, Tabasco, and chili powder in a 1 quart casserole.

3. Arrange the sausage over the rice and bake, uncovered, for 30 minutes until the sausages are brown.

CHICKEN DIVAN

Makes: 2 servings
Groundwork: 10 minutes
Bake: 25 to 30 minutes
Oven Temp: 350°
Need: colander
medium mixing bowl
2 qt. flat baking dish

Remember!
All can sizes may vary
slightly according to
the brand. An ounce
or so difference
usually will not matter.

Turkey can always be
used in place of
chicken.

3 (5 oz.) cans boneless chicken (drained)
1 (8 oz.) pkg. frozen broccoli cuts
1 (10¾ oz.) can cream of chicken soup
¼ cup mayonnaise
¼ cup sour cream
2 teaspoons lemon juice
¼ teaspoon curry powder
⅛ teaspoon salt
¼ teaspoon pepper
½ cup (½ of 4 oz. pkg.) shredded Cheddar cheese

1. Preheat the oven to 350°.

2. Thaw the broccoli in a colander under cold running water.

3. While the broccoli is thawing, combine the soup, mayonnaise, sour cream, lemon juice, curry powder, salt, and pepper in a mixing bowl.

4. Grease the baking dish, drain the broccoli well, and spread the broccoli over the bottom.

5. Sprinkle ½ the cheese over the broccoli.

6. Drain the chicken and flake it evenly over the cheese.

7. Pour the sauce evenly over the chicken and top with the remaining cheese.

8. Bake, uncovered, 25 to 30 minutes until it is bubbly.

CHICKEN HURRY CURRY

Makes: 2 servings
Groundwork: 5 minutes
Cook: 5 minutes -
  MEDIUM
Need: medium
  saucepan

Serve over 4 cups hot
cooked rice.

Do not omit the
condiments! Curry isn't
curry without them.

Start cooking the rice
first. The curry sauce
will be ready before it
is.

1 (10¾ oz.) can cream of shrimp soup
1 Tablespoon butter
1 cup sour cream
2 Tablespoons instant minced onion
¾ teaspoon curry powder
2 (5 oz.) cans boneless chicken (drained)

TOP WITH 2 or MORE CURRY CONDIMENTS:

Diced green onions
Chopped peanuts
Grated coconut
Raisins
Crumbled bacon
Mandarin orange slices
Chutney
Grated hard-cooked eggs

1. Combine the soup, butter, sour
   cream, onion, and curry powder in
   a medium saucepan on MEDIUM.

2. Drain and flake the chicken in the
   saucepan.

3. Cook 5 minutes, stirring frequently,
   until the mixture begins to bubble.

CHICKEN ORIENTAL

Makes: 2 servings
Groundwork: 3 minutes
Cook: 5 min. - MEDIUM
Need: medium
 saucepan

Serve Over:
Cooked rice or
 noodles
Baked puff pastry shell
Toast or toasted
 English Muffins
Chow Mein noodles

---

1 (10¾ oz.) can cream of chicken soup
2 (5 oz.) cans boneless chicken (drained)
1 (4 oz.) can sliced mushrooms (drained)
¼ cup sliced water chestnuts (drained)
2 Tablespoons (diced) pimiento
¼ cup cashews, sliced almonds or
 peanuts
¼ cup sherry

1. Heat the soup in a medium saucepan on MEDIUM.

2. Drain the chicken, mushrooms and chestnuts, and add to the soup.

3. Add pimiento and cashews and cook until very hot but not boiling, stirring frequently.

4. Stir in the sherry just before serving.

CHICKEN AND RICE

Makes: 4 servings
Groundwork: 3 minutes
Bake: 60 minutes
Oven Temp: 350°
Need: 2 quart
 casserole

2 (5 oz.) cans boneless chicken (drained)
1 (10¾ oz.) can cream of chicken or
 mushroom soup
½ soup can water
½ cup uncooked rice
¼ teaspoon salt
¼ teaspoon pepper
2 Tablespoons instant bell pepper
1 Tablespoon instant minced onions
2 Tablespoons diced pimiento
2 Tablespoons mushrooms (diced or
 sliced)

1. Preheat the oven to 350°.

2. Lightly grease the casserole.

3. Drain the chicken and combine all the ingredients in a 2 quart casserole.

4. Cover and bake 60 minutes until the rice is tender.

LE CHIC POULETTE

Makes: 6 servings
Groundwork: 15
  minutes
Bake: 50 minutes
Oven Temp: 350°
Need: medium mixing
  bowl
2 qt. baking dish
small mixing bowl

For easier slicing,
allow the casserole to
stand 4 to 5 minutes
before serving.

1 cup boiling water
3 chicken bouillon cubes
1 (6 oz.) pkg. seasoned cornbread
  stuffing mix
½ cup (1 stick) butter
½ cup mayonnaise
¼ teaspoon pepper
3 (5 oz.) cans boneless chicken or
  turkey (drained)
2 eggs
1½ cups milk
1 (10½ oz.) can cream of mushroom soup
1 cup (4 oz. pkg.) shredded Cheddar
  cheese

1. Combine the boiling water, bouillon cubes, and vegetable seasoning packet (from the stuffing mix box) in a medium mixing bowl.

2. Cut the butter into small pieces (for easier melting) into the bowl of hot water mixture and stir to melt.

3. Stir in the stuffing mix; add the mayonnaise and pepper and mix well.

4. Grease baking dish.

5. Spread one-half of the stuffing mixture evenly over the bottom of the dish, cover with the chicken, and top with the remaining one half of the stuffing mixture.

6. Combine the eggs and milk thoroughly in a small mixing bowl and pour evenly over the mixture.

7. Dot the mushroom soup over the top and gently spread the dots evenly over the casserole with the back of a spoon.

8. Bake uncovered 40 minutes, sprinkle with the cheese and bake 10 additional minutes.

CHICKEN SPAGHETTI

Makes: 4 servings
Groundwork: 5 minutes
Bake: 40 to 45 minutes
Oven Temp: 350°
Need: 2 quart
casserole with lid

The two serving dot on the spaghetti measure (inside back cover) equals 4 ounces uncooked spaghetti.

Serve with warm, crusty Italian bread (pages 257-259) and a tossed salad (page 58).

1 (15½ oz.) jar spaghetti sauce
*¾ to 1 cup water
1 teaspoon Italian seasoning
¼ teaspoon garlic powder
½ teaspoon salt
½ (4 oz.) can sliced mushrooms (drained)
4 oz. uncooked spaghetti
2 (5 oz.) cans boneless chicken (drained)
¼ cup Parmesan cheese

1. Preheat the oven to 350°.

2. Place the spaghetti sauce, water, Italian seasoning, garlic, salt, and mushrooms in the casserole and stir to mix well.

3. Break the spaghetti into pieces (approximately 2½ inches) and stir into the sauce.

4. Drain the chicken and flake it into the mixture, stirring to mix thoroughly. (The spaghetti should be completely submerged in the mixture to insure proper cooking.)

5. Cover and bake 35 to 40 minutes until the spaghetti is cooked.

6. Top with the Parmesan cheese, re-cover, and bake an additional 5 minutes until the cheese melts.

* If the spaghetti sauce is very thick, it will require an extra ¼ cup of water.

HEN IN THE GARDEN

Makes: 4 servings
Groundwork: 2 minutes
Bake: 30 minutes
Oven Temp: 375°
Need: colander
1½ quart casserole
with lid

If your casserole does
not have a lid, just
seal it with foil.

**2 (5 oz.) cans boneless chicken
(drained)
1 (16 oz.) pkg. frozen mixed vegetables
1 (10¾ oz.) can cream of chicken soup
½ cup milk + 2 Tablespoons
⅛ teaspoon pepper
1 (2.8 oz.) can French fried onions**

1. Preheat the oven to 375°.

2. Thaw the vegetables under cold,
   running water and drain well.

3. Drain the chicken and combine all
   the ingredients in the casserole
   except ¼ of the onions.

4. Cover and cook 25 minutes until it is
   bubbly.

5. Top with the remaining onions and
   cook, uncovered, an additional 5
   minutes.

OPTIONS:

A. Replace the chicken with 2 cups
   cooked ham (cubed).

B. Replace the frozen mixed
   vegetables with 1 (16 oz.) can of
   mixed vegetables, green peas,
   or green beans (drained).

C. Add ½ cup shredded Cheddar
   cheese to the soup mixture.

D. Replace the onion rings with
   crushed potato chips.

Note:
Bake the unused
biscuits on a cookie
sheet and serve with
the pie.

E. Chicken pie:
   Ten minutes before the end of
   the baking time, add the onion
   rings. Separate 1 (5 count) pkg.
   of flakey refrigerator biscuits,
   divide each into thin rounds,
   place on top of the hot chicken
   mixture and bake, uncovered,
   10 additional minutes until
   biscuits are brown.

QUICK CRAB AU GRATIN

Makes: 2 servings
Groundwork: 3 minutes
Bake: 20 minutes
Oven Temp: 400°
Need: 1 qt. casserole

1 (6½ oz.) can crab meat (drained)
1 (10¾ oz.) can cream of shrimp soup
½ cup (½ of 4 oz. pkg.) grated
   Cheddar cheese
½ cup sliced water chestnuts (optional)
½ teaspoon Worcestershire
2 Tablespoons white wine
½ cup bread crumbs
2 Tablespoons butter

1. Preheat the oven to 400°.

2. Lightly grease the casserole.

3. Rinse the crab meat under cold water, drain well, and remove any bits of shell or cartilage.

Crab Au Gratin can also be baked in individual serving-sized casseroles or seashells.

Canned Seafood Flavor-Savor:
To improve the flavors of both crab and shrimp, first drain the liquid from the can and refill with iced water. Soak for 15 minutes, drain again, and pat dry with paper towels.

4. Combine the crab, soup, cheese, water chestnuts, Worcestershire, and wine in the casserole.

5. Pour the mixture into the baking dish and sprinkle evenly with bread crumbs and dot with butter.

6. Bake 20 minutes until very hot and light brown.

SIMPLE SHRIMP CREOLE

Makes: 2 servings
Groundwork: 2 minutes
Cook: 15 min. - MED. LOW
Need: medium
   saucepan with lid

1 (4¼ oz.) can shrimp (drained)
1 (15 oz.) can Spanish rice
1 teaspoon instant minced onions
4 drops Tabasco
pinch garlic powder
pinch chili powder

1. Drain the shrimp, rinse in cold water, and drain thoroughly.

2. Combine all the ingredients in the saucepan and stir to mix.

3. Cover and simmer on MEDIUM LOW 15 minutes stirring occasionally.

NEPTUNE'S NEWBERG

Makes: 2 servings
Groundwork: 3 minutes
Cook: 8 to 10 minutes -
  LOW
Need: medium
  saucepan

2 (6½ oz.) cans crab meat (drained)
1 (10¾ oz.) can cream of shrimp soup
¼ soup can milk
¼ teaspoon instant minced onions
**½ cup (½ of 4 oz. pkg.) shredded
  Cheddar cheese**
⅛ teaspoon pepper
2 Tablespoons sherry

FOUNDATIONS:
Serve over your
choice of:
Baked puff pastry
  shells
Hot cooked rice or
  noodles
Toast or English muffins
Chow Mein noodles or
Waffles

Garnish with paprika

Good with a green
veggie and fruit salad.

1. Prepare **"Foundation"** from side
   column.

2. Rinse the crab meat under cold
   water, drain well, and remove any
   shell or cartilage.

3. Combine the crab, soup, milk,
   onion, cheese, and pepper in a
   medium saucepan on MEDIUM.

4. Reduce to LOW and cook uncovered
   8 to 10 minutes, stirring frequently, until
   the cheese has melted and the
   Newberg is hot but not boiling.

5. Stir in the sherry and serve
   immediately.

OPTIONS:

A. Replace the crab with 2 (4¼ oz.)
   cans shrimp or 1 (16 oz.) pkg.
   frozen shrimp (shelled) prepared
   according to the directions on
   the package.

B. **Fish and Fowl**
   Replace the crab with 1 (4¼ oz.)
   can shrimp (drained), and 1 (6½
   oz.) can boneless chicken
   (drained), and add 1 (4 oz.) can
   sliced mushrooms (drained).

SALMON CROQUETTES

Makes: 2 servings
Groundwork: 10 minutes
Cook: 6 to 8 min. -
  MED. HIGH
Need: medium mixing
  bowl
medium skillet

Salmon Error:
Did you know that the
"l" in salmon is **always**
silent? The correct way
is to say sam' on.

These are a special
treat when served with
white or cheese sauce
(SAUCES AND GRAVIES).

Simple Salmon Sauce:
Combine
2 Tablespoons
  mayonnaise
¼ cup sour cream
⅓ cup cucumbers
  (peeled and finely
  diced)

1 (15½ oz.) can pink or red salmon
  (drained)
1 egg
¼ cup milk
¼ cup flour
½ teaspoon salt
¼ teaspoon pepper
oil for frying

1. Drain the salmon, remove the skin
   and bones, and flake the meat into
   a medium mixing bowl.

2. Add all the other ingredients and
   mix **thoroughly.**

3. Firmly pack the mixture into balls,
   ovals, or patties.

4. Heat ¼ inch of oil in a medium skillet
   on MEDIUM HIGH.

5. Carefully add the croquettes and
   brown on all sides.

OPTIONS:

A. Add 1 Tablespoon each of
   instant minced onions and
   parsley flakes.

B. Replace the flour with ½ cup
   cracker meal or bread crumbs.

C. Replace the milk with the liquid
   from the salmon.

D. Add ½ teaspoon lemon juice.

TUNA CASSEROLE

Makes: 3 servings
Groundwork: 3 minutes
Bake: 30 minutes
Oven Temp: 350°
Need: 1½ quart
  casserole

1 (6½ oz.) can tuna (drained)
1 (10¾) can cream of mushroom soup
¼ cup milk
¼ teaspoon pepper
½ teaspoon parsley flakes
1 Tablespoon instant minced onions
¾ cup potato chips (crushed)

1. Preheat the oven to 350°.

2. Lightly grease a 1½ quart casserole.

3. Drain and flake the tuna and combine all the ingredients except ¼ cup of the chips in the casserole, stirring to mix well.

4. Top with the remaining ¼ cup of chips.

5. Bake, uncovered, 30 minutes until bubbly.

OPTIONS:

A. Sprinkle with ¼ cup shredded Cheddar cheese before topping with the potato chips.

B. Add 1 (8 oz.) can green peas (drained).

C. **Tuna Chow Mein**
    1. Replace the potato chips with ¼ cup cashew nuts and add:
        1 Tablespoon instant celery flakes
        1 teaspoon instant bell pepper
        2 teaspoons soy sauce

    2. Cover the top with Chow Mein noodles 5 minutes before the end of the baking time, and return to the oven for 5 minutes.

To reduce the calories in oil-packed tuna, drain in a colander, rinse under cold water and drain well.

130

UNCANNY VEGGIES

Canned or frozen vegetables do not have to taste like the container! With a minimum of time and a little wizardry, you can create the illusion of their fresh counterparts.

Some canned vegetables are more "tinny" than others and are better when not "stewed in their own juice". Replace the liquid with ½ cup water for:

Carrots   Greens
Green Beans   White potatoes
Squash

Other veggies may be heated in their own liquid:

Asparagus   Corn
Beets   Green Peas
Black-eyed peas   Spinach
Butter or lima beans

ALL vegetables are improved when some additions are made to the liquid:

FOUNDATION FORMULA

1 (16 oz.) can vegetables   **⅛ teaspoon salt**
1 Tablespoon butter   **⅛ teaspoon pepper**

1. Combine all the ingredients in a small saucepan on MEDIUM and heat to just below the boiling point.

2. Reduce the heat to LOW, cover, and cook 20 minutes, stirring occasionally.

VIVACIOUS VEGETABLES

Many veggies can be turned into a real gourmet dish simply by replacing or discarding the liquid and making a few additions:

Follow the Foundation Formula EXCEPT:

Beans (Butter or Lima): Replace the butter with bacon drippings and add ¼ teaspoon hot pepper sauce.

Beans (Green): Skinny — Replace the liquid with ½ cup water and add 1 beef bouillon cube, 1 (4 oz.) can sliced mushrooms (drained), and 1 teaspoon Chef's Spice. (The Creole Cottage, DINNER).

Beans (Green): Down Home — Replace the butter with 1 or 2 slices of bacon. Cut the bacon into small pieces and fry in the saucepan until crisp. Replace the liquid with ½ cup water and add to the bacon drippings. Add ⅛ teaspoon sugar and (optional) 1 (16 oz.) can whole potatoes (drained).

Carrots: Replace the liquid with ½ cup water or orange juice and add 2 teaspoons brown sugar or maple syrup and a pinch of nutmeg.

Greens (Turnips or Collard): Replace the liquid with ½ cup water, replace the butter with bacon drippings, and add ¼ teaspoon hot pepper sauce.

Peas (Black-eyed): Replace the butter with bacon drippings and add ¼ teaspoon hot pepper sauce.

Peas (Green): Add 1 Tablespoon instant minced onions and/or ¼ cup instant celery flakes, 1 (4 oz.) can sliced water chestnuts (drained), 1 (8 oz.) jar pearl onions.

Potatoes (Whole white): Add 1 (8 oz.) jar pearl onions (drained).

Spinach: Garnish with 1 hard-cooked egg (sliced).

Corn (whole kernel or Hominy): Ignore the Foundation Formula: Cut 1 or 2 slices of bacon into small pieces and fry in a saucepan until enough drippings have accumulated to sauté the vegetable. Drain the corn or hominy, add to the bacon and drippings, season with salt and pepper, and sauté until it is thoroughly heated and the bacon is cooked.

COBBLED CARROTS

Makes: 4 servings
Groundwork: 2 minutes
Bake: 15 minutes
Oven Temp: 350°
Need: 1 quart
  casserole

1 (16 oz.) can sliced carrots, drained
1 (21 oz.) can apple pie filling

1. Preheat the oven to 350°.

2. Lightly grease the casserole.

3. Drain the carrots and combine with the pie filling in the casserole, stirring gently to mix.

4. Bake, uncovered, 15 minutes until very hot.

GREEN BEAN CASSEROLE

Makes: 4 servings
Groundwork: 5 minutes
Cook: 20 to 25 minutes
Oven Temp: 350°
Need: small sauce-
pan, ½ quart
casserole

SPICY GREEN BEANS:
Replace the cheese
spread with 2 to 3 oz. of
garlic cheese roll cut
into small chunks to
speed melt time.

⅔ can cream of mushroom soup
3 to 4 oz. cheese spread (Cheese Whiz,
Old English, etc.)
¼ cup (2 oz.) white wine
½ can (2 oz.) chopped pimientos
1 Tablespoon instant minced onion
¼ teaspoon pepper
1 (14½ or 16 oz.) can green beans
(drained)
½ stack (approx. 17) Ritz Crackers
(crushed)
½ to 1 Tablespoon butter

1. Mix soup, cheese, wine, pimientos
and seasonings in a small saucepan
on medium-low until the cheese melts
(stir occasionally to mix).

2. Drain the beans.

3. Crush the crackers in a plastic sandwich bag while the cheese melts.

4. Pour the soup mixture over the beans
and stir to mix.

5. Top with crumbs and dot with butter.

6. Cook 20 to 25 minutes until bubbly.

CAMOUFLAGED CARROTS

Makes: 2 servings
Groundwork: 1 minute
Cook: 5 min. - MEDIUM
Need: small saucepan

1 (8 oz.) can carrot fingerlings
(drained)
⅛ cup water
2 Tablespoons butter
¼ to ½ teaspoon dill weed
salt & pepper to taste

1. Drain the carrots and combine with
the water in a small saucepan on
MEDIUM.

2. Add the butter, dill weed, salt and
pepper and heat until very hot and
most of the water has evaporated.

ASPARAGUS PARMESAN

Makes: 2 servings
Groundwork: 3 minutes
Oven Temp: BROIL
Need: small saucepan
medium baking dish

1 (10½ oz.) can asparagus spears
  (drained)
2 Tablespoons butter
1 teaspoon lemon juice
¼ cup grated Parmesan cheese

1. Preheat the oven to BROIL.

2. Drain the asparagus and arrange in
   a single layer in the baking dish.

3. Melt the butter in a small saucepan
   on MEDIUM, add the lemon juice, stir
   and pour evenly over the asparagus.

4. Sprinkle evenly with Parmesan.

5. Broil until hot and very light brown.

BROCCOLI EXTRAORDINAIRE

Makes: 2 servings
Groundwork: 5 minutes
Bake: 1 hour
Oven Temp: 350°
Need: colander
1 quart casserole with
  lid

1 (10 oz.) pkg. frozen chopped
  broccoli
½ can cream of shrimp soup
½ (8 oz.) container soft cream cheese
1½ teaspoons instant minced onions
¼ cup sliced almonds

1. Thaw the broccoli in a colander
   under running water until separated
   and press out any excess water.

2. Preheat the oven to 350°.

3. Combine the soup, onion, and
   cream cheese in a 1 quart
   casserole and melt in the oven while
   it preheats, stirring once to mix.

4. Add the broccoli to the melted
   mixture and stir to mix well.

5. Top with the almonds.

6. Cover, and bake 1 hour until the
   broccoli is tender and the casserole
   is bubbly.

BAKED BEANS

Makes: 2 servings
Groundwork: 5 minutes
Bake: 30 minutes
Oven Temp: 350°
Need: 1 quart
  casserole

Create a main dish by adding 4 to 8 hot dogs or 1 (7 oz.) can luncheon meat (sliced and pan fried) to the top of the beans before baking.

---

2 slices bacon (cooked & crumbled)
1 (16 oz.) can pork and beans
1½ teaspoons instant minced onions
1 teaspoon mustard
¼ cup catsup
1 Tablespoon brown sugar

1. Preheat the oven to 350°.

2. Cook the bacon until crisp, drain and crumble.

3. Grease the baking dish.

4. Combine all ingredients in the casserole.

5. Bake, uncovered, for 30 minutes.

OPTIONS:

A. Spice it up by stirring in 1 teaspoon chili powder before baking.

B. Replace the brown sugar with molasses or pancake syrup.

C. Top the beans with 2 slices uncooked bacon before baking.

BEETS PIQUANT

Makes: 2 servings
Groundwork: 2 minutes
Cook: 5 min. - MED.
  HIGH
15 min. - LOW
Need: small saucepan

Beets Piquant will keep for a month refrigerated in an airtight container (a jar is best as plastic will stain eventually).

---

1 (16 oz.) can whole beets (undrained)
1 teaspoon whole cloves
¼ cup vinegar
½ cup sugar

1. Combine all ingredients in a small saucepan on MEDIUM HIGH and stir gently to dissolve the sugar.

2. Bring to a boil, reduce the heat to LOW, and cook, uncovered, 15 minutes until the liquid is reduced to half.

3. Serve hot or cold.

HOPPING JOHN

Makes: 4 servings
Groundwork: 5 minutes
Cook: 20 min. - LOW
Need: medium
  saucepan with lid

The aroma coming
from the kitchen will
make Ol' John hop to
it every time!

---

3 slices bacon
½ small onion (diced)
1 (16 oz.) can blackeyed peas
  (undrained)
¼ teaspoon Tabasco
1 Tablespoon Worcestershire
½ cup uncooked rice
¼ cup water
salt and pepper to taste

1. Cut the bacon into 1 inch pieces into the saucepan and cook on MEDIUM, stirring frequently until it is crisp and brown.

2. While the bacon is cooking, peel and dice the onion.

3. Remove the bacon from the saucepan, add the diced onions to the bacon drippings and cook just until transparent but not browned.

4. Add the peas, and add the remaining ingredients, and stir to mix.

5. Cover, reduce to LOW, and cook 20 minutes stirring occasionally until the rice is tender.

6. Top with crumbled bacon, serve hot.

POTATO CRISPS

Makes: 2 servings
Groundwork: 2 minutes
Broil: 4 to 6 minutes
Need: 9" x 13" baking
  dish

1 (16 oz.) can sliced potatoes (drained)
¼ cup (½ stick) butter
2 teaspoons paprika
¾ teaspoon garlic salt

1. Preheat the oven to BROIL.

2. While the oven is preheating, melt the butter in the baking dish under the broiler.

3. Drain the potatoes, add to the melted butter, stir to coat completely.

4. Arrange the slices in a single layer and sprinkle with ½ of the paprika and garlic salt.

5. Broil 2 to 3 minutes until brown and crispy, turn each slice, sprinkle with remaining paprika and garlic salt, and broil an additional 2 to 3 minutes.

OPTIONS:

Replace the garlic salt with:

A. ¼ teaspoon onion powder and ½ teaspoon salt.

B. ¾ teaspoon Chef's Spice. (The Creole Cottage, DINNER), Italian, or Greek seasoning.

C. Replace ½ the butter and all the spices with 2 Tablespoons Italian salad dressing.

HOT GERMAN POTATO SALAD

Makes: 2 servings
Groundwork: 5 minutes
Cook: 5 min. - MEDIUM
Need: medium skillet

2 slices bacon (diced)
1 teaspoon flour
2 teaspoons onion soup mix
¼ teaspoon pepper
1 Tablespoon sugar
3 Tablespoons vinegar
1 (16 oz.) can sliced potatoes (drained)

1. Dice the bacon into a medium skillet and cook on MEDIUM until crisp, stirring frequently.

2. Remove the bacon and discard all but 2 teaspoons of the drippings.

3. Add the flour, onion soup mix, pepper, and sugar, and stir to mix.

4. Add the vinegar, mix, and cook 1 minute until hot and thick.

5. Drain the potatoes, add to the sauce and cook, stirring frequently until very hot.

6. Top with crumbled bacon.

POTATOES PAPRIKA

Makes: 2 servings
Groundwork: 5 minutes
Bake: 25 minutes
Oven Temp: 400°
Need: 9" x 13" baking
  dish

1 (16 oz.) can whole potatoes (drained)
¼ cup (½ stick) butter
2 teaspoons paprika
½ teaspoon salt
¼ teaspoon pepper
2 teaspoons parsley flakes

1. Preheat the oven to 400°.

2. Melt the butter in the baking dish in the oven while it preheats.

3. Drain the potatoes, add to the melted butter and stir to coat completely.

4. Sprinkle with salt, paprika, pepper, and parsley flakes.

5. Bake, uncovered, 25 minutes until golden brown.

OPTIONS:

A. Replace the canned potatoes with 6 tiny new red potatoes, (peeled or unpeeled), reduce the oven temperature to 375°, and increase the cooking time to 40 minutes.

1 cup uncrushed corn
flakes makes ½ cup
finely crushed.

B. Combine ½ cup crushed cornflakes and 2 Tablespoons Parmesan cheese in a small mixing bowl. Roll the potatoes in the melted butter, then in the cornflake mixture, return to the baking dish, and bake 20 minutes at 375°.

COUNTRY CLUB SQUASH CASSEROLE

Makes: 3 to 4 servings
Groundwork: 4 minutes
Bake: 40 to 45 minutes
Oven Temp: 350°
Need: 1 quart
　casserole

¾ cup mayonnaise
1 egg
1 cup (4 oz. pkg.) shredded Cheddar
　cheese
1 Tablespoon instant minced onions
¼ teaspoon salt
¼ teaspoon pepper
1 (16 oz.) can yellow squash (drained)

TOPPING:

¼ cup Italian bread crumbs
2 Tablespoons butter

1. Preheat the oven to 350°.

2. Lightly grease the casserole.

3. Combine the mayonnaise, egg, cheese, onions, salt, and pepper in the casserole.

4. Drain the squash, and add to the casserole, stirring to mix thoroughly.

5. Bake, uncovered, 35 minutes until slightly firm.

6. Top with the stuffing or bread crumbs, **dot with** butter and bake 5 to 10 additional minutes until light brown.

SPINACH SOUFFLÉ

Makes: 4 servings
Groundwork: 5 minutes
Bake: 30 minutes
Oven Temp: 350°
Need: colander
1 quart casserole with lid

Elegant Additions:
Before baking add:
1 Tablespoon sherry
1 (14 oz.) can artichoke hearts (drained and quartered)
1 (4 oz.) can sliced mushrooms (drained)

1 (10 oz.) pkg. frozen chopped spinach
1 (8 oz.) carton sour cream & onion dip
½ cup Parmesan cheese
½ teaspoon garlic powder
½ cup sliced water chestnuts

1. Preheat the oven to 350°.

2. Lightly grease the casserole.

3. Thaw the spinach in a colander under hot running water to separate and press to remove the excess water.

4. Combine all ingredients in the casserole and stir to mix thoroughly.

5. Bake, covered, 30 minutes until hot and light brown.

TIPSY YAMS

Makes: 2 servings
Groundwork: 5 minutes
Bake: 25 minutes
Oven Temp: 350°
Need: 1 quart casserole with lid

In certain parts of the country, sweet potatoes are called "yams."

1 (17 oz.) can whole sweet potatoes (drained)
1 Tablespoon butter
⅓ cup orange juice
2 teaspoons flour
⅓ cup brown sugar
pinch salt
1 Tablespoon sherry

1. Preheat the oven to 350°.

2. Melt the butter in the casserole in the oven while it preheats.

3. Add all the other ingredients except the potatoes, stir, and return to the oven.

4. Cook 2 to 3 minutes, stirring **frequently** until the mixture thickens.

5. Add the potatoes and stir to coat.

6. Bake, covered, 15 minutes, uncover and bake an additional 10 minutes.

SWEET POTATO CASSEROLE

Makes: 4 servings
Groundwork: 10
  minutes
Bake: 25 to 30 minutes
Oven Temp: 350°
Need: 9" pie plate,
  small mixing bowl

1 (14½ oz.) can mashed sweet potatoes
1 egg
1½ Tablespoons butter
⅓ cup sugar
2 Tablespoons milk
½ teaspoon vanilla

1. Preheat the oven to 350°.

2. While the oven is heating, melt the butter in the pie plate in the oven.

3. Combine all the other ingredients except the topping in the pie plate, and stir to mix well.

TOPPING:

3 Tablespoons butter (room temp.)
⅓ cup brown sugar
1 Tablespoon flour
⅓ cup shelled pecans (chopped)
10 to 12 pecan halves

TOPPING:

1. Combine the butter, sugar and flour with a fork in a small mixing bowl.

2. Add the chopped pecans and combine with your hands.

3. Dot the topping evenly over the potato mixture and top with the pecan halves.

4. Bake, uncovered, 25 to 30 minutes until bubbly and the topping is crystalized.

OPTIONS:
Replace the topping
with enough of one of
the following to cover
the top:
Miniature marshmallows
Pecans
Raisins
Pineapple
Coconut

Replace the pecans in
the topping with
walnuts.

WINTER TOMATOES

Makes: 2 servings
Groundwork: 3 minutes
Bake: 50 minutes
Oven Temp: 350°
Need: 1 quart
  casserole

2 Tablespoons butter
1 Tablespoon flour
1 (16 oz.) can stewed tomatoes
  (undrained)
½ teaspoon instant minced onions
¼ teaspoon salt
¾ teaspoon oregano
¾ cup herb-seasoned croutons
½ cup (½ 4 oz. pkg.) shredded
  Cheddar cheese

1. Preheat the oven to 350°.

2. Melt the butter in the casserole in the oven while it preheats.

3. Add the flour and stir to combine.

4. Add the tomatoes and liquid, onions, salt, and oregano and stir.

5. Spread the croutons evenly on top.

6. Bake, uncovered, 45 minutes until the tomatoes are hot.

7. Sprinkle evenly with cheese and bake 5 additional minutes until the cheese has melted.

DINNER

STARTING FROM SCRATCH

THE INSTANT CHEF has even simplified cooking with fresh foods, making traditional meals easier for life in the fast lane. These streamlined versions of old favorites use short-cuts and time-saving ingredients for the fastest foods in town.

THE MEAT OF THE MATTER
AND
HOW TO COOK IT

'Tis a sad fact of life that all cuts of meat cannot be cooked alike. Non-believers may as well eat dinner in a shoe factory. For insured success, just match your cut of meat with the proper cooking technique. For FISH, see Fish Facts.

COOKING TECHNIQUES	
For Tender Cuts Only **No Liquid Added; Short Cooking Time**	
BROIL	Move the oven rack to the top position so the surface of the meat will be about 2 to 4 inches below the broiling unit. Preheat the oven on BROIL (550°F) for 10 minutes with the door slightly open on an electric oven and closed on a gas one. Grease the broiler pan and rack. Center the meat on the rack. Broil until the meat is brown; basting occasionally, turn and repeat.
GRILL	See THE PATIO CHEF.
PAN BROIL	Very lightly grease a **heavy** skillet or griddle and preheat on HIGH or MEDIUM HIGH until it is sizzling hot. Add the meat, brown quickly on both sides, reduce to MEDIUM LOW, and cook, uncovered, until done, draining the fat as it accumulates.
PAN FRY **(Stir-Fry or Saute)**	In a heavy skillet melt enough butter or preheat enough oil on MEDIUM HIGH to cover the bottom ⅛ inch deep. Brown all sides, turning or stirring as needed. See the STIR-FRY CHEF.
SKILLET OR **CHICKEN FRY**	In a heavy skillet, melt enough butter or preheat enough oil on MEDIUM HIGH to cover the bottom ½ to 1 inch deep. Season and flour or bread the meat. Brown the meat on both sides. Reduce to MEDIUM, cover and cook until done, turning as needed. (Do not cover seafood.) Remove the lid and cook briefly on both sides until meat re-crisps.

DEEP FRY **(French Fry)**	Use a deep, heavy saucepan, Dutch oven, or electric deep-fat fryer. Fill only ½ full with any vegetable-based oil or shortening. (Animal fats smoke and burn!) Heat the oil to 350° to 400° or until the grease is in motion (halfway between a waltz and a jitterbug) with no smoking. Season and flour or bread the food if needed. Add only enough food to make one layer. Fry until the food floats and is brown. Allow the oil to return to the correct temperature before adding the next batch.
OVEN FRY	Preheat the oven to 375° for meat and poultry and 450° for seafood. In a shallow baking pan, heat enough butter or oil to barely cover the bottom of the pan. Season and flour or bread the food. Place it in the pan with the skin-side down. For seafoods, spoon a small amount of melted butter or oil on the top since it is not necessary to turn these over. Cook seafoods for approximately 10 to 15 minutes or until done. (Do not overcook.) Most meats and poultry require one hour to oven fry and must be turned after 30 minutes or halfway through the time indicated in the recipe.
STEAM **(Mostly used for poultry and seafood)**	Use a deep pan with a tightly fitting lid and a lightly greased wire rack, metal colander, or basket insert. Add enough water or liquid to completely cover the bottom of the pan, but not the rack. Bring the water to a rapid boil on HIGH. Place the food in a single layer on the metal insert. Cover and reduce to MEDIUM HIGH. Steam until tender.
ROAST (Bake) **(Place a strip of bacon over very lean cuts.)**	Preheat the oven to 325° (350° for pork). Place seasoned meat fat-side up on the roasting pan, insert a meat thermometer, and cook, uncovered, until done. For roasting in a covered pan, do not insert a meat thermometer.

FOR TOUGH CUSTOMERS **Liquid Added, Long Cooking Time**	
BRAISE **(Pot Roast)**	In a heavy Dutch oven or deep skillet, heat on MEDIUM HIGH enough oil or butter to cover the bottom ⅛ inch deep. Season the food and flour it, if desired. Add the meat or poultry and brown well on all sides. If the pan juices do not completely cover the bottom of the pan, add a small amount of water or other liquid. Cover tightly and simmer on LOW or in a 325° oven until the meat is tender.
FRICASSEE **(Smother)**	Follow the directions for BRAISING, except flour all pieces before browning. Remove the pieces, make a gravy or add cream, return the pieces to the liquid, cover, reduce the heat to LOW, and cook until tender.
STEW	Follow the directions for BRAISING, except add enough water or broth to completely cover the food.

THE MATCH MAKERS

Match your cut of Meat, Fish, or Poultry with the correct cooking technique and use the directions in THE MEAT OF THE MATTER for perfect results every time.

BEEF	CUTS	COOKING TECHNIQUES
Steaks:	Sirloin, Porterhouse, T-Bone, Ribeye (Delmonico), Filet Mignon (tenderlion) . .	Broil, Grill, Pan Broil, Pan Fry
	Round, Flank, Blade	Braise
	Tenderized Round (also called Cubed or Minute), Flank	Pan Broil, Pan Fry, Fricassee
	Marinated Round, Chuck, Flank	Broil, Grill, Pan Broil
	Ground	Broil, Grill, Pan Broil, Pan Fry, Oven Fry, Bake
Roasts:	Filet of Tenderloin, Eye of Round, Rib (Standing or Rolled)	Roast, Grill
	Sirloin Tip, Rump, Top Round (Pike's Peak)	Roast, Grill, Braise
	Blade, Arm, Chuck, Shoulder, English Cut, Top or Bottom Round	Braise
Special Cuts:	Short Ribs, Brisket, Stew, Corned Beef . . .	Stew,
	Liver	Braise, Pan Fry (quickly)
PORK	CUTS	COOKING TECHNIQUES
Chops:	Loin, Rib, Butterfly	Broil, Pan Broil, Grill, Bake, Pan Fry, Oven Fry, Fricassee
Steaks:	Arm	Braise,
	Blade, Ham	Broil, Grill, Pan Broil, Pan Fry, Braise
Ribs:	Spareribs (loin or country style)	Braise, Roast, Grill, Broil
Roasts:	Loin (Sirloin, Tenderloin, Blade, Center), Boston Butt, Crown	Roast
Ham:		Roast, Grill, Boil
Special Cuts:	Canadian Bacon (Whole)	Roast
	Canadian Bacon (Sliced)	Broil, Grill, Pan Fry
	Tenderloin (Slices, Medallions)	Pan Fry, Smother, Grill
VEAL	CUTS	COOKING TECHNIQUES
Roasts:	Crown, Rib (Rack)	Roast
	Rump, Round, Arm, Blade, Rolled, Shoulder, Loin, Sirloin, Leg	Roast, Braise
Chops:	Leg	Roast, Braise, Smother
	Loin, Rib	Pan Fry, Braise, Smother

Steaks: (Cutlets)	Blade, Arm	Pan Fry, Braise, Smother
	Round, Sirloin	Braise, Smother
Special Cuts:	Ribs, Stew, Heel of Round, Shank	Braise, Stew
	City Chicken or Mock Chicken	Pan Fry, Braise
	Liver (Calf's)	Broil, Pan Broil, Pan Fry, Braise, Deep Fry

LAMB	CUTS	COOKING TECHNIQUES
Roasts:	Leg (American & French have bone removed), Rib (Crown has 12-15 ribs; Rack has 6-7 ribs), Sirloin, Loin, Rolled or Cushion Shoulder	Roast, Grill, Broil, Braise, Stew
Chops or Patties:	Rib, Loin, Sirloin, Tenderloin (T-Bone), Ground Patties	Broil, Grill, Pan Broil, Pan Fry, Oven Fry,
	Shoulder, Round, Blade	Braise, Broil, Grill, Pan Broil
Special Cuts:	Riblets, Shanks, Stew, Rolled or Stuffed Breast	Braise, Stew
	Liver	Broil, Pan Broil, Pan Fry, Braise

POULTRY	CUTS	COOKING TECHNIQUES
Chicken:	**Fryer:**	
	Whole	Roast
	Halves	Broil, Grill
	Pieces	Chicken fry, Pan fry, Deep fry, Oven fry, Broil, Grill, Steam
	Hen:	
	Roaster or Baker	Roast, Stew, Braise, Fricasee
	Stewing	Stew, Fricasee
Turkey:	Whole	Roast
	Breast, Boneless Breast Hindquarter	Roast, Grill
	Pieces (young, tender)	Chicken Fry, Pan Fry, Grill
Cornish Hens:		Roast, Grill
Duckling:		Roast
SEAFOOD	**See Fish Facts (DINNER)**	

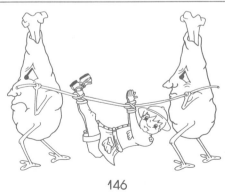

THE MEAT THERMOMETER

This gadget will earn its "board and keep" with the first roast that is neither burned, dry, raw, tough, or otherwise inedible. There are two types available: one works like a medical thermometer with a red, black, or sliver indicator line inside a metal or glass tube; the other has a round gauge with a moveable arrow that tops the tube. This type tends to break easily, and cannot be read as accurately.

HOW TO USE IT

Simple! Insert the pointed end into the thickest part of the meat. For a glass thermometer, first make a hole with a metal skewer or sharp knife. Push the tip halfway through the meat. Use the "drumstick" portion of poultry or the center of the stuffing if it is stuffed. Make sure the point does not touch any bones. That's all Folks!

HOW TO READ IT

When the indicator line or arrow reaches the desired temperature, remove the meat from the oven or grill. But remember, with **large** cuts of meat like a ham, turkey, or roast, the temperature will continue to rise up to 5° after it is removed from the heat. No wonder many restaurants often overdo a good thing!

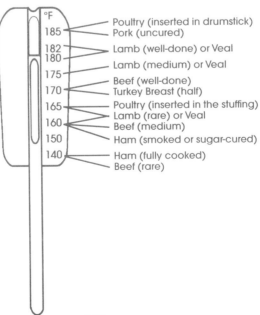

°F	
185	Poultry (inserted in drumstick) / Pork (uncured)
182	Lamb (well-done) or Veal
180	Lamb (medium) or Veal
175	
170	Beef (well-done) / Turkey Breast (half)
165	Poultry (inserted in the stuffing) / Lamb (rare) or Veal
160	Beef (medium)
150	Ham (smoked or sugar-cured)
140	Ham (fully cooked) / Beef (rare)

147

BEEF

Average Serving Size Per Person for Beef, Pork, Lamb or Veal:
Boneless or lean cuts (very little fat) - ¼ to ⅓ lb.
Moderate amount of fat and bone - ½ lb.
Very bony - ¾ to 1 lb.

ROAST BEEF

Makes: (Servings per pound)
Boneless: 4
Bone-in: 3
Groundwork: 2 minutes

Bake:	
Minutes Per Lb.	Meat Thermometer
Rare:	
22 - 26	140°
Medium:	
26 - 30	160°
Well Done:	
33 - 35	170°
For Rolled Roast: Add 10 minutes per pound.	

Oven Temp: Preheat 500°
Bake: 325°
Need: Baking pan with rack or broiler pan
meat thermometer

FOR STANDING RIB: No rack is needed - the bones keep it out of the drippings.

Tender cuts such as: Standing Rib, Rolled Rib, Sirloin Tip, Eye of Round, or Rolled Rump (Use only the highest quality rump roast.)

1 (2 to 3 lb.) roast
Salt
Pepper
Garlic powder (optional)

1. Preheat the oven to 500°.

2. Lightly grease the bottom of the roasting pan if you plan to use the pan drippings for gravy.

3. Season the meat on all sides.

4. Place the roast, fat-side up, on a rack in a shallow baking or broiler pan.

5. Insert the meat thermometer, place the roast in the oven, **immediately** turn it down to 325,° and cook according to the side column.

OPTIONS:

A. Serve with Au Jus (the drippings in the bottom of the pan or the Elegant Au Jus (SAUCES AND GRAVIES).

BEEF ROAST

Makes: (Servings per
  pound)
Boneless: 4
Bone-in: 3
Groundwork: 2 minutes
Cook: Browning time:
  5 minutes - HIGH
Bake or cook:
Bone-in - 1½ hr. per lb.
Boneless - Allow 20-25
  additional minutes
  per pound
Oven Temp: 325°
Cook Temp: LOW
Need: Dutch oven or
  electric skillet

POT ROAST:
Add to the Beef Roast
ingredients:
4 small onions
4 small carrots
4 small potatoes
1 small bell pepper
1 rib celery
¾ to 1¾ cups water
salt and pepper

Follow the directions
for Beef Roast EXCEPT:

Add the water (1 to 2
cups total) to the
browned meat and
cook 30 minutes
before adding the
washed, peeled
veggies.

Less tender cuts such as: Blade, Chuck, Shoulder, Round, or Rump.

1 (2 lb.) roast
Salt
Pepper
Garlic powder
1 Tablespoon vegetable oil
½ cup water

1. Preheat the oven to 325°

2. Season the roast on all sides.

3. Heat the vegetable oil in the Dutch oven or electric skillet on MEDIUM HIGH.

4. Brown the meat on all sides.

5. Turn off the heat and carefully add the water (be careful not to singe your whiskers with the steam!).

6. Cover, place it in the oven, (or turn the heat down to LOW), and cook 2 to 2½ hours until the roast is tender.

7. Turn the roast once or twice during cooking and add more water if necessary (be sure not to let all the liquid cook away or the roast will scorch.).

Serve the gravy in a separate bowl.

OPTIONS:

A. Coat the roast lightly with flour before browning.

B. Thicken the gravy (SAUCES AND GRAVIES).

SPICED EYE OF ROUND

Makes: 6 servings
Groundwork: 3 minutes

Bake:	
Minutes Per Lb.	Meat Thermometer
Rare: 45	135-140°
Medium: 60	155-160°
Well: 1¼ hr.	170°

Oven Temp: 375°
Need: waxed paper
baking pan with a
    rack
meat thermometer

Some eye of round
roasts are short and
fat while others are
long and skinny,
making a meat
thermometer the safest
bet for perfect
doneness.

Slice the cooked roast
very thinly, serve warm
or at room
temperature with
Horseradish Sauce
(SAUCES AND GRAVIES).

Makes: 2 servings
Groundwork: 5 minutes
Bake: 2 hours
Oven Temp: 325°
Need: Dutch oven with
    lid

Serve over: Hot cooked
rice or noodles.

Large amounts of stew
beef cubes will brown
more quickly if they
are dipped in flour first.

---

1 (2½ lb.) eye of round roast
1 Tablespoon vegetable oil
2 Tablespoons Italian seasoning

1. Preheat the oven to 375°.

2. Remove any excess fat from the roast and coat the entire roast with the oil.

3. Sprinkle a strip of waxed paper with the Italian seasoning.

4. Roll the roast in the seasoning until it is completely coated.

5. Insert the meat thermometer into the center of the thickest part of the meat and center the roast on the rack in the baking pan.

6. Bake 45 minutes to 1¼ hours to desired doneness.

OPTIONS:

A. Omit the oil and replace the Italian seasoning with ¼ teaspoon garlic powder and 1 teaspoon coarse-ground black pepper, and place a slice of uncooked bacon over the top.

BEEF TIPS

1 Tablespoon butter
1 lb. lean stew beef (cut into ½" cubes)
1 (10¾ oz.) can mushroom soup
1 (10¾ oz.) can French onion soup
½ cup white wine or water

1. Preheat the oven to 325°.

2. Melt the butter in a Dutch oven on MEDIUM HIGH, add the beef cubes, and brown well.

3. Add all other ingredients, mix well, cover and bake 2 hours.

INDOOR STEAKS

Makes: 1 serving
Groundwork: 3 minutes
BROIL
1" thick - 15 to 20 min.
1½" thick - 20 to 25 min.
2" thick - 30 to 35 min.
Need: broiler pan

For easy clean-up, line the bottom of the broiler pan with foil and trash it when the steak is ready.

Garnish with mushrooms (lightly browned in butter) or spread each steak with seasoned butter (THE BREAD BASKET).

Steaks on the grill are in THE PATIO CHEF.

¾ to 1 lb. Sirloin, T-Bone, Porterhouse, Rib OR ¼ to ⅓ lb. Fillet or Ribeye
½ to 1 teaspoon Worcestershire
¼ teaspoon salt
¼ teaspoon pepper
⅛ teaspoon garlic powder
1 Tablespoon butter (pan broiled only)

1. Slash the fat at 1" intervals to prevent curling, but do not cut into the meat.

2. Sprinkle each side of the steak evenly with Worcestershire, garlic, salt, and pepper.

OVEN BROILED: (1 to 2 inch steaks)

A. Adjust the rack so the top of the steak is 5 inches from the heat for **rare** or **medium** or 3 inches from the heat for **well done** and turn the oven to BROIL.

B. Place the steak on the broiler pan rack and broil to the desired doneness, turning only once.

PAN BROILED: (½ to ¾ inch steaks)

A. Heat a heavy skillet on MEDIUM HIGH until very hot.

B. Add the butter and stir until melted.

C. Add the steak and brown well on both sides.

D. Reduce the heat to MEDIUM and continue cooking to the desired doneness, turning several times and removing the pan juices as they accumulate.

OPTION:

A. Pan drippings from oven or pan broiled steak can be used to make Au Jus gravy (SAUCES AND GRAVIES).

SHIPWRECK STEW

Makes: 4 servings
Groundwork: 7 to 10
  minutes
Cook: 5 min. - MED. HIGH
30 to 45 min. - LOW
Need: small paper
  bag
large saucepan with
  lid OR Dutch oven

2 medium onions (peeled)
2 medium potatoes (peeled)
2 medium carrots (peeled)
1 pound lean stew beef
4 Tablespoons vegetable oil
½ cup flour
1½ teaspoons salt
1½ teaspoons pepper
1 Tablespoon parsley flakes
½ teaspoon celery salt
2 cups warm water

1. Peel and cut the vegetables into bite-sized chunks.

2. Add the flour, 1 teaspoon each of salt and pepper, and meat to a small paper bag, and shake to coat.

3. Heat the vegetable oil in a large saucepan or Dutch oven on MEDIUM HIGH.

4. Brown the meat on all sides and remove from the pan.

5. Add 4 Tablespoons of the seasoned flour to the hot oil and stir constantly until the roux is a rich brown.

6. Remove the saucepan from the heat, gradually add the water, stirring constantly until well mixed.

7. Return the saucepan to the heat, add the meat, vegetables, and the remaining spices, and return the stew **just** to barely bubbling.

8. Reduce to LOW, stir, cover, and cook, stirring occasionally for 30 to 45 minutes until the meat is done and the veggies are tender. (Add additional water if the gravy thickens too much or cooks away.)

MAMA'S HOMEMADE VEGETABLE BEEF SOUP

Makes: 4 servings
Groundwork: 5 minutes
Cook: 1 hour - LOW
Need: large saucepan
or stockpot

1 (16 oz.) can whole tomatoes (undrained)
1 lb. lean stew beef
6 cups water
1 Tablespoon minced onions
1 teaspoon salt
¼ teaspoon pepper
1 Tablespoon parsley flakes
2 Tablespoons celery flakes
1 (16 oz.) pkg. frozen mixed vegetables
¼ cup uncooked rice or elbow macaroni

1. Cut the tomatoes into bite-size pieces.

2. Combine the cut tomatoes and juice from the can, beef, water, and spices in a large saucepan or stockpot on HIGH.

3. Bring to a boil, reduce the heat to LOW, cover and cook 20 to 30 minutes until the beef is tender.

4. Add the vegetables and rice or pasta and continue cooking 30 additional minutes.

OPTION:

A. Replace the stew beef with ground beef (crumbled), diced cooked ham, turkey, or chicken.

Stone Soup:
Like the old fable, a little bit of nothing can turn into soup. Just keep a labeled container in the freezer and add your leftover vegetables and meat to add to the next pot.

Don't add seafood, asparagus, mashed or sweet potatoes or any food in a sauce or marinade.

153

PORK

PORK ROAST

Makes: (Servings per pound)
Boneless: 3-4
Bone-in: 2-3
Groundwork: 1 minute
Bake: 35-40 min. per lb.
Meat Thermometer:
  Loin: 170°
Rib or Shoulder: 185°
Need: baking pan (no rack required)
meat thermometer

Add 10 to 15 minutes per lb. to the cooking time for a rolled boneless pork roast.

Properly cooked pork roast is completely gray with no pink remaining.

---

1 loin, rib, or shoulder pork roast
salt, pepper and garlic powder to taste

1. Preheat the oven to 325°.

2. Lightly grease the baking pan (only if you plan to make gravy).

3. Sprinkle the roast with salt and pepper, place it fat-side up in a baking pan, and insert the meat thermometer.

4. Bake the pork roast until well done — not medium or rare!

OPTION:

A. Pork roasts can also be braised like beef roasts (The Meat of the Matter).

PORK CHOPS

Makes: 2 servings
Groundwork: 3 minutes
Broil: 20 to 26 minutes
Oven Temp: BROIL
Need: broiler pan or shallow baking pan with rack

Basting sauces are in SAUCES AND GRAVIES.

Chops are great sauteed, skillet or chicken fried (The Meat of the Matter.)

---

4 small to medium OR 2 large pork chops
¼ teaspoon salt
¼ teaspoon pepper
1½ cups basting sauce

1. Preheat the oven to BROIL.

2. Slash the fat at 2 inch intervals to prevent curling; salt and pepper both sides of the chops.

3. Choose a basting sauce.

4. Place the chops on the broiler pan, baste on both sides, and broil 3 to 5 inches from the heat until light brown, basting frequently and turning once.
½ - ¾ inch thick - 10 to 11 min. per side
¾ - 1 inch thick - 11 to 13 min. per side

BARBECUED SPARERIBS

Makes: 2 servings
Groundwork: 3 minutes
Bake: 1 hour 45 minutes
Oven Temp: 450° - 15 minutes
350° - 1½ hours

To remove excess fat and make them more tender, ribs may be boiled 2 to 4 minutes before baking.

Country Style ribs are meatier and require longer cooking time (15 to 30 minutes).

1½ to 2 pounds spareribs
¼ teaspoon salt and pepper
1 cup barbecue sauce

1. Preheat the oven to 450°.

2. Sprinkle both sides of the meat with salt and pepper.

3. Arrange the ribs in a single layer on broiler pan, cover loosely with foil, and bake 15 minutes.

4. Reduce the oven temperature to 350°, baste the ribs on both sides with the sauce, cover, and continue to cook 1 hour, basting and turning frequently.

5. Uncover the pan, baste, and cook an additional 30 minutes until the ribs are tender.

SPARERIBS AND SAUERKRAUT

Makes: 2 servings
Groundwork: 5 minutes
Cook: 30 min. - MED. HIGH
45 minutes - LOW
Need: large skillet with lid or electric skillet

Add your choice: ½ teaspoon carraway seeds OR 1 apple, cut into small wedges.

1 Tablespoon vegetable oil
1½ to 2 pounds spareribs
¼ teaspoon salt and pepper
½ (12 oz.) can beer
1 (16 oz.) can sauerkraut (drained)
1 Tablespoon brown sugar

1. Cut the ribs apart into 2 or 3-rib pieces, and salt and pepper both sides.

2. Heat the oil in a large skillet on MEDIUM HIGH. Brown the ribs, remove them from the skillet, and drain off the drippings.

3. Combine the ribs and beer in the skillet, reduce the heat to LOW, cover, and simmer 30 minutes.

4. Drain the sauerkraut, add it and the brown sugar to the skillet and continue to cook, covered, for an additional 45 minutes until tender.

155

BAKED HAM

Read all the directions on the package first! Some hams are fully cooked and need no additional baking. Some have to be refrigerated before opening while others can be stored on the pantry shelf.

UNCOOKED WHOLE, HALF, BONED-AND-ROLLED, OR PICNIC HAM:

HAM	MINUTES PER POUND (325°)	MEAT THERMOMETER
Whole, Half	20 (30 if larger than 10 lbs.)	160°
Boned & Rolled	25 to 30	170°
Picnic	20	170°

I. The No-Baste Way:

1. Preheat the oven to 325°.

2. Remove all wrapping from the ham including the paper strip on some hams that proudly announce "water has been added."

3. Wrap the ham in foil (optional) and place it fat-side-up on a rack in the baking pan.

4. Insert the meat thermometer and bake 20 minutes **per pound.**

5. About 30 minutes before the end of the baking time, remove the ham from the oven and remove the thermometer.

6. With a sharp knife, cut off the skin and all but a thin layer of fat.

7. If desired, cut the top of the ham into a checker board or diamond pattern ¼ inch deep. Insert 1 whole clove in the center of each diamond or square.

8. Cover the top and sides of the ham with one of the Great Ham Glazes that follows.

9. Replace the meat thermometer and continue baking the ham for the remaining 30 minutes.

10. Cool 10 to 15 minutes before slicing.

II. The Basted Way:

1. Follow the directions for the No-Baste-Way except before baking remove the skin and all but a thin layer of the fat.

2. Insert a meat thermometer and baste the ham with your choice of basting liquids every 30 minutes during the baking time.

3. Glaze, if desired, 30 minutes before the end of the baking time

Best Basting Bets:

A. Coca-Cola or 7-Up

B. Pineapple, orange, apricot or apple juice or cider.

FULLY COOKED (READY-TO-EAT):

While these hams can be sliced and enjoyed "as-is," both the taste and texture are vastly improved with additional baking. Before baking canned hams, remove the jellied juice and wrap the ham in foil.

HAM	MINUTES PER POUND	MEAT THERMOMETER
WHOLE	12 to 15	140°
HALF	15 to 17	140°
BUFFET	15	140°
BONED,	20	140°
ROLLED CANNED	20 - up to 6 pounds 15 - over 6 pounds	130°

ROYAL HAMS

Crown the cooked ham by either glazing or garnishing (or both) and return it to the hot oven for 5 minutes. For a regal touch, serve ham with Royal Cherry Sauce (SAUCES AND GRAVIES, PAGE 253).

I. **Great Ham Glazes**

   A. Brown sugar and orange juice or mustard (plain, Dijon, spicy, or Creole)

   B. Seedless jelly: apricot, currant, raspberry, orange marmalade

   C. Barbecue sauce

II. **Great Ham Garnishes**

Top the cooked ham (with the skin removed and scored if desired) with either:

   A. Pineapple or apple rings with a red or green maraschino cherry in the center of each and sprinkle the finished product with brown sugar.

   B. Insert one whole clove in the center of each diamond score before glazing.

HAM SLICES

Makes: 3 to 4 servings per lb.
Groundwork: 2 minutes
Bake: 45 to 60 minutes
Oven Temp: 350°
Need: shallow baking dish or pan with lid.

For Spiffy Slices add one of the Great Ham Glazes or Garnishes (Royal Hams).

½ **to 1 inch thick center-cut ham slice**
½ **cup fruit juice or cider**

1. Preheat the oven to 350°.

2. Slash the fat at 2-inch intervals to prevent curling.

3. Lightly grease the baking dish.

4. Center the ham in the dish and pour the apple juice over the ham slice.

5. Cover and bake, basting several times, 45 to 60 minutes until tender.

POLISH, GERMAN, ITALIAN, CAJUN, OR SMOKED SAUSAGES

Makes: 3 to 4 servings per lb.
Groundwork: 2 minutes
Bake: 30 to 45 minutes
Oven Temp: 325°.
Need: baking pan with rack boil

All of these sausages are terrific on the grill (Patio Chef), Pan Fried or Pan Broiled (The Meat of the Matter).

Sausage
Universal Sauce/Marinade (SAUCES AND GRAVIES)

1. Preheat the oven to 325°.

2. Baste the sausages with Universal Sauce and arrange them in a single layer on a rack in the baking pan.

3. Lightly cover with foil.

4. Bake, basting the sausages every 10 minutes for 30 to 45 minutes until thoroughly cooked and a rich brown color.

OPTION:

   A. Replace the Universal Sauce with garlic butter (The Bread Basket).

LAMB AND LIVER

LAMB CHOPS

Makes: 1 serving
Groundwork: 2 minutes
Marinate: 1 to 12 hours
 (optional)
Broil: 12 to 18 min.
Need: broiler pan

2 lamb chops per person
Pineapple juice
Tarragon or rosemary

1. Trim the excess fat from each chop and slash the remaining fat.

2. Place the chops in a plastic bag, cover with pineapple juice, seal tightly, and refrigerate 1 to 12 hours.

No time to marinate? Just dip the chops in pineapple juice before broiling and baste several times during broiling.

3. Drain the chops and sprinkle each with a pinch of tarragon or rosemary.

4. Broil 4 to 5 inches from the heat, turning once:

   Time for **each** side (medium doneness):

   1 inch thick - 6 minutes
   1½ inches thick - 9 minutes

BREADED CHOPS

Makes: 2 servings
Groundwork: 5 minutes
Cook: 5 to 7 min. -
 MEDIUM
Need: skillet
small mixing bowl

1 egg
1 cup plain cracker crumbs
2 Tablespoons Parmesan cheese
½ teaspoon rosemary or tarragon
⅛ teaspoon pepper
4 lamb chops
1 Tablespoon butter

1. Beat the egg in a small mixing bowl.

2. Combine the crumbs, cheese, and spices in a plastic bag.

3. Dip each chop first in the beaten egg, then shake in the crumb mixture and pan fry 2½ to 3½ minutes on each side in melted butter.

LIVER AND ONIONS

Makes: 2 servings
Groundwork: 2 minutes
Cook: onions - 5 min.
  MEDIUM
liver - 5 min. MEDIUM
Need: medium skillet

1 Tablespoon butter or bacon
  drippings (for the onions)
1 medium onion (peeled and sliced)
1 Tablespoon butter or bacon
  drippings (for the liver)
½ lb. calf's liver (cut into ½ inch slices
  and all membranes removed)
2 Tablespoons flour
¼ teaspoon salt
⅛ teaspoon pepper
4 slices crisp bacon (optional)

Over-cooking liver will toughen it quickly. It is best cooked only to medium doneness - still pink in the center.

The onions can be kept warm in the oven on 200° while the liver is cooking. An added plus — a warm serving platter!

1. Melt the butter in a medium skillet on MEDIUM.

2. Peel and slice the onion into the melted butter, cook 4 to 5 minutes until they are tender but not brown, and remove them to a serving platter.

3. Melt the additional butter in the skillet.

4. Salt and pepper the liver slices and coat both sides with flour.

5. Cook the slices for 2 to 2½ minutes on each side until brown and crisp.

6. Top with the cooked onions and crisp crumbled bacon (optional).

**AVERAGE SERVING
SIZES PER PERSON:**
Chicken
Broiler - ½ chicken
Fryer - ¾ to 1 lb.
Hen - ¾ lb.
Turkey:
Whole - ¾ lb.
Boneless Breast - ⅓ lb.

Definition Dilemma:
Technically, "one chicken breast" means one half of the whole (double) chicken breast. Rarely will any recipe use the entire breast.

Makes: 2 servings
Groundwork: 5 minutes
Cook: 15 to 20 min. - MED. HIGH
20 to 30 min. - MEDIUM
Need: small paper or plastic bag
medium skillet with lid

Chicken Livers:
These are fried the same as chicken pieces except:

1. Puncture both sides several times with a fork before cooking or they will explode!
2. Reduce the cooking time to 5 to 10 minutes.

To prevent the breading or batter from falling off, the oil must be very hot when the chicken is first added.

POULTRY

IMPORTANT INFO! Always rinse fresh, raw poultry under cold water and pat it dry with paper towels before cooking. Then, wash your hands and any used utensils thoroughly before handling any other foods! Bacterial contamination from raw poultry is one of the most common forms of food poisoning.

FRIED CHICKEN

4 medium chicken pieces
Vegetable oil
⅛ teaspoon salt
⅛ teaspoon pepper
½ cup flour

1. Rinse the chicken under cold water and pat dry with paper towels.

2. Pour enough oil in a medium skillet to 1⅛ inches deep and heat on MEDIUM HIGH.

3. While the oil is heating, add the flour to a paper or plastic bag and salt and pepper on both sides of the chicken.

4. Shake the chicken in the bag of flour (1 piece at a time) to coat thoroughly.

5. Brown the floured chicken pieces 7 to 10 minutes on each side.

6. Cover, reduce the heat to MEDIUM, and cook approximately 20 to 30 minutes until the chicken is tender.

7. Remove the lid and cook 5 to 8 more minutes to re-crisp.

OPTION:

A.   Replace the flour with Beer Batter or Backwater Breading (Seafood).

Makes: ½ to ¾ lb. per
serving
Groundwork: 4 minutes
Bake: 50 minutes
Oven Temp: 425°
Need: baking pan
plastic bag

Use any extra Chicken
Cruncher to make a
quick side dish! Wash
and slice a whole
potato ½ inch thick.
Coat the slices and
dip in the mix. Bake in
a separate greased
pan while the chicken
bakes.

Crunchy Oven Fried:
In place of melted
butter, dip or coat the
chicken in buttermilk,
mayonnaise, Ranch or
Italian salad dressing.
Roll in one of the
Crunchers and bake
in a lightly greased
pan.

OVEN FRIED CHICKEN

4 medium chicken pieces
¼ cup (½ stick) butter
1 choice of Chicken Crunchers

1. Preheat the oven to 425°.

2. Melt the butter in the baking pan
   while the oven preheats.

3. Prepare your choice of Chicken
   Cruncher.

4. Dip the chicken on both sides in the
   melted butter, roll in the Chicken
   Cruncher and arrange the pieces
   skin-side down in the baking pan.

5. Bake, uncovered, for 35 minutes, turn
   each piece over, and bake 15
   additional minutes until the chicken
   is tender and golden brown.

CHICKEN CRUNCHERS

Mix the ingredients in a plastic bag,
drop in the chicken one piece at a
time, and shake to coat completely.

A. ½ cup self rising flour or biscuit mix
    1½ teaspoons poultry seasoning
    ¼ teaspoon salt (omit with biscuit
    mix)
    ¼ teaspoon pepper

B. ½ cup cheese crackers (crushed)
    1 teaspoon taco seasoning

C. ½ cup (plain or Italian) bread
    crumbs
    ¼ cup Parmesan cheese

D. ½ cup saltine crackers (crushed)
    ½ teaspoon dry herb salad
    dressing mix
    ½ teaspoon paprika

EASY OVEN BAKED CHICKEN PIECES
(Take your choice of favorite cuts)

Makes: ½ to ¾ lb. per serving
Groundwork: 1 to 2 minutes
Bake: 1¼ - 1½ hours
Oven Temp: 350°
Need: baking dish with lid

Chicken halves or pieces are also great broiled. Simply follow the "Broil" directions (The Meat of the Matter), basting frequently with one of the SAUCES.

For a change use chicken in place of fish in Fish Amandine (SEAFOOD).

---

1. Preheat the oven to 350°.

2. Arrange the chicken, skin-side up, in a single layer in a baking dish.

3. Coat the chicken with your choice of Baking Makings.

4. Cover and bake 60 minutes until the chicken is tender.

5. Uncover and bake 15 to 30 minutes until the chicken is brown.

BAKING MAKINGS

A. Universal Sauce (SAUCES AND GRAVIES), Italian Dressing, or Barbecue Sauce.

B. Combine either of the following in a small mixing bowl:

   1. 1 (8 oz.) bottle Russian dressing
      1 (¼ oz.) envelope dry onion soup mix
      1 (8 oz.) jar apricot jam

   2. 1 (10¾ oz.) can cream of mushroom or chicken soup
      ½ (1¼ oz.) dry onion soup mix

CHICKEN CACCIATORE

Makes: 2 servings
Groundwork: 2 minutes
Bake: 1 hour
Oven Temp: 350°
Need: 8 x 8 inch
baking dish

Calorie Counter:
Remove the skin and
bones from the
chicken to reduce
both the calorie and
cholesterol count.

---

1 (5 oz.) can of
boneless chicken is
equal to 1 large
chicken breast half
(cooked, with the skin
and bones removed).

2 chicken breast halves (skinned and boned)
1 (8 oz.) jar spaghetti sauce
½ cup bread crumbs
¼ cup Parmesan cheese

1. Preheat the oven to 350°.

2. Lightly grease the baking dish.

3. Arrange the chicken in a single layer in the baking dish.

4. Cover the chicken evenly with spaghetti sauce and sprinkle with bread crumbs and Parmesan cheese.

5. Bake, uncovered, for 1 hour until the chicken is tender.

CHICKEN DIJON

Makes: 2 servings
Groundwork: 5 minutes
Bake: 1 hour
Oven Temp: 350°
Need: small mixing
bowl
waxed paper
baking dish

Chicken Cuts: in most
recipes using a
specific cut of
chicken, **any other cut**
may be substituted.
The cooking time will
be slightly altered, if
the pieces are larger
or smaller than the
original ones.

2 chicken breast halves
2 Tablespoons Dijon mustard
1 slice of bread (finely crumbled)
¼ cup Parmesan cheese
2 teaspoons butter

1. Preheat the oven to 350°

2. Grease the baking dish.

3. Crumble the bread finely into a small mixing bowl, add the cheese, mix well, and pour the mixture onto a large sheet of waxed paper.

4. Coat the chicken pieces with mustard on all sides and roll in the bread crumb mixture, pressing the crumbs firmly on both sides.

5. Arrange the chicken in the baking dish meat-side up, and top each with a slice of butter.

6. Bake, uncovered, 1 hour until tender and brown.

OVEN CHICKEN CORDON BLEU

Makes: 2 servings
Groundwork: 4 minutes
Bake: 20 to 25 minutes
Oven Temp: 425°
Need: plastic wrap
medium mixing bowl
baking dish or pan
toothpicks

2 chicken breast halves (skinned and boned)
2 Tablespoons butter
¼ cup bread crumbs
¼ cup Parmesan cheese
¼ teaspoon garlic powder
2 oz. Monterey Jack or Swiss cheese (cut into strips)
2 slices boiled ham
⅛ teaspoon salt

Pseudo Cordon Bleu:
Cook 2 frozen
breaded chicken
patties as directed on
the package and top
each with a slice of
ham and a slice of
cheese 5 minutes
before the end of the
baking time.

Top with Marquery
Sauce (SAUCES AND
GRAVIES).

Freebie Time Saver:
Ask your butcher to
run the chicken
through the meat
tenderizer machine.

1. Preheat the oven to 425°.

2. Melt the butter in the baking dish in the oven while it preheats.

3. Place the chicken breast halves between 2 sheets of plastic wrap and flatten each with a meat mallet or the edge of a saucer (held vertically).

4. Combine the bread crumbs, Parmesan, garlic, and salt in bowl.

5. Cut the cheese and ham into 2 strips, place one strip of each in the center of each piece of chicken, fold each end of the chicken over the strips, fold in both sides totally to encase the cheese and ham, and fasten it securely with toothpicks.

6. Dip each bundle into the melted butter and roll in the bread crumb mixture.

7. Place each, seam-side down, in the baking dish and bake 20 to 25 minutes until golden brown. (Cooking time depends on the size and thickness of the chicken.)

CHICKEN PICCATA

Makes: 2 servings
Groundwork: 3 minutes
Cook: 6 to 8 minutes
Need: plastic wrap
medium skillet

2 **chicken breast halves (skinned & boned)**
⅛ **teaspoon salt**
⅛ **teaspoon pepper**
2 **Tablespoons flour**
2 **Tablespoons butter**
1 **Tablespoon vegetable oil**
2 **Tablespoons white wine**
1 **Tablespoon capers (drained)**
4 **thin slices of lemon (seeds removed) OR 1 to 2 teaspoons lemon juice**

Serve with a crisp green salad with Italian dressing and hot garlic bread (THE BREAD BASKET).

Buy the chicken breasts already skinned and boned and don't complain about the cost of capers — you would pay a small fortune for this meal in a good Italian restaurant.

1. Place the chicken between two sheets of plastic wrap and flatten to ¼ inch thick with a meat mallet or the edge of a saucer (held vertically).

2. Sprinkle each with salt and pepper, coat each with flour on both sides and shake off the excess.

3. Melt the butter and oil together in the skillet on MEDIUM HIGH and heat until the butter bubbles disappear.

4. Add the chicken and cook 4 to 5 minutes, turn, and cook 2 to 3 minutes, turn again and cook 1 to 2 additional minutes until golden brown.

5. Add the wine, and continue cooking until the mixture is slightly thickened.

6. Add the capers and lemon slices and cook 1 minute until hot.

7. Serve each piece of chicken topped with lemon slices and the caper sauce.

ROAST TURKEY

Makes: 5 to 7 servings
Thaw Time:
Refrigerator - 2 to 2½ days
Cold water - 5 hours
Groundwork: 10 minutes
Bake: see below
Oven Temp: 325°
Need: covered dark enamel roasting pan OR shallow open roasting pan with rack.

Roasting Times:
Open Pan: 3¾ hrs. (stuffed) 185° (165° if inserted in stuffing)
3 hrs. (unstuffed) 185°
Covered Dark Enamel Pan: (no meat thermometer) 3¼ hrs. (stuffed)
2¾ hrs. (unstuffed)

Roast Chicken or Cornish Hen
Prepare and cook the same as turkey.
1-2 lb. Cornish Hen (stuffed or unstuffed):
Open pan 1½ hrs. - 185°
Covered dark pan - 1 hr.

5 Lb. Chicken
Open pan 2½ hrs. - 185°
Covered dark pan - 2 hrs.

How do you know if it is done?
If the drumstick-thigh joint moves easily and the meat feels soft, she is ready to eat!

10 lb. turkey (thawed)
5 Tablespoons butter or vegetable oil
½ teaspoon salt
½ teaspoon pepper
½ cup water (optional)
***stuffing (optional)**

1. Preheat the oven to 325°.

2. Remove the giblets (gizzard, heart, liver, neck) from the neck and/or body cavity of the thawed turkey.

3. Rinse the bird thoroughly inside and out with cold water.

4. Salt and pepper both the inside of the body cavity and the outside of the bird.

5. Place 1 Tablespoon of the butter in the neck cavity underneath the skin flap.

6. Either put 2 Tablespoons of butter in the body cavity or fill with dressing (*stuffing).

7. Reposition the legs either under the skin flap that is usually left at the opening of the body cavity for that purpose, in the metal wire (if one was provided), or tie the legs to the tail with clean twine. (The ol gal will kick her cover off as she cooks if you don't.)

8. Dot the breast-side of the bird with the remaining 2 Tablespoons of butter and place her in the roasting pan.

9. When using a covered roaster, add the water to the bottom of the pan, cover, and roast at 325°.

10. When roasting uncovered, cover the breast lightly with foil. Remove it when the bird is ¾ done to allow browning.

11. Baste her occasionally with the drippings in the bottom of the roaster.

WHAT IN THE WORLD DO YOU DO WITH THE GIBLETS (Gizzard, Heart, Liver, Neck)?

Giblets from turkey
4 cups water
2½ teaspoons salt
1 teaspoon pepper
1 Tablespoon parsley flakes

1. Wash the giblets in cold water.

2. Bring the water, giblets (except the liver), salt, pepper, and parsley to a boil in a medium saucepan on HIGH.

3. Reduce to MEDIUM LOW, cover, and simmer 1 hour.

4. Add the liver and continue cooking for 30 minutes until tender.

5. Remove as much meat as possible from the neck bone, chop the giblets and neck meat and use in making Giblet Gravy (SAUCES AND GRAVIES), or add to the Dressing (Accompaniments).

Leftovers:
Refrigerate the turkey and dressing (stuffing) separately, removing any left inside the bird. Cover both tightly and use within 3 to 4 days or freeze for longer storage.

SEAFOOD

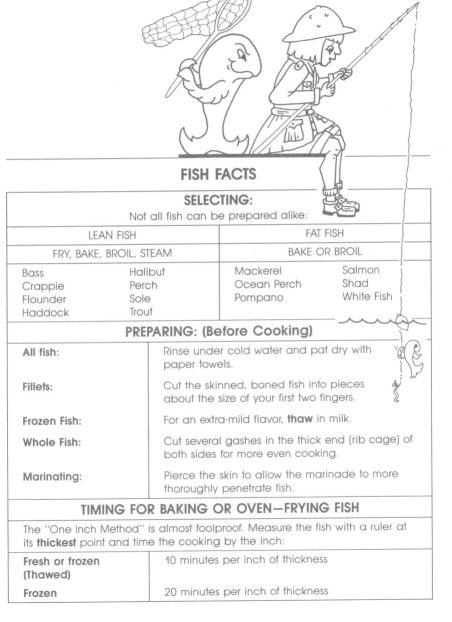

FISH FACTS

SELECTING:
Not all fish can be prepared alike:

LEAN FISH		FAT FISH	
FRY, BAKE, BROIL, STEAM		BAKE OR BROIL	
Bass	Halibut	Mackerel	Salmon
Crappie	Perch	Ocean Perch	Shad
Flounder	Sole	Pompano	White Fish
Haddock	Trout		

PREPARING: (Before Cooking)

All fish:	Rinse under cold water and pat dry with paper towels.
Fillets:	Cut the skinned, boned fish into pieces about the size of your first two fingers.
Frozen Fish:	For an extra-mild flavor, **thaw** in milk.
Whole Fish:	Cut several gashes in the thick end (rib cage) of both sides for more even cooking.
Marinating:	Pierce the skin to allow the marinade to more thoroughly penetrate fish.

TIMING FOR BAKING OR OVEN—FRYING FISH

The "One Inch Method" is almost foolproof. Measure the fish with a ruler at its **thickest** point and time the cooking by the inch:

Fresh or frozen (Thawed)	10 minutes per inch of thickness
Frozen	20 minutes per inch of thickness

BAKED FISH
(Fillets, Whole Fish or Steaks)

Oven Temp: 400°
Need: baking dish or
   pan

Average Serving Size
Per Person:
Fillets - ⅓ to ½ lb.
Steaks: ½ lb.
Whole: ¾ to 1 lb.

---

1. Preheat the oven to 400°.

2. Lightly grease a shallow baking dish.

3. Sprinkle both sides of the fish with salt and pepper and coat with melted butter or vegetable oil.

4. Bake according to the ONE-INCH TIME, basting occasionally with pan drippings, melted butter, or a sauce. (SAUCES AND GRAVIES).

OPTIONS:

A. Replace the butter or vegetable oil with Italian Dressing, mayonnaise, OR one of these sauces found in SAUCES AND MARINADES: Lemon Butter, Amandine, Shrimp, Marquery, or Mustard Dill Sauce.

B. **Crunchy:** Dip the fish in French dressing, coat in crushed cheese crackers (¼ cup dressing and ¾ cup crackers for 1 pound of fillets), and top each with a pat of butter. When using this or the Fish Camp Breading, turn to BROIL for 1 or 2 extra minutes to crisp.

BROILED FISH
(Fillets or Steaks at Least 1 inch Thick)

Need: broiler pan or
   baking pan with
   rack

1. Preheat the oven to BROIL.

2. Lightly grease the broiler rack.

3. Salt and peppr both sides of the fish and coat them with butter, vegetable oil, Italian Dressing, or lemon-butter.

4. Broil 4 to 7 minutes on each side until the fish flakes easily.

DEEP-FRIED FISH

Groundwork: 5 to 10
   minutes
Cook: 3 to 6 minutes
   Fryer - 350° to 400°
   Pan - MED. HIGH
Need: deep fat fryer
   OR deep saucepan

1. Preheat to 350° to 400° enough vege-table oil to make at least 4 inches in a deep fat fryer or saucepan.

2. Choose a coating from Batters and Breadings.

3. Carefully slide the coated fish into the hot oil (do not crowd them - they need room to float freely) and cook 3 to 6 minutes until they are golden brown and float to the top.

Remember to let the oil reheat a minute or two between "cookings" if you're cooking more than one batch.

4. Drain on paper towel on an oven-proof platter and place in a **warm** oven to stay hot until all are cooked.

PAN-FRIED FISH

Groundwork: 5 minutes
Cook: 6 to 12 min. -
   MED. HIGH
Need: large heavy
   skillet

Follow the directions for Deep-Fried EXCEPT:

1. Preheat on MEDIUM HIGH a mixture of ½ butter and ½ vegetable oil to cover the bottom of the skillet ⅛ inch deep.

2. Fry 6 to 12 minutes, turning once, until golden brown and flakes easily.

COATINGS, BATTERS, AND BREADINGS
(For 1 Pound of Fish Fillets)

BEER BATTER:

Groundwork: 5 minutes
Need: medium mixing
   bowl
wire whisk

1 cup biscuit mix
1 egg
½ cup beer

1. Combine all ingredients in a mixing bowl with a wire whisk until smooth.

OPTIONS:

A. Replace the baking mix with self-rising flour.

Groundwork: 5 minutes
Need: paper or
plastic bag

The fish may be
breaded or coated
ahead of time,
covered with plastic
wrap, and refrigerated
until you are ready to
cook them.

Groundwork: 15 minutes
Need: medium mixing
  bowl
plastic wrap OR large
  baking dish

Tip: Use one end of a
baking dish for
"crumbing" the fish,
and place the coated
fillets in the other end.
Then simply cover and
refrigerate until ready
to use.

Groundwork: 10 minutes
Need: 2 medium
  mixing bowls

For crisper breading
use cracker crumbs in
place of the corn meal.

CORN-MEAL COATING:

2 cups corn meal mix OR
1½ cups corn meal and ½ cup flour
½ teaspoon salt
¼ teaspoon pepper
¼ teaspoon cayenne pepper

1. Combine the corn meal mixture, salt
   and peppers in a small paper or
   plastic bag and shake to mix well.

2. Drop the fish into the bag and coat thoroughly by shaking the bag vigorously.

FISH CAMP BREADING:

2 cups saltine crackers
½ cup sour cream
¼ cup prepared mustard
¼ teaspoon salt
¼ teaspoon black pepper
¼ teaspoon cayenne pepper

1. Crush the crackers into fine crumbs,
   and place on a long piece of
   plastic wrap or at one end of a
   large baking dish.

2. Combine the sour cream, mustard, salt,
   and peppers in a small mixing bowl.

3. Dip the fillets into the sour cream
   mixture and roll them in the cracker
   crumbs until they are entirely coated.

BACK WATER BREADING:

1 egg
2 Tablespoons water
¼ teaspoon salt
½ cup flour
½ cup corn meal

1. Combine the egg, water, and salt in a
   medium mixing bowl until blended.

2. Combine the flour and corn meal in
   another medium mixing bowl.

3. Dip the fish into the egg mixture and
   then roll in the flour mixture.

FISH AMANDINE

Makes: 2 servings
Groundwork: 5 minutes
Cook: 6 to 8 min. -
  MED. HIGH
Need: small paper
  bag
large skillet

Omit the flour to cut
the cals!

Amandine Chicken
Fillets are winners as
well.

---

4 fish fillets (trout, bass, etc.)
⅛ teaspoon salt
⅛ teaspoon pepper
½ cup flour
¾ cup (1½ sticks) butter
4 Tablespooons lemon juice or white
** wine**
dash paprika
½ cup sliced almonds
1 Tablespoon parsley flakes

1. Rinse the fish under cold water and pat them dry with paper towels.

2. Add the flour, salt, pepper, and fish to a small paper bag and shake to coat the fish.

3. Melt 1 stick of butter in a large skillet on MEDIUM HIGH. (Allow this to get hot before adding the fish so the flour will not fall off.)

4. Cook the fish 6 to 8 minutes (turning carefully) until they are golden brown.

5. Place the cooked fillets on an heat-proof plate and place it in the oven on WARM.

6. Add the remaining butter, lemon juice, and paprika and heat until the butter melts.

7. Reduce the heat to MEDIUM, add the almonds and parsley and stir until the almonds are brown, scraping the bottom of the pan to release the browned flour residue.

8. Pour the sauce over the fillets to serve.

LOW COUNTRY FILLETS

Makes: 2 to 3 servings
Groundwork: 5 minutes
Bake: 5 to 10 minutes
Oven Temp: 500°
Need: 9" x 13" baking
    pan

1 (16 oz.) pkg. frozen fish fillets
½ cup (1 stick) butter
¼ teaspoon salt
⅛ teaspoon pepper
¼ teaspoon paprika
3 Tablespoons white wine
2 Tablespoons lemon juice
¼ cup Parmesan cheese

1. Preheat the oven to 500°.

2. Melt the butter in the oven while it preheats and leave it for 4 to 5 minutes until it is well browned, but not burned.

3. Sprinkle both sides of the fillets with salt and pepper and arrange them in a single layer skin-side up in the browned butter.

4. Bake 4 to 5 minutes and remove the pan from the oven.

5. Carefully turn each fillet over, sprinkle each with wine and lemon juice, and top with Parmesan and paprika.

6. Return the pan to the oven and bake an additional 5 minutes until the thickest part of the fillet flakes easily with a fork and serve the fillets topped with the sauce from the pan.

GULF COAST FISH FILLETS

Makes: 2 servings
Groundwork: 2 minutes
Marinate: 20 to 30
  minutes
Bake: 10 to 12 minutes
Broil: 8 to 10 minutes
Oven Temp: 400°
  BROIL
Need: plastic bag
large baking pan

½ pound fish fillets (¼ to ½ inch thick)
¼ cup Italian salad dressing
¼ cup (½ stick) butter (melted)

1. Rinse the fish in cold water and dry on paper towels.

2. Combine the fish and Italian dressing in a plastic bag, seal, shake to coat, and marinate 20 to 30 minutes, turning at least once.

3. Preheat the oven to 400° or BROIL.

4. Pour ⅛ of a cup of salad dressing into a large baking pan, add the butter, and melt in the oven as it preheats.

5. Coat both sides of the fish thoroughly in the warm mixture, and arrange them in a single layer.

6. Bake 10 to 12 minutes or BROIL 8 to 10 minutes, basting occasionally, until the fish is light brown and flakes easily with a fork. Top with the sauce from the pan.

LIVE SHELLFISH

Groundwork: 10
  minutes
Cook: See timing
  below
Need: large saucepan
  or stockpot with lid

Serve Hot With:
melted butter
lemon wedges

Live lobsters or crabs
can be kept up to 24
hours in a deep
cardboard box in a
cool place. Putting
them in water will kill
them!

Tantalize your taste
buds by trying Lobster
on the Grill (THE PATIO
CHEF).

**Average Serving Size
Per Person:**
Crabs - 2 to 4
Lobsters - 1 to 2 lb.
Scallops - 1 dozen

Live lobsters or crabs
Water
Lemon juice (crab only)
Salt (1 Tablespoon per quart of water)

1. Fill the saucepan with enough water to cover the shellfish and bring to a rolling boil on HIGH.

2. Add the salt and lemon juice (crab only) and stir.

3. Hold the lobster by the middle of its back or use tongs to hold the crab, plung it, head first, into the boiling water and cover.

4. Return the water to a rolling boil before adding more shellfish, and begin the timing.

LOBSTER:
1 to $1\frac{1}{2}$ pounds - 10 to 12 minutes
$1\frac{1}{2}$ to 2 pounds - 15 to 18 minutes
$2\frac{1}{2}$ to 5 pounds - 20 to 25 minutes

HARDSHELL CRAB:
$\frac{1}{3}$ to $\frac{1}{2}$ pound - 5 to 10 minutes (until the shell turns bright red)

5. Drain and cool slightly before handling and shucking.

SHUCKING SHELLFISH

SHRIMP (raw or cooked): Remove the head by holding the body just below the rib cage with one hand and, with the other hand, twisting the upper torso to pop it off.

Then, hold the little fellow (legs up) in one hand; pinch the legs between your thumb and index finger of the other hand and, with a twist of the wrist, remove the legs and shell. Remove the dark vein by making a shallow cut down the center of the back with a small sharp knife. With the knife tip, lift or cut out the vein. A real salty dog will make short work of deveining with a quick thumb nail down its back. The vein is harmless and tasteless, but the shrimp is more appealing if it is removed. **Rock shrimp must have the vein removed.**

WHOLE LOBSTER (cooked only):
CLAWS: Twist off the claws and crack the shells with a nutcracker, hammer, or pliers, and remove the meat. **TAIL:** With its feet up, hold the body in one hand and the tail in the other. Press the tail down until it cracks loose from the body. Break the flippers off of the tail, insert a fork where the flippers were and push the meat out. OR, make a cut down the center of the underside with a sharp knife, pull the sides apart to crack the shell open, loosen the meat, and remove the meat with a fork. Place the meat striped-side down, and cut lengthwise down the center just deep enough to expose the dark vein and remove it. **BODY:** Pull the shell off the body and open it by cracking the body in half lengthwise. Remove the white meat with a small fork or tweezers, and discard any gray or spongy matter. There are some surprises hidden in a lobster! The tomally is lobster liver which

turns green during cooking and is considered a delicacy by seafood lovers around the world. In female lobsters, there may be red roe called "coral." This lobster caviar can be added to lobster salad or crumbled to use as a garnish. **LEGS:** These are small and almost impossible to crack, but they also contain tasty meat. Just remove them from the body, put the open end in your mouth, and pretend they are straws!

OYSTERS (raw): Scrub the shells with a stiff brush under cold running water. Beginners need a thick mitt or folded towel to pad the hand holding the unopened oyster. **Firmly** hold the oyster with the thickest part of the shell in a cupped palm. Insert a thin, strong knife between the shells and run the knife around the entire circumference of the oyster until the strong muscle holding the shells together has been severed and the shells can be opened.

Oysters and clam shells will open very easily if first washed in cold water, placed in a plastic bag and put in the freezer for 1 hour.

For "On-the-Half-Shell": Discard the empty shell half and loosen the oyster from the other half with a knife tip.

For Other Uses: Have a strainer or colander with a bowl underneath at hand and pour in oysters and liquid to separate.

CLAMS (raw): Open the clams the same as oysters. Do not eat the neck (or syphon).

Discard any clams or mussels that are not tightly closed.

MUSSELS (raw): Open the mussels the same as oysters. Cut off and discard the horny "beard."

FRIED SHRIMP

Makes: 2 servings
Groundwork: 10 to 15
  minutes
Cook: 3 to 5 minutes
Fryer: 350° to 400°
Pan: MED. HIGH
Need: small plastic
  bag
deep fat fryer OR
  deep saucepan
small mixing bowl

"Butterfly" large or
extra-large shrimp by
cutting ⅔ of the way
through down the
back and open like a
book.

Also try the "Great
Beer Batter."

**1 pound shrimp (peeled and
  deveined)**
¼ teaspoon baking powder
4 Tablespoons flour
1 egg
1 cup cracker crumbs
Vegetable oil

1. Rinse shrimp under cold water.

2. Combine the baking powder and
   flour in a small plastic bag.

3. Beat the egg in small mixing bowl
   and crush the crackers.

4. Shake the shrimp (a few at a time) in
   the bag of flour to coat.

5. Heat enough oil to allow the shrimp
   to float freely in a large saucepan
   on MEDIUM-HIGH until bubbly.

6. Dip in the egg; roll in the crumbs.

7. Fry 3 to 4 minutes on MEDIUM-HIGH.

SHRIMP SCAMPI

Makes: 2 servings
Groundwork: 2 minutes
Bake: 10 to 12 minutes
Oven Temp: 400°
Need: medium baking
  dish

Great with rice pilaff
and Caesar salad.

---

1 lb. shrimp (uncooked, peeled)
¼ cup (½ stick) butter (melted)
1 Tablespoon lemon juice
¾ teaspoon garlic powder
1 Tablespoon parsley flakes

1. Preheat the oven to 400°

2. Combine all ingredients except the
   shrimp in a baking dish and melt in
   the oven as it preheats.

3. Coat the shrimp in the mixture and
   bake 10 to 12 minutes, basting
   occasionally.

BOILED SHRIMP

Makes: 2 servings
Groundwork: 10
 minutes
Cook: 5 to 15 min. -
 MED. HIGH
Need: large saucepan
 or stockpot
colander

**Average Serving Size
Per Person:**
in the shell - ½ lb.
shelled - ¼ to ⅓ lb. (for
"heads on" double
the amount)

Check the Creole
Cottage, page 201, for
more shrimp dishes.

**2 quarts water
1 Tablespoon salt
1 Tablespoon ground seafood
 seasoning (or 1 teaspoon liquid
 shrimp boil)
1 (12 oz.) can beer (optional)
1 pound shrimp (with shells, headless)**

1. Combine the water, salt, seasoning
   and beer in a large saucepan on
   HIGH and bring to a rolling boil.

2. Rinse the shrimp under cold water
   and carefully add to the boiling
   water.

3. Return to a boil, reduce to MEDIUM
   HIGH and cook until the shrimp are
   bright pink and tender:

   small shrimp - 4 to 6 minutes
   medium shrimp - 6 to 8 minutes
   large shrimp - 8 to 10 minutes

4. Immediately pour the shrimp into a
   colander in the sink, and rinse them
   under cold running water until they
   are no longer hot to stop the
   cooking process. (Toss in a handful
   of ice cubes for quicker cooling
   when serving cold.)

OPTIONS:

A. **HOMEMADE SHRIMP BOIL** (for 1 pound
   of shrimp and 2 quarts of water)

**1 Tablespoon salt
¼ teaspoon coarse ground black pepper
1¼ teaspoons carraway seed
⅛ teaspoon red or cayenne pepper
¼ teaspoon marjoram
¼ teaspoon thyme
1 teaspoon rosemary
1 (12 oz.) can beer**

1. Add all the ingredients to the boiling
   water.

Be sure to rinse the
cooked shrimp well to
remove the loose
spices.

FRIED OYSTERS

Makes: 2 servings
Groundwork: 10 to 12
minutes
Cook: 3 to 5 minutes
Fryer - 350° to 400°
Pan - MED. HIGH
Need: small paper or
plastic bag
deep fat fryer OR
deep saucepan
small mixing bowl

Approximately 28
crackers will make 1
cup of crumbs. Just
zap them in a blender
or pop them in a
small plastic bag and
roll them with a rolling
pin.

The oysters, shrimp,
and fish will float
when they are done.

**Average Serving Size
Per Person:**
Large - ½ to 1 dozen
Medium - 1 dozen (12
per pint)

12 oysters (1 pint shucked)
¼ teaspoon baking powder
4 Tablespoons flour
1 egg
4 drops Tabasco
1 cup cracker crumbs
Vegetable oil

1. Rinse the oysters under cold water and pat dry with paper towels.

2. Combine the baking powder and flour in a small paper or plastic bag and shake to mix.

3. Beat the egg and Tabasco in a small mixing bowl with a wire whisk, and crush the crackers into crumbs.

4. Shake the oysters (2 or 3 at a time) in the bag of flour to coat.

5. Heat enough oil to allow the oysters to float freely in a large saucepan on MEDIUM HIGH until bubbly.

6. Dip each oyster in the egg mixture, and roll in the cracker crumbs.

7. Fry 3 to 5 minutes on MEDIUM HIGH until puffy and golden brown.

BARBECUED OYSTERS

Makes: 2 servings
Groundwork: 2 to 4
minutes
Bake: 10 to 15 minutes
OR
Broil: 5 to 8 minutes
Oven Temp: 425° or
BROIL
Need: large baking
pan OR broiler pan

12 large oysters (in shells) or 1 pint (shucked)
¾ cup barbecue sauce, Italian dressing, or a seafood sauce

1. Preheat the oven to 425° or BROIL.

2. Remove the oysters from the shell and wash the shells thoroughly to remove grit and sand or rinse the shucked ones under cold water and pat them dry with paper towels.

3. Place the oysters in the half-shells (or shucked) in the pan and cover with the sauce of your choice.

4. Bake 10 to 15 minutes or BROIL 5 to 8 minutes until the edges begin to curl.

OYSTERS BIENVILLE

Makes: 2 servings
Groundwork: 10
  minutes
Broil: 3 min. AND
Bake: 15 min. or BROIL
  5 min.
Oven Temp: 350°
Need: small saucepan
medium baking dish
and 12 shells
  (optional)

If using oysters in the shells, remove them and wash the shells thoroughly to remove grit and sand. Purchased shells may be used if oysters in their shells are not available.

For elegant serving and to keep the oysters hot, fill the bottom of an ATTRACTIVE baking dish or pan with rock salt. Place the oysters in individual shells and nestle the shells in the salt. Cook as the recipe directs and serve in the baking dish.

1 (10¾ oz.) can cream of mushroom
  soup
1 (4¼ oz.) can shrimp (drained)
1 Tablespoon instant minced onions
1 Tablespoon parsley flakes
1 teaspoon instant celery flakes
¼ teaspoon garlic powder
1¼ teaspoons Worcestershire
3 Tablespoons white wine
12 large (or 1 pint) oysters
⅛ cup Parmesan cheese
¼ cup cracker crumbs
Paprika
12 thin slices of butter

1. Preheat the oven to BROIL.

2. Drain the shrimp and rinse in cold water.

3. Heat the soup, shrimp, onion, parsley, celery, garlic, Worcestershire, and wine in a small saucepan on MEDIUM, stirring frequently.

4. Spread the oysters in the baking dish in one layer and broil 3 minutes (or until the edges begin to curl); pour off the liquid.

5. Either spread the oysters again in a single layer or place them in individual shells and arrange the shells in the baking dish.

6. Sprinkle each with Parmesan cheese, cover with the sauce, top with cracker crumbs, sprinkle with paprika, and top each with a thin slice of butter.

7. Bake, uncovered, 15 minutes OR Broil 5 minutes.

THE FRESH VEGETABLE PATCH

RULES OF THE RANGE

Cook vegetables in the smallest possible amount of water for the shortest length of time to retain maximum vitamin and mineral content and preserve color and texture.

The two simplest ways to cook vegetables are:

I. SIMMER

A. **Boil** — Start vegetables that grow **below** the ground (potatoes, carrots, beets) in a pan of cold, salted water. Bring to a boil on HIGH, reduce the heat to LOW, cover, and begin the timing.

For vegetables that grow **above** ground (peas, beans, spinach) add to 1 inch of **rapidly boiling** salted water. When the water returns to boiling, reduce to LOW, cover, and begin the timing.

B. **Southern Style** — Add vegetables to 2 to 3 inches of rapidly boiling salted water. Reduce to LOW and cover tightly. Increase the cooking time to between two hours and half the day.

II. STEAM

Place a steamer basket inside a saucepan with a tightly fitting lid. Add water to just below the bottom of the steamer, cover, and bring to a rapid boil on HIGH. Spread the vegetables evenly in the steamer basket, cover, reduce to MEDIUM, and begin timing. Steaming usually takes 10 to 15 minutes longer than Simmering.

THE CHEF'S COLLEGE

NAME IT:	PREPARE IT:	COOK IT:
ARTICHOKES **French** **Italian**	Cut off the stem and any damaged leaves; cut 1" off the top with a knife; remove the thorny leaf tips with scissors, rinse in cold water; tie a string or foil strip around it to keep leaves together.	SIMMER: 30 - 40 min. STEAM: 40 - 50 min.

Jerusalem	Wash, peel, and either slice or leave whole; add 1 teaspoon vinegar to the water to preserve the color. Do not overcook Jerusalem artichokes, they re-toughen.	SIMMER: 15 min., sliced
		    20 min., whole
		STEAM: 20 min. sliced
		    45 min., whole

ASPARAGUS	Break off the stalks as far down as they will snap easily. Peel all white and large green stalks to remove bitterness. Rinse in cold water to remove any sand (if the stalks are large, **either** cut off the bottom 1½" and cook stalks 5 minutes before adding the tops, or tie the bundle together with string or foil strip and simmer (covered) standing up in 2" of water in a tall saucepan).	SIMMER: 12 - 18 min. STEAM: 17 - 30 min.

BEANS
Green
Snap
Wax
Pole
	Rinse in cold water; remove strings and ends; snap or cut into 1"-2" pieces, leave whole, or cut lengthwise into thin strips (French style). Bacon drippings (or slices) or butter may be added for seasonings. For Southern Style, use the above or ham hock, salt pork, or fat back.	SIMMER:
		  Whole: 15 - 20 min.
		  Snapped: 10 - 15 min.
		  French: 5 - 10 min.
		STEAM:
		  Whole: 25 - 30 min.
		  Snapped: 20 - 25 min.
		  French: 15 - 20 min.

Lima **Forkhook** **Baby Lima** **Butter Beans**	Pop open the pods and remove the beans; rinse in cold water and season as for green beans.	SIMMER: 20 - 30 min. SOUTHERN STYLE: minimum 2 hours

BEETS	Leave whole and unpeeled; cut off all but 1" of the root and stem; after cooking, remove peeling, roots and stems before slicing. For quick cooking, peel and slice or dice.	SIMMER:
		  Whole: 30 - 45 min.
		  Sliced: 15 - 20 min.
		STEAM:
		  Sliced: 20 - 25 min.

BROCCOLI	Remove all leaves and tough part of stalk; split stalk lengthwise into halves or quarters (or cook the stalk separately), or standing up like asparagus.)	SIMMER: 10 - 15 min. STEAM: 15 - 20 min.
BRUSSELS SPROUTS	Leave whole; trim off any wilted leaves and discolored part of the stem; rinse in cold water.	SIMMER: 10 - 15 min.

OF VEGETABLE KNOWLEDGE

NAME IT:	SERVE IT WITH:	ALSO TRY IT:
ARTICHOKES **French** **Italian**	Melted butter Hollandaise Sauce Vinaigrette or French Dressing Lemon Butter	Marinated
Jerusalem	Salt and Pepper Butter Lemon Butter Minced Parsley French Dressing	
ASPARAGUS	Salt and Pepper Lemon Butter Hollandaise Sauce Cheese Sauce Herb Butter Vinaigrette Dressing Au Gratin Sauce	Stir-Fried
BEANS **Green** **Snap** **Wax** **Pole**	Chopped Onion Whole Green Onions Bacon (Cooked, Crumbled) Toasted Slivered Almonds Pearl Onions Cashew Nuts	Stir Fried Marinated
BEETS	Salt and Pepper Butter Herb Butter	
BROCCOLI	Salt and Pepper Melted Lemon or Herb Butter Hollandaise or Cheese Sauce Au Gratin Sauce Parmesan or Cheddar Cheese	Batter Fried Marinated Stir Fried Raw
BRUSSELS SPROUTS	Salt and Pepper Lemon Butter Hollandaise or Cheese Sauce	

THE CHEF'S COLLEGE

NAME IT:	PREPARE IT:	COOK IT:
CABBAGE **Green** **Red** **Savory** **Chinese**	Remove outer leaves and either shred or cut wedges (do not use the core - it is bitter!). Bacon drippings or butter may be added for seasoning.	SIMMER: 10 - 12 min. STEAM: 15 - 20 min. SIMMER: 7 - 9 min. STEAM: 10 - 15 min.

CARROTS	Peel or scrape and leave whole or cut into dresired sizes; rinse in cold water. A bay leaf, pinch of sugar, orange or lemon peel (or juice), or a slice of apple may be added for seasoning. Times are given for small, young carrots. Double the time for large, old ones.	SIMMER:
		  Whole: 15 - 20 min.
		  Halved: 10 - 15 min.
		  Quartered: 8 - 10 min.
		  Thinly Sliced: 6 - 10 min.
		STEAM:
		  Whole: 20 - 30 min.
		  Halved: 15 - 25 min.
		  Quartered: 10 - 15 min.
		  Sliced: 10 - 15 min.

CAULIFLOWER	Remove all leaves and tough part of stalk; leave whole or separate into flowerettes; rinse in cold water.	SIMMER:
		  Whole: 25 - 30 min.
		STEAM:
		  Flowerettes: 10 - 15 min.

CORN **On the Cob** **Off the Cob**	Remove all the husks, stems and silks, (a dry brush gets more off than a wet one); rinse in cold water. **EXCEPTION TO RANGE RULE: Do Not** add salt to cooking water; add sugar instead to keep the kernels tender.	SIMMER: 5 - 6 min. STEAM: 10 - 12 min. SIMMER: 5 - 6 min. STEAM: 10 - 12 min.
EGGPLANT	Rinse in cold water; peel only if the skin is tough; slice, dice, or cut into strips. Slice eggplant just before cooking — it discolors quickly! Bay leaf, onion, or garlic may be added to cooking water to flavor.	SIMMER: 10 - 15 min.
GREENS **Beet** **Bok Choy** **Chicory** **Dandelion** **Kale** **Spinach** **Swiss Chard**	Remove root ends, damaged leaves, and large stems. Wash **thoroughly** in cold water. Smooth leaves may need only one washing. **EXCEPTION TO RANGE RULE:** Young, tender greens may be cooked with **no water** except what clings to the leaves after washing. Bacon drippings, bouillon cubes, or butter may be added for seasonings.	SIMMER: 5 - 15 min.
Collard **Mustard** **Turnip**	For Southern Style, fatback, ham hock, or salt pork may be used for seasoning in place of butter or bacon drippings.	SIMMER: 5 - 15 min. SOUTHERN STYLE: Minimum of 2 hours

OF VEGETABLE KNOWLEDGE

NAME IT:	SERVE IT WITH:	ALSO TRY IT:
CABBAGE **Green** **Red** **Savory** **Chinese**	Butter Salt and Pepper Lemon Juice Soy Sauce Herb Butter Cheese Sauce	Raw Stir-Fried
CARROTS	Salt and Pepper Lemon Butter Dill Butter Lemon Juice Chopped Mint Parsley, Nutmeg or Cinnamon	Baked Braised Marinated Raw Stir Fried
CAULIFLOWER	Salt and Pepper Parmesan or Shredded Cheddar Cheese Melted, Herb or Lemon Butter Cheese, Hollandaise Sauce or Au Gratin Sauce	Baked Batter Fried Marinated Stir-Fried Raw
CORN **On the Cob**	Salt and Pepper Butter Herb Butter Lemon or Lime Butter	Baked Grilled Fried
Off the Cob	Same As Above	Creamed Fried
EGGPLANT	Salt and Pepper Chives Parmesan or Gruyere Cheese Parsley Tomato Sauce	Baked Batter Fried Broiled (slices only) Oven Fried Sautéed Stir-Fried
GREENS **Beet** **Bok Choy** **Chicory** **Dandelion** **Kale** **Spinach** **Swiss Chard**	Salt and Pepper Bacon, (Cooked, Crumbled) Butter Hard-Cooked Egg Slices	Raw Sautéed Stir Fried
Collard **Chard** **Turnip**	Bacon, (Cooked, Crumbled) Hot Pepper Sauce	

THE CHEF'S COLLEGE

NAME IT:	PREPARE IT:	COOK IT:
MUSHROOMS	Wash, pat dry, cut off end of stem. Leave whole or slice.	SAUTÉ: 4 to 5 minutes until tender
OKRA	Leave whole. Remove stem caps after cooking, if desired.	SIMMER: 7 - 12 min.
ONIONS	Peel and leave whole, or slice ¼ inch thick.	STEAM: 15 min. (small or sliced only)
PEAS **Green**	Shell; rinse in cold water. Butter and ⅛ teaspoon sugar may be added to cooking water.	SIMMER: 3 - 5 min. STEAM: 10 min.
Black-eyed **Crowder** **Purple Hull**	Bacon slices or drippings, ham hock, salt pork, and ⅛ teaspoon sugar may be added to cooking water.	SIMMER: Southern Style Minimum of 45 minutes
POTATOES **Sweet**	Leave whole with the skin on; wash thoroughly in cold water; remove skin after cooking.	SIMMER: 30 - 40 min. STEAM: 30 min. (sliced only)
White **Red** **New** **Irish**	Rinse and scrub thoroughly in cold water and cook whole, halved, or sliced in the skins or peel.	SIMMER: Whole: 35 - 40 min. Sliced: 20 - 25 min. STEAM: 30 min. (sliced or small whole)
SQUASH **Yellow,** **Pattypan** **Zucchini**	Wash in cold water, remove both ends; cut if desired.	SIMMER: 10 - 15 min. STEAM: Whole: 20 - 25 min. Sliced or small whole 5 - 10 min.
Acorn **Butternut** **Hubbard** **Turban**	Wash in cold water; cut in half, remove seeds.	STEAM: 40 min.
Spaghetti	Wash in cold water, cut in half lengthwise.	SIMMER - (cut-side up): 20 - 30 min. STEAM - (cut-side up): 30 - 40 min.
TOMATOES	Peel, chop into quarters, and cook **without** adding any water.	SIMMER: 10 - 15 min.
TURNIPS	Peel and slice into ¼" slices or dices. (Can be cooked along with the turnip greens.)	SIMMER: 20 - 30 min. (covered)

OF VEGETABLE KNOWLEDGE

NAME IT:	SERVE IT WITH:	ALSO TRY IT:	
MUSHROOMS	Butter Parsley, Nutmeg or Curry Powder Lemon Juice	Baked Batter Fried Broiled	Grilled Marinated Raw
OKRA	Salt and Pepper Butter	Batter Fried Pan Fried	
ONIONS	Salt and Pepper Bacon (Cooked, Crumbled) Butter Garlic Salt	Baked Batter Fried Braised Broiled	Marinated Oven Fried Pan Fried Raw
PEAS Green Black-eyed Crowder Purple Hull	Salt and Pepper Butter Cheese or White Sauce Pepper Sauce Tomato or Onion (chopped) Hot Pear Relish Bacon (Cooked, Crumbled)	Sauteéd Stir Fried	
POTATOES Sweet White Red New Irish	Salt and Pepper, Butter Brown Sugar, Cinnamon, Maple Syrup Pecans, Allspice, Marshmallows Au Gratin Butter or Herb Butter Bacon (Cooked, Crumbled)	Baked Deep Fried Pan Fried Baked Broiled Deep Fried The Great Baked Potato (Irish and White, only)	 Pan Fried Stir Fried Oven Fried
SQUASH Yellow Pattypan Zucchini Acorn Butternut Hubbard Turban Spaghetti	Salt and Pepper, Butter, Herb Butter, Lemon Butter Shredded Cheddar Cheese, Bacon (Cooked, Crumbled), Parmesan Cheese Brown sugar, Cinnamon, Maple Syrup Lemon Juice, Crushed Pineapple, Pecans Marshmallows Butter Parmesan Cheese Spaghetti Sauce	Baked Batter Fried Broiled Grilled Marinated Baked (THE CHEF'S PREFERENCE) Baked (THE CHEF'S PREFERENCE)	Oven Fried Pan Fried Raw Sauteéd Stir Fried
TOMATOES	Salt and Pepper Onion (Chopped) Thyme, Basil, Oregano Parmesan Cheese Bacon (Cooked, Crumbled)	Baked Broiled Marinated Oven Fried	Pan Fried Raw Stir Fried
TURNIPS	Salt and Pepper Bacon (Cooked, Crumbled) Onions (Chopped) Butter	Sauteéd Stir-Fried	

BAKED ACORN SQUASH

Makes: 2 servings
Groundwork: 2 minutes
Bake: 60 minutes
Oven Temp: 350°
Need: small baking
dish

___

Fabulous Fillings:
2 Tablespoons butter
2 Tablespoons brown
  sugar or honey
cinnamon, nutmeg or
cloves

¼ cup applesauce
⅛ teaspoon cinnamon

___

1 acorn squash
1 choice of filling
water

1. Preheat the oven to 350°.

2. Pour ½ inch of water into the baking dish.

3. Cut the squash in half lengthwise (from stem to flower end) and remove the seeds.

4. Place the two halves cut-side down in the water and bake 45 minutes.

5. Turn the halves over, fill with your choice of filling and bake 15 additional minutes until the squash is tender and the filling is hot.

SAUTEÉD MUSHROOMS

Makes: 2 servings
Groundwork: 3 minutes
Cook: 10 to 12 min. -
  MEDIUM
Need: medium skillet

___

Sauteéd mushrooms
may also be used as
a topping for meat.

___

½ lb. fresh mushrooms
2 Tablespoons butter
½ teaspoon lemon juice
⅛ teaspoon salt and pepper

1. Rinse the mushrooms in cold water, trim off the brown end of the stem, and dry on paper towels.

2. Melt the butter in a medium skillet on MEDIUM, add the mushrooms, cover and cook 10 minutes, stirring frequently.

3. Turn off the heat and leave the mushrooms in the skillet for several minutes to absorb the butter.

4. Add the lemon juice, salt, and pepper and mix well.

EGGPLANT PARMESAN

Makes: 4 servings
Groundwork: 4 minutes
Bake: 20 minutes
Oven Temp: 350°
Need: small mixing
  bowl
9" x 13" baking dish.

½ **small eggplant**
½ **cup bread crumbs**
¼ **cup Parmesan cheese**
½ **teaspoon garlic powder**
½ **teaspoon salt**
¼ **teaspoon pepper**
1 **(15¼ oz.) jar spaghetti sauce**
1 **cup (4 oz. pkg.) shredded mozzarella cheese**

1. Preheat the oven to 350°

2. Lightly grease the baking dish.

3. Peel and slice the eggplant into ¼ inch thick slices.

4. Combine the bread crumbs, Parmesan cheese, garlic, salt, and pepper in a small mixing bowl and stir to blend well.

5. Layer into the baking dish: spaghetti sauce to barely cover the bottom, the eggplant slices in one layer over the sauce, the remaining sauce, ½ of the cheese, and the bread crumb mixture.

6. Bake, uncovered, 20 minutes until the eggplant is tender and the cheese is light brown.

7. Top with the remaining cheese and bake 5 additional minutes until the cheese melts.

BAKED ONIONS

Makes: 2 servings
Groundwork: 5 minutes
Bake: 50 to 60 minutes
Oven Temp: 350°
Need: foil
small baking dish

CAUTION:
Open the foil packets
carefully.

These are great on the
grill! Place the packets
on the side of the
cooking rack away
from the hot coals and
cook 50 to 60 minutes.

---

2 large onions
2 slices bacon
2 (1 teaspoon) pats butter
Salt and pepper

1. Preheat the oven to 350°.

2. Cut a thin slice off the top and
    bottom of each onion, remove the
    outer skin, and rinse in cold water.

3. Salt and pepper thoroughly.

4. Put a pat of butter in the center
    opening of each onion.

5. Cut the bacon in half and place in
    an "X" over the top of each onion.

6. Seal each onion in foil and place
    upright in a small baking dish.

7. Bake 50 to 60 minutes until the
    onions are tender and the bacon is
    cooked.

OVEN CORN ON THE COB

Makes: 2 servings
Groundwork: 5 minutes
Bake: 20 to 30 minutes
Oven Temp: 350°
Need: Foil
shallow baking dish

These love to be
grilled. Just place the
packets on the
cooking rack directly
over **warm** to **medium
coals** (or on one side
for HOT COALS) and
cook 20 to 30 minutes,
turning and rotating
their position often.

---

2 ears corn (fresh or frozen)
2 Tablespoons butter
¼ teaspoon garlic powder
¼ teaspoon salt
¼ teaspoon pepper
1 teaspoon lime juice

1. Preheat the oven to 350°.

2. Butter the corn and sprinkle with
    garlic powder, salt, pepper, and
    lime juice, and seal.

3. Place the packets on a shallow
    baking dish and bake 20 to 30
    minutes.

HASH BROWNS

Makes: 2 servings
Groundwork: 8 minutes
Cook: 4 to 5 min. -
  MED. HIGH
5 to 8 min. - LOW
10 min. - MED.
TOTAL - 20 min.
Need: medium skillet
  with lid

2 large or medium potatoes (diced)
2 Tablespoons (¼ stick) butter,
   vegetable oil, or bacon drippings
¼ cup onion (chopped)
¼ teaspoon salt
¼ teaspoon pepper
¼ teaspoon paprika (optional)

1. Peel and dice the potatoes and onions.

2. Heat the butter in a medium skillet on MEDIUM HIGH.

3. Sprinkle the potatoes with salt and pepper.

4. Stir the potatoes and onions into the hot butter and brown lightly (about 4 to 5 minutes).

5. Reduce the heat to LOW, cover and cook 5 to 8 minutes.

6. Remove the lid, sprinkle with paprika, increase to MEDIUM and continue to cook, uncovered, 10 more minutes, stirring occasionally.

OPTIONS:

   A. Oven Hash Browns

      1. Preheat the oven to 425°.

      2. Heat 3 Tablespoons vegetable oil in a baking pan in the oven while it preheats.

      3. Add the remaining ingredients, stir to coat, and spread them into a single layer.

      4. Bake 35 minutes, stirring at least once, until the potatoes are brown and tender.

MASHED POTATOES

Makes: 2 servings
Groundwork: 6 minutes
Cook: 20 to 25 min. -
  MED. LOW
Need: medium
  saucepan
potato masher
mixer

Mash potatoes while they are hot to avoid lumps. Heating the milk before adding it will also reduce lumping.

2 large or medium potatoes
Water to cover
¼ cup (½ stick) butter
¼ teaspoon salt
⅛ teaspoon pepper
½ cup milk

1. Peel and cut the potatoes into chunks (or ¼ inch slices for quicker cooking).

2. Cover the potatoes with water in a medium saucepan and heat to boiling on HIGH.

3. Reduce to MEDIUM LOW, cover, and cook 20 to 25 minutes until tender.

4. Drain off the water, leaving the cooked potatoes in the warm saucepan.

5. Immediately add the butter, salt, and pepper and mash the potatoes with a potato masher (or fork) until the lumps are gone.

6. Add the milk and mix them with a mixer or rotary beater until they are smooth and fluffy.

LEFTOVER OPTIONS:

  A. **Potato Pancakes**
    1. For one cup of leftover mashed potatoes, add 2 eggs, ¼ cup flour, and 2 teaspoons baking powder and mix well.

    2. Form into 4 patties and pan fry in ¼ inch oil until brown on both sides.

THE GREAT BAKED POTATO

Makes: 1
Groundwork: 1 minute
Bake: 45 to 60 minutes
Oven Temp: 400°
Need: shallow baking
pan

When baking two or more, select potatoes of similar size for uniform doneness.

For faster baking, just insert a **metal** skewer or fork prongs into the center of the potato and reduce the cooking time by 10 to 15 minutes.

SWEET POTATOES are baked exactly the same, and are topped with butter, salt, and pepper.

For a light, fluffy texture, roll the hot baked potato on the countertop using gentle pressure and a hot pad.

Imitation bacon chips can be used in place of cooked and crumbled bacon.

For any toppers containing cheese, return the completely assembled potato to the hot oven for 5 minutes to melt the cheese.

1 Irish or Russet potato (no cuts or spots)

1. Preheat the oven to 400°.

2. Scrub the potato under running water to remove all dirt.

3. Pierce the skin in several places with the tip of a knife to allow the steam to escape.

4. **For soft skins** (use for topping): wrap the potato tightly in foil and place it directly on the oven rack.

   For crisp skins (use for stuffing): Coat the potato completely with oil, butter, or shortening and place it in a shallow baking pan. Do not wrap with foil.

5. Bake 45 minutes to 1 hour until the potato feels soft in the center when gently squeezed with a hot pad.

SUPER TOPPED SUPPER SPUDS

TOPPERS

Seafood Special: shrimp cocktail
Italian: pizza sauce, sliced pepperoni, sliced black olives, shredded mozzarella cheese
Bacon-Cheese: bacon (cooked and crumbled), chopped onion, shredded Cheddar cheese
South of the Border: taco sauce, chopped onion, diced green chili pepper, Monterrey Jack cheese with jalapeño pepper
Chili: chili with beans, chopped onions, shredded Cheddar cheese
Taco: ground beef cooked in taco sauce, chopped onion, nacho cheese dip
Broccoli: broccoli with cheese sauce, diced cook ham

TWICE BAKED POTATO

Makes: 2 servings
Groundwork: 8 minutes
Bake: 45 to 60 minutes
5 minutes
Oven Temp: 400°

2 hot baked potatoes
¼ cup butter (½ stick)
¼ cup milk
¼ cup sour cream
¼ teaspoon curry powder
½ teaspoon salt
½ teaspoon pepper

These may be made ahead of time and either refrigerated or frozen. Just remember to increase re-heating time.

1. Bake the potato 45 to 60 minutes (See The Great Baked Potato), cut in half lengthwise and scoop out the pulp.

2. Add the butter and mash with a potato masher until the butter is melted and the pulp is smooth.

3. Add the remaining ingredients and beat with a rotary or electric mixer until fluffy and smooth.

4. Stuff into the shells, return to the oven, and bake 5 minutes.

FRIED OKRA OR GREEN TOMATOES

Makes: 2 servings
Groundwork: 10 minutes
Resting Time: 5 to 10 min. (okra)
Cook: 7 to 9 min. - MEDIUM
Need: medium skillet plastic wrap

½ pound okra or 2 green tomatoes
Salt
1 cup corn-meal mix
3 to 4 Tablespoons vegetable oil

Do Ahead Okra:
Stop at the end of Step 2, seal the sticky okra in plastic wrap, and refrigerate up to 24 hours.

1. Wash the vegetables thoroughly, cut off the stem ends and slice them into ¼ inch slices.

2. Omit this step for green tomatoes! Spread the slices on a piece of plastic wrap, sprinkle with salt, and allow to stand 5 to 10 minutes. (This makes the okra sticky).

3. Coat the slices in the corn-meal mix thoroughly on all sides.

4. Heat the vegetable oil in a medium skillet on MEDIUM. Cook, stirring or turning frequently, 7 to 9 minutes until golden brown.

BROILED TOMATOES

Makes: 2 servings
Groundwork: 2 minutes
Broil: 3 to 5 minutes
Oven Temp: Broil
Need: baking pan
small mixing bowl

1 large, firm, ripe tomato
¼ teaspoon salt
⅛ teaspoon pepper
1 tomato topper

1. Preheat the oven to BROIL.

2. Prepare your choice of topper.

3. Slice the tomato in half across the middle. Sprinkle the cut-side with salt and pepper and add a topper.

4. Arrange them, cut-side up, in the baking dish and broil 3 to 5 minutes until hot and light brown.

TOPPERS:

Combine in small mixing bowl:

A. 1 Tablespoon soft butter
    ¼ cup bread crumbs
    ½ teaspoon Italian seasoning

B. 2 slices bacon (cooked and crumbled)
    1 Tablespoon onion (chopped)
    1 Tablespoon Parmesan cheese
    2 teaspoons parsley flakes

C. ¼ cup herb seasoned stuffing mix
    1 Tablespoon shredded Cheddar cheese
    2 teaspoons green onions (chopped)
    1 Tablespoon soft butter

RICE

Rice probably originated in Southeast Asia and is as old as Methusela. The ceremonial custom of serving rice was established in China by the Emperor Chin Mung in 2800 B.C. It was brought to the U.S. by accident in the 1600's when bad weather forced a Madagascan ship into the Charleston Harbor and it took America by a storm!

Makes: 2 to 3 (⅔ cup) servings
Groundwork: 1 to 3 minutes
Cook: 15 to 20 min. - LOW
Need: medium saucepan with lid colander

---

1 cup uncooked rice = 3 cups cooked.

Never lift the lid during cooking!

To reheat, place the leftover rice in a saucepan (with a lid), add a small amount of water (about 1 Tablespoon for 2 cups of rice), stir, cover, and heat on LOW 5 to 8 minutes.

To keep warm, place it in a metal colander, place the colander in the top of a saucepan, cover, and steam it over boiling water.

Store leftover rice in plastic bags in the freezer to use for any recipe needing "cooked rice."

WHITE:

Always use **long-grained** or **converted rice** (the short grained is sticky!). Use short grained for pudding, fried rice, etc. "Converted" means that the rice has been parboiled slightly — **not** to be confused with "Instant."

Method I - Cold-Water Start:

½ cup uncooked long grain rice
1 cup water
½ teaspoon salt
½ teaspoon butter (optional)

1. Place the rice, cold water, salt, and butter in a medium saucepan, cover, and heat on HIGH until it comes to a full boil.

2. Reduce to LOW and simmer 15 more minutes until the water is almost absorbed.

3. Drain the rice in a colander and rinse with hot water.

Method II - Boiling Water Start:

½ cup uncooked rice (long grain or converted)
2 cups water (1⅓ cups for converted)
½ teaspoon salt
½ teaspoon butter (optional)

1. Bring the water, salt, and butter to a boil in a medium saucepan on HIGH.

2. Add the rice and return it to boil.

3. Cover, reduce to LOW, and cook 15 to 20 minutes until the rice is tender and the water is absorbed.

Bake: 25-30 min.
Oven Temp: 35°
Need: 1 qt. casserole

Method III - Oven Steamed:
½ cup uncooked long grained rice
1 cup water
½ teaspoon salt
1 teaspoon butter (optional)

Rice is done if a grain can be mashed between your thumb and index finger.

1. Preheat the oven to 350°.

2. Mix all the ingredients in a 1 quart casserole and cover it tightly.

3. Bake 25 to 30 minutes until the rice is tender and the water is absorbed.

CONVERTED:

Always follow the directions on the package. The cooking times and water amounts vary. **Use the boiling water start.**

BROWN:

Follow the directions for white EXCEPT: increase the water to 1¼ cups for Cold-Water Start and 2¼ cups for Boiling-Water Start, and increase the cooking time to 30 to 45 minutes.

The Great Pretender
Wild rice isn't rice at all! It is the seed of a marsh plant that is not related to rice.

WILD:

½ cup wild rice
2 cups water
½ teaspoon salt
1 Tablespoon butter (optional)

OPTION:
Reduce the salt to ¼ teaspoon, increase butter to 2 Tablespoons and add 1 (4 oz.) jar mushroom stems and pieces (drained) and 1 teaspoon instant chicken bouillon.

1. Rinse the rice **well** in a colander under cold water.

2. Bring the water, salt, and butter to a full boil on HIGH.

3. Gradually stir in rice, reduce to LOW.

4. Cover and cook 40 to 50 minutes (without stirring or uncovering) until rice is tender and water absorbed.

FRIED RICE

Makes: 2 servings
Groundwork: 3 minutes
Cook: 8 to 10 min. -
  MED. HIGH
Need: medium skillet

Try this as a side dish
for stir-fry meals.

Add (and cook with
the rice and soy
sauce):
1 to 1½ cups cooked,
  diced chicken, ham
  or pork; ¾ to 1 lb.
  cooked shrimp; or 4
  slices cooked,
  crumbled bacon for
  an entreé.
⅓ cup sliced water
  chestnuts and/or ¼
  cup canned sliced
  mushrooms.

Makes: 2 servings
Groundwork: 5 minutes
Cook: 20 min. - LOW
Need: medium
  saucepan with lid

Remember: You can
substitute ½ can beef
bouillon and ½ soup
can water for the
water and bouillon
cubes.

---

2 Tablespoons butter
2 cups cooked rice
1 Tablespoon soy sauce
¼ cup chopped onions
1 egg

1. Melt the butter in a medium skillet
   on MEDIUM HIGH.

2. Add the rice, onions and soy sauce
   and cook until hot and light brown,
   stirring constantly.

3. Reduce to LOW, push the rice to one
   side of the skillet, break the egg into
   the other side, and quickly scramble
   to medium firmness.

4. Stir to combine.

PILAFF RICE

½ cup uncooked long grain or
   converted rice
2 Tablespoons butter
1 cup water (1⅓ cups for converted)
⅛ teaspoon salt
⅛ teaspoon pepper
1 Tablespoon instant minced onions
1 Tablespoon instant bell pepper
1 Tablespoon parsley flakes
2 beef bouillon cubes

1. Melt the butter in a medium
   saucepan on MEDIUM.

2. Add the rice and cook until the rice
   is brown, stirring constantly.

3. Stir in the remaining ingredients.

4. Cover, bring to a boil on MEDIUM
   HIGH, reduce the heat to LOW and
   cook 20 minutes:

THE CREOLE COTTAGE

THE CREOLE COTTAGE introduces a blend of Acadian and Creole dishes that have been modified from the usual 1 to 2 days of preparation to less than one hour. At first glance they may seem long and complex, but, like the mysterious land of their origin, looks are amazingly deceptive.

THE CHEF'S SPICE

Groundwork: 2 minutes
Need: 8 oz. container
(a large empty spice jar is perfect).

½ cup salt
1½ Tablespoons black pepper
2 Tablespoons cayenne pepper
1 Tablespoon garlic powder
1 Tablespoon chili powder

Use in place of salt to spice up any dish.

1. Combine all the ingredients in a container and shake well to mix.

SAUCEPAN SHRIMP CREOLE

Makes: 2 servings
Groundwork: 3 minutes
Cook: 3 min. - MED. HIGH
20 min. - LOW
Need: medium saucepan with lid

1 (8 oz.) can tomato sauce
¾ cup water
½ teaspoon Tabasco
¼ to ½ teaspoon chili powder
½ teaspoon garlic powder
3 Tablespoons instant minced onions
1 Tablespoon instant celery flakes
1 Tablespoon instant bell pepper
½ cup uncooked rice
1 teaspoon salt
½ pound peeled shrimp (uncooked)

1. Combine all the ingredients except the shrimp in a medium saucepan on MEDIUM HIGH until bubbling.

2. Reduce to LOW, cover, and continue cooking for 10 minutes without lifting lid.

3. Increase to MEDIUM HIGH, add shrimp, bring to a boil, stirring constantly.

4. Reduce to LOW, cover, and continue cooking for 10 minutes until the shrimp is pink and tender.

SHRIMP GUMBO TOUT de SUITE

ROUX:

Makes: 4 servings
Groundwork: 15
  minutes
Cook: Gumbo 45 min.
  - LOW
Need: large heavy
  saucepan or Dutch
  oven with lid.

Serve over: 2 cups hot
cooked rice.

Roux: The key to great
gumbo is the Roux - it
must be **very** dark, but
not scorched.

Spices: Gumbo should
be extremely spicy
before serving over
rice!

**CROWD PLEASER -
GUMBO PARTY:**
To make gumbo for 12,
triple this recipe and
serve with hot garlic
bread and a crisp
green salad.

If time is no problem,
do this the old
fashioned way:
Replace the instant
with fresh onion and
bell pepper.

2 Tablespoons butter
2 Tablespoons flour
⅛ teaspoon pepper
⅛ teaspoon salt

GUMBO:

2 (14½ oz.) cans chicken broth
3 oz. water
1 Tablespoon instant minced onions
1 Tablespoon parsley flakes
1 Tablespoon instant bell pepper
⅛ teaspoon salt
½ teaspoon garlic powder
⅛ teaspoon thyme
⅛ teaspoon cayenne pepper
pinch The Chef's Spice
⅛ teaspoon Tabasco
½ small tomato (chopped)
½ cup frozen okra (cut)
1 bay leaf
1 pound peeled shrimp (uncooked)
*file' to taste

1. Melt the butter in a large, heavy sauce-
    pan or Dutch oven on MEDIUM.

2. Add the flour, salt, and pepper,
    reduce to MEDIUM LOW, and stir **con-
    stantly** until the roux is very **dark** brown,
    being careful not to let it scorch.

3. Gradually add the broth and water, stir-
    ring constantly until thoroughly mixed.

4. Stir in the onion, parsley, bell pepper,
    salt, garlic, thyme, cayenne pepper,
    The Chef's Spice, bay leaf and Tabasco.

5. Increase the heat to MEDIUM HIGH
    and bring to a boil, stirring frequently.

6. While the mixture is returning to a boil,
    chop the tomato and cut the okra (if
    necessary); add both to the mixture.

7. Cover, reduce to LOW, and simmer
    30 minutes.

*Filé may be moistened or used dry. It may be added to the pot rather than to the individual servings, but it will make the gumbo stringy if it is reheated.

Makes: 4 servings
Groundwork: 5 minutes
Cook: 15 minutes -
  LOW
Ignore: 10 minutes
Need: medium
  saucepan

Great served with E'toufée but is NOT compatible with Gumbo.

8. Add the shrimp, return to a boil on MEDIUM HIGH, re-cover, reduce the heat again to LOW and simmer an additional 15 to 20 minutes.

9. Moisten the filé with a small amount of water, if desired.

10. Serve the gumbo in individual bowls over hot rice and top with a pinch of the filé.

LOUISIANA RICE

2 Tablespoons butter
¾ cup uncooked rice
1 (10½ oz.) can chicken broth
1 Tablespoon instant minced onions
2 teaspoons parsley flakes
⅓ teaspoon marjoram
⅓ teaspoon savory
¾ teaspoon rosemary
⅓ teaspoon salt

1. Melt the butter in a medium saucepan on MEDIUM.

2. Add the rice and cook, stirring constantly until it is a medium brown.

3. Add the broth and the remaining ingredients and bring to a boil on HIGH stirring to mix thoroughly.

4. Cover, reduce the heat to LOW and cook 15 minutes.

5. Remove the pan from the heat (do not remove the lid) and ignore it for at least 10 minutes.

6. Stir before serving.

SHRIMP E'TOUFÉE

Makes: 4 servings
Groundwork: 5 minutes
Cook: 35 min. - LOW
Need: Dutch oven or
   heavy saucepan with
   lid

3 Tablespoons butter or oil
3 Tablespoons flour
⅛ teaspon salt
¾ teaspoon pepper
1 cup warm water
2 chicken bouillon cubes
1 Tablespoon instant minced onions
¼ Tablespoon instant bell pepper
1 Tablespoon instant celery flakes
¼ teaspoon garlic powder
2 Tablespoons parsley flakes
4 drops Tabasco
¼ teaspoon Worcestershire
2 Tablespoons cream of mushroom or
   celery soup
3 drops of red food coloring
dash of lemon juice
1 pound peeled shrimp (uncooked)

Serve over: Louisiana
Rice or 2 cups hot
cooked rice.

E'toufée is a French
word meaning
smothered.

1. Heat the butter or oil in a Dutch
   oven or large saucepan on MEDIUM.

2. Add the flour, salt, and pepper and
   stir constantly until the roux is
   medium brown.

3. Remove the pan from the heat and
   gradually stir in the warm water,
   stirring constantly to prevent
   lumping.

4. Return the pan to the heat and stir
   in the bouillon cubes, onions, bell
   pepper, celery, garlic, parsley,
   Tabasco, Worcestershire, soup, food
   coloring and lemon juice.

5. Reduce the heat to LOW, cover, and
   simmer 20 minutes, stirring
   occasionally. (This will seem too thick
   and too spicy at this point, but
   adding the shrimp corrects that.)

6. Add the shrimp, bring to a boil on
   MEDIUM, quickly reduce to LOW, and
   simmer an additional 15 minutes,
   stirring occasionally.

SHRIMP JAMBALAYA

Makes: 4-6 servings
Groundwork: 10
    minutes
Cook: 30 min. - LOW
Need: large skillet or
    saucepan with lid

Red pepper sauce is
not the same as
Tabasco! It is not as
hot and has a different
taste.

**Chicken or Ham
Jambalaya:** Replace
the shrimp with 2 cups
cooked chicken
(skinned, boned, and
diced) or ham.

8 pieces of bacon
¾ cup uncooked long grained rice
1 (10½ oz.) can beef bouillon
2 Tablespoons instant minced onions
½ soup can water
2 Tablespoons instant celery flakes
2 Tablespoons instant bell pepper
1 Tablespoon parsley flakes
½ teaspoon garlic powder
⅛ teaspoon chili powder
⅛ teaspoon pepper
2 Tablespoons Worcestershire
2 Tablespoons red pepper sauce
1 bay leaf (optional)
1 lb. peeled shrimp (uncooked)

1. Cut the bacon into 1 inch squares
    and cook in a large skillet or
    saucepan on MEDIUM until the
    bacon begins to brown.

2. Add the rice and cook, stirring
    frequently until the rice is golden
    brown and the bacon is done.

3. Add the liquids and all the other
    ingredients **except the shrimp** and
    bring quickly to a boil on HIGH,
    stirring constantly.

4. Reduce to LOW, cover, and simmer
    15 minutes.

5. Stir in the shrimp and turn the heat
    to MEDIUM HIGH to quick start them.

6. Again, reduce the heat to LOW,
    cover, and continue to cook 10
    minutes until the shrimp are done.

PIRATES' POT

Makes: 2 servings
Groundwork: 10
minutes
Cook: 20 min. - MED.
HIGH
6 min. - HIGH
Need: stock pot OR
large saucepan

1 **pound shrimp (uncooked, headless
shrimp in shells)**
2 **quarts water**
1 **(12 oz.) can beer**
5 **Tablespoons The Chef's Spice**
2 **Tablespoons garlic powder**
1 **teaspoon coarse ground black
pepper**
1¼ **teaspoons salt**
2 **small onions (peeled)**
2 **small red potatoes**
¼ **pound Smoked, Cajun, Italian, or
Polish sausage**
2 **small ears corn (frozen or fresh,
shucked and washed)**

Adjust the spices to
taste — but remember
you are seasoning
through the shells of
the shrimp and the
skins of the potatoes.

Pirate Party:
Wonderful for a crowd!
Just provide lots of
napkins and a bowl
for the shells and
cobs. Be careful with
the spices when
increasing this recipe.
When doubling, only
increase the spices by
half.

1. Bring the water, beer, and spices to
   a boil in a stock pot or large
   saucepan.

2. While the water is heating (8 to 10
   minutes), cut the root and top end
   off the onions and peel off the first
   thin outer layer; wash the potatoes;
   cut the sausage into 1 inch pieces;
   add these to the boiling water.

3. Allow this to return to a **full** boil, (2 to
   3 minutes) reduce to MEDIUM HIGH,
   and cook 10 minutes.

4. While the vegetables and sausage
   are cooking, rinse the shrimp under
   cold water.

5. Increase to HIGH, add the corn,
   allow it to return to a **full** boil,
   reduce to MEDIUM HIGH, and cook 5
   minutes.

6. Again increase to HIGH, add the
   shrimp, allow to return to a **full** boil,
   reduce to MEDIUM, and cook 5 to 7
   minutes depending on the size of
   the shrimp.

NEW ORLEANS BARBECUED SHRIMP

Makes: 2 servings
Groundwork: 5 minutes
Bake: 10 minutes
Oven Temp: 400°
Need: shallow baking
    pan

This has a lot of ingredients but don't let that scare you off! It is quick, easy, and **well** worth the effort.

Serve with crisp French rolls for dipping in the sauce. This is a messy meal, so provide lots of napkins and consider covering the table with yesterday's newspapers!

These are great on the grill! Set the baking pan directly over MEDIUM coals and grill, COVERED or UNCOVERED, 10 minutes until the shrimp are pink.

For a Princely Potato entrée:
Peel the shrimp before cooking. Split 2 large baked potatoes and fill with the cooked shrimp and lots of the sauce.

½ **cup (1 stick) butter**
2 **teaspoons liquid crab boil OR 1 Tablespoon ground seafood seasoning**
¼ **cup olive oil**
3 **Tablespoons lemon juice**
½ **teaspoon Tabasco**
1 **Tablespoon parsley flakes**
¾ **teaspoon basil**
¾ **teaspoon garlic powder**
1 **teaspoon oregano**
¾ **teaspoon salt**
1 **teaspoon coarse ground black pepper**
2 **teaspoons paprika**
1 **pound fresh shrimp (unpeeled)**

1. Preheat the oven to 400°.

2. Melt the butter in the baking pan in the oven while it preheats.

3. Wash the shrimp under cold water and drain well.

4. Add the spices to the melted butter, and stir to combine.

5. Add the shrimp, stir to coat each, and arrange them in a single layer.

6. Bake 10 minutes until the shrimp are hot and tender. DO NOT OVERCOOK!

OPTIONS:

A. Replace the shrimp with fish fillets.

B. Replace the oil with 3 to 5 oz. lite beer and ½ cup lower fat margarine or liquid butter substitute such as reconstituted Butter Buds for a lighter, low-cal meal.

RED BEANS AND RICE

Makes: 4 servings
Groundwork: 2 minutes
Cook: 8 to 10 min. -
  HIGH
35 min. - LOW
Need: large saucepan
  with lid

Serve with a tossed
salad (page 58) and
hot garlic bread (page
257, 259)

2 cups water
1 (3 oz.) bag seafood boil
2¼ teaspoons Tabasco
1 teaspoon pepper
⅛ teaspoon cayenne pepper
⅛ teaspoon garlic powder
1 Tablespoon parsley flakes
1 Tablespoon instant minced onions
¼ lb. ham (diced)
¾ lb. Cajun, smoked, Polish, or Italian
  sausage (sliced)
1 (15 oz.) can red kidney beans
  (drained)
1 cup cooked rice

1. Place the water, seafood boil,
   Tabasco, peppers, garlic, onion,
   and parsley in a large saucepan on
   HIGH, bring to a boil, reduce to
   MEDIUM, and boil 8 to 10 minutes
   (uncovered).

2. While the spices are boiling, cut the
   ham into ½-inch cubes or chunks.

3. Carefully remove the bag of
   seafood boil and discard.

4. Add the ham to the spicy water,
   reduce to LOW, cover and simmer
   20 minutes.

5. While the ham is simmering, cook
   the rice according to the directions
   on the package.

6. Slice the sausage into ½ inch
   rounds.

7. Add the sausage and simmer 15
   minutes.

8. Drain the beans, add to the mixture,
   and simmer an additional 10
   minutes until the beans are heated
   and slightly soft.

9. Either mix with or serve over the hot
   rice.

CREOLE DRESSING

Makes: 5 servings
Groundwork: 20
 minutes
Cook: 15 to 20 min. -
 MEDIUM
Need: medium skillet
medium saucepan
large double boiler

Important Note:
You may need to add
more spices once the
oysters and rice are
combined with the
pork.

A wonderful
accompaniment to
festive holiday dinners
or a main dish for
cozy winter suppers.

½ cup uncooked long grain rice
1 lb. ground lean pork
4 to 5 green onions & tops (chopped)
3 Tablespoons parsley flakes
1 teaspoon pepper
1 teaspoon salt
2 teaspoons poultry seasoning
1 pint raw oysters (drained)

1. Cook the rice as directed on the
   package.

2. While the rice is cooking, wash and
   chop the onion.

3. Crumble the pork into a medium
   skillet, add the seasonings, cook on
   MEDIUM until it begins to brown,
   stirring frequently to break up the
   larger pieces.

4. Add the chopped onions to the
   skillet and continue cooking until the
   pork is brown and the onions are
   soft. Drain on paper towels.

5. Bring enough water to a boil on
   HIGH in the lower section of a
   double boiler to just touch the
   bottom of the top section.

6. Drain the oysters.

7. Mix the cooked rice, pork, oysters,
   and parsley flakes together in the
   top section, cover, and steam on
   MEDIUM just until the oysters are
   puffy and done, stirring frequently.

THE PASTA PUZZLE

Like wines, pastas can be intimidating with their old-world names and traditions. The simple truth is that all cream-colored pastas are just flour and eggs made into different shapes for convenience and variety. The tastes are identical and the shapes are interchangeable within limits. Small pasta shapes accept sauces well, medium shapes combine with other ingredients beautifully, and large shapes easily lend themselves to stuffing or layering. Colored pastas have added ingredients: green pasta includes spinach, red pasta has tomatoes, and other hues may be made from a variety of flours (rye, buckwheat, whole wheat, etc.). The taste differences are extremely subtle, and the colors are mainly for eye appeal. Only tradition and practicality dictates which pasta shape is used.

THE PASTA PROCESS

Preparing purchased pasta is refreshingly simple:

1. For each quart of water, add 1 teaspoon of salt. To prevent boil-over and keep pasta from sticking together, add 1 teaspoon oil or butter.

2. Use **enough** rapidly boiling water so that pasta is never crowded. . .at least 4 quarts per pound.

3. Never let the water stop boiling rapidly. Add the raw pasta slowly and stir frequently to keep it separated.

4. For use in hot or cold pasta **salads** or any dish that will need **baking,** undercook (Al Dente) pasta by one fourth the recommended time.

5. For both hot or cold **salads**, rinse pasta in cold water and drain well.

6. When serving with **heated sauces,** rinse the pasta in **hot** water. Keep the pasta warm in a colander or strainer placed over a small amount of hot water in a saucepan on LOW.

7. Cooked pasta can be frozen for one month. Just toss it lightly with a small amount of oil before freezing.

PASTA PARTNERS

Pasta Salads are in LUNCH and casseroles are in SUPPER. In some recipes, THE CHEF cooks pasta directly in the sauce to save time and clean-up!

Traditionally, many pasta sauces are inseparable from their partner shapes. Sigmond Freud might have mentally collapsed if served Alfredo sauce atop the lasagna noodles! The following combos are ancient classics:

Warm the pasta serving bowl by filling it with very hot water and draining it well just before serving.

Groundwork: 5 minutes
Cook: 5 minutes - MED. HIGH
Need: small saucepan

A hardy addition for hot, cooked angel hair pasta.

SAUCED OR TOSSED PASTA

Olive oil or butter is a natural with hot cooked pasta, but simple sauces send it soaring. The following sauces are for 2 (2 oz.) servings of cooked pasta:

BROWN BUTTER SAUCE

¼ **cup (½ stick) butter**
¼ **cup Parmesan cheese**
¼ **teaspoon garlic salt**

1. Melt the butter in a small sauce pan on MEDIUM HIGH and stir frequently until the butter browns to a rich chocolate color.

2. Pour over the hot cooked pasta, add the cheese and garlic salt, and toss gently to combine.

211

WHITE CLAM SAUCE

Groundwork: 2 minutes
Cook: 2 min. - MEDIUM
Need: medium
saucepan

¼ cup (½ stick) butter
¼ teaspoon garlic powder
1 Tablespoon instant minced onions
1 (6½ oz.) can minced clams
(undrained)
½ teaspoon salt
⅛ teaspoon pepper
¼ cup dry white wine
¼ cup Parmesan cheese

Garnish with parsley
and lemon slices.

Perfect with vermicelli.

1. Melt the butter in a medium saucepan on MEDIUM.

2. Add the garlic powder, minced onions, clams and ½ of the clam liquid, salt, and pepper and heat until very hot but not boiling.

3. Add the wine and heat until very hot.

4. Toss with the pasta and top with Parmesan cheese.

ALFREDO SAUCE

Groundwork: 2 minutes
Need: measuring cup

¼ cup whipping cream (unwhipped) or milk (room temp.)
1½ teaspoons parsley flakes
1 Tablespoon butter (room temp.)
1½ Tablespoons Parmesan cheese
pinch garlic powder

Traditionally served
with hot fettucini.

PASTA PRIMAVERA:
Sauté the following in
1 Tablespoon of
vegetable or olive oil
and toss with Alfredo-
sauced pasta:

6 to 8 snow pea pods
2 Tablespoons frozen
green peas
1 small green onion
(sliced)
¼ cup sliced
mushrooms

1. Combine the whipping cream (or milk) and parsley flakes in a measuring cup while the pasta cooks.

2. Drain the pasta and return it to the pan.

3. Add the butter to the hot pasta and stir until it has melted.

4. Add the remaining ingredients and toss gently to combine.

CARBONARA

Add to Alfredo Sauce:

1 egg yolk (uncooked)
4 strips bacon (cooked & crumbled)

GARLIC SAUCE

Groundwork: 1 minute
Cook: 2 min. - MEDIUM
Need: small saucepan

¼ cup olive oil
¼ teaspoon garlic powder
2 Tablespoons parsley flakes
½ teaspoon salt
¼ teaspoon pepper
¼ cup Parmesan cheese

A great sauce for
spaghetti!

1. Combine the oil, garlic powder, and parsley flakes in a small saucepan on MEDIUM and heat until very hot.

2. Add the salt and pepper to the sauce, toss with the pasta and top with Parmesan cheese.

RED CLAM SAUCE

Goundwork: 1 minute
Cook: 3 min. - HIGH
14 to 15 min. - MEDIUM
Need: medium
   saucepan

2 (6½ oz.) cans minced clams
   (drained with liquid reserved)
½ cup spaghetti sauce
¼ teaspoon garlic powder
1 Tablespoon parsley flakes
2 Tablespoons Chablis OR
   other white wine (optional)

Garnish with parsley.

Serve with hot, cooked
linguine.

1. Drain the clam liquid into a medium saucepan; bring to a boil on HIGH (3 minutes). Reduce heat to MEDIUM and cook until the liquid is reduced to ½ cup (about 14 to 15 minutes), stirring occasionally.

2. Add the spaghetti sauce, garlic powder, and parsley; stir until well blended and heat until very hot.

3. Add the clams and wine, heat 1 minute until hot, and toss with the pasta.

THE STIR FRY CHEF

The cooking time is very fast but the preparation of the food for stir-frying can be time-consuming. Some supermarkets carry pre-cut meats and vegetables but charge more for the convenience.

THE PAN

A WOK is wonderful but not necessary. Any heavy skillet will work well, electric or otherwise.

THE OIL

Each type adds its own flavor — take your choice to find your favorite.

DO TRY: any pure vegetable oil — corn, peanut, safflower. Use olive oil only as a flavoring mixed with another oil. Its strength can overwhelm a delicate dish.

DO NOT TRY: any animal based oil — butter, margarine, drippings, or hydrogenated shortening! These hate high temperatures and are guaranteed to activate your smoke alarm.

THE TEMPERATURE

The ideal temperature for stir-frying is 350° to 375°. Heat the oil in a wok or skillet on MEDIUM HIGH for 2 to 3 minutes.

THE FOODS

Most fresh or frozen vegetables and meats can successfully be stir-fried. Frozen vegetables will not be as crisp as fresh ones and should be added to the wok while still frozen. Select 2 or 3 choices of vegetables and 1 or more meats with compatible flavors.

THE CUTS

Cutting foods diagonally will expose more food surface to the heat and make cooking faster. Always use a diagonal cut for less tender cuts of meat and crunchy or stalky vegetables. Partial freezing of meats makes slicing easier.

THE PROCESS

1. Purchase or prepare a sauce.

2. Prepare all foods for cooking.

3. Pour enough oil in the wok or skillet to completely coat all foods. (One tablespoon per serving is usually enough.)

4. Heat the oil on HIGH until it is very hot but not smoking.

5. As each food is added, stir it quickly to coat, and stir constantly while it cooks. Keep it hot and keep it moving! If needed, reduce to MEDIUM HIGH to prevent the outside of the food from browning before the inside is hot and tender.

6. As each food is cooked, push it up the side and out of the way in a wok, or remove from the skillet to a warm (150°) oven.

7. Cook the foods in this order:

    Pork — stir until no pink remains

    Beef or poultry — stir until tender

    Seafood - stir gently to avoid breaking

    Vegetables - stir until crisp-tender (cover for 30 seconds to steam)

    Sauce - stir until hot and thickened

THE TIMING

Texture and doneness is a matter of choice, but these general guides may help:

3 to 4 minutes — Pork, poultry, beef

2 to 3 minutes — Seafoods, and crunchy vegetables (carrots, celery, cabbage)

1 to 2 minutes — Tender vegetables (bean sprouts, snow peas, peppers)

THE FRUITS AND VEGETABLES

TYPE	PREPARATION
Apple	Fresh; peel, remove core; cut in wedges
Asparagus	Fresh; cut diagonally into 1" pieces Frozen: thaw slightly and cut into 1" pieces
Bamboo shoots	Fresh: cut in half lengthwise Canned: drain well
Beans (green)	Fresh: remove stem ends and cut diagonally into 1" pieces Frozen: do not thaw
Bean Sprouts	Fresh: rinse in cold water, pat dry Canned: drain well
Bell Pepper (green, red, yellow)	Fresh: remove ends and seeds; cut in thin strips or rings
Bok Choy (Chinese cabbage)	Fresh: rinse in cold water; pat dry; chop or slice thinly
Broccoli	Fresh: rinse in cold water; remove all leaves and cut apart; diagonally slice into $\frac{1}{2}$" pieces all stems larger than $\frac{1}{2}$" in diameter Frozen: rinse in cold water to slightly thaw and separate, pat dry
Cabbage	Fresh: cut into quarters; remove core: slice coarsely
Carrots	Fresh: peel; remove ends; slice diagonally into $\frac{1}{8}$" slices or grate coarsely
Cauliflower	Fresh: rinse in cold water; cut into flowerettes; discard large stems Frozen: rinse in cold water to separate, pat dry
Celery	Fresh: rinse in cold water, remove strings; cut diagonally into $\frac{1}{2}$" pieces
Cucumber	Fresh: peel; cut into $\frac{3}{4}$" thick rounds; remove large seeds
Eggplant	Fresh: peel and cut into $\frac{1}{2}$" slices (1" length)
Mushrooms	Fresh: rinse in cold water; pat dry; slice or leave whole Canned: drain well
Onions	Fresh: peel and slice into $\frac{1}{4}$" rings or thin wedges
Oranges (mandarin)	Canned: drain well
Peas (green)	Fresh: remove from pod, discard blemished ones Frozen: do not thaw
Pineapple	Fresh: peel and cut into $\frac{1}{2}$" cubes Canned chunks: drain well

Scallions (green onions)	Fresh: remove root end; slice diagonally into 1" pieces
Snow Peas (pea pods)	Fresh: remove stem ends & strings; leave whole Frozen: do not thaw
Spinach	Fresh: rinse in cold water, remove large stems; tear into smaller pieces, if desired
Squash	Fresh (summer): remove stem & flower ends; slice into ¼" rounds; remove large seeds Fresh (winter): don't bother — it will not stir-fry
Tomatoes	Fresh: remove stem end; cut into ½" thick wedges; cut cherry (patio) tomatoes in half.
Tofu (bean curd)	Fresh: cut into ½" cubes
Water chestnuts	Canned: drain; slice thinly
Zucchini	Fresh: remove stem & flower ends; cut into ½" thick slices or 2" long strips (½" thick)

THE MEATS

TYPE	PREPARATION
Beef or Veal	Very tender cuts: (sirloin or top round) slice into ½" to ¾" pieces Less tender cuts: (round, flank) slice diagonally across the grain ¼" thick (do not use shank or brisket)
Pork	Slice thinly into ¼" to ½" strips: cut ham into ½" to ¾" cubes
Chicken	Cut into 1" pieces
Lamb	Cut into ½" to 1" pieces

THE SEAFOODS

TYPE	PREPARATION
Clams and oysters	Fresh: rinse the shell in cold water; open shell & remove clam or oyster Canned: drain well Frozen: thaw and drain
Crab and lobster	Fresh: cook and remove from shell Frozen: thaw and cut into bite-size pieces, if needed Canned: rinse in cold water; drain well
Shrimp	Fresh: remove shell, tail & veins; cut large shrimp in half lengthwise Frozen: thaw and pat dry Canned: drain well

THE EXTRAS	
PREPARATION	**TYPE**
Nuts	Raw or cooked: leave whole for peanuts, pecans, cashews, walnuts: thinly slice chestnuts
Seeds	Toast sesame seeds in 350° oven until light brown (optional)
Rice (white, brown or wild) OR Pasta	Cook until barely done; rinse under hot water to remove starch; drain well and refrigerate until chilled before stir-frying DO NOT stir-fry rice or pasta when serving over hot cooked rice.

THE SEASONINGS

Your choice of herbs and spices can be added to either the food or the oil. The standards include: soy sauce, ground ginger, finely grated fresh ginger root, garlic powder, peeled garlic cloves, sherry, curry or basil.

For a **Szechwan** taste (hot & spicy) add Tabasco, or cayenne pepper to the sauce. Or crushed red peppers can be added to the oil while it's heating and removed before adding the foods.

FOR TERIYAKI:

Marinate the meat in teriyaki sauce 20 to 30 minutes before cooking; use Thai Fry Sauce to finish.

THE SAUCES

These make the difference between good and great! No need to cook — just mix well, add to the food in the hot wok, and stir until thickened.

Many sauces can be purchased in most supermarkets: Black bean, Hoisin, Sweet and Sour, Oyster, Stir Fry.

Or, make your own:

THAI-FRY SAUCE
(Everybody's Favorite! It goes with any combination)

½ cup chicken or beef broth
2 tablepoons soy sauce
1 Tablespoon cornstarch
2 Tablespoons cold water

1. Dissolve the cornstarch in water and stir in the soy sauce and broth.

SWEET AND SOUR SAUCE (Great for Shrimp)

½ cup pineapple juice
3 Tablespoons vinegar
3 Tablespoons brown sugar
1 teaspoon soy sauce
1 Tablespoon cornstarch
2 Tablespoons cold water

1. Dissolve the cornstarch in cold water and stir in other ingredients.

THE SIDE DISHES

Stir-fry can be served with any or all of the following:

Chow Mein Noodles
Egg Rolls (purchased)
Rice (steamed or fried)
Vegetables (steamed or marinated)
Wonton Rolls (purchased)

Serve with soy sauce and Hot Chinese Mustard.
(mix and let stand 10 minutes):

1 teaspoon ground mustard
1 teaspoon water
2 teaspoons ketchup or mayonnaise (or half of each)

A FEW CLASSIC COMBINATIONS	
(Or use any combination of your favorite Meats and Veggies)	
Burmese Beef	Beef, broccoli, bell pepper, celery, onions, Thai Fry Sauce
Chinese Pepper Steak	Beef, bell pepper, celery, onion, tomato, Thai Fry sauce with ginger added
Moo Goo Gai Pan	Chicken, boc choy, mushrooms, snow pea pods, water chestnuts, Stir Fry Sauce
Shanghai Shrimp	Shrimp, pineapple, water chestnuts, green onions, Thai Fry Sauce with sherry added
Seoul Food	Pork, zucchini, tomatoes, mushrooms, onion, celery, Black Bean Sauce with garlic added
Sweet and Sour Pork	Pork, snow pea pods, mandarin oranges, Sweet and Sour Sauce
Sukiyaki	Beef, bok choy, green onions, celery, bean sprouts, bamboo shoots, mushrooms, water chestnuts, tofu (optional), Oyster Sauce topped with cashew nuts

THE PATIO CHEF
The cavemen never had it so easy!

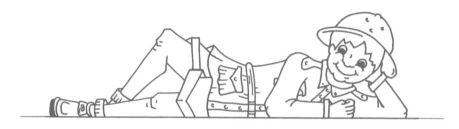

TOOLS AND EQUIPMENT

1. Grill (habachi, brazier, covered grill, smoker, or gas grill)
2. Long handled fork and spatula.
3. Pair of tongs
4. Basting brush (a small paint brush or pastry brush is fine)
5. Plastic bottle filled with water (try a **clean** detergent bottle)
6. Hot pads or mitts
7. Skewers (for kabobs)

IMPORTANT INFORMATION

1. Choose a **level well-ventilated place** far enough from shrubs or flammables so that a flame-up will not ignite anything. **Never** use a charcoal or gas grill inside a home or garage.

2. Use only charcoal lighter fluid (unless you have good accident insurance!) and **never** add more fluid after the fire has been started.

3. Keep a bottle of water handy to **extinguish those stubborn flame-ups** that cannot be controlled by either closing the cover and vents, removing some of the coals, or spacing them farther apart. The chance of flame-ups can be reduced by using lean meats, trimming off as much of the visible fat as possible, or reducing the amount of oily basting sauce.

4. Keep charcoal dry. A **wet** bag of charcoal produces a very flammable gas that can ignite spontaneously and explode if exposed to direct sun or heat!

5. Grease the cooking rack with vegetable oil before cooking to **keep foods from sticking.**

T.L.C. (MAINTENANCE)

To keep your grill working properly, prolong its life, and generally maintain its respectability, always keep it clean (but never use oven cleaners!). Cover the cooled, clean grill to protect it until your next cookout.

THE FIRE STARTERS

Always start a charcoal fire **at least 45 minutes** before you plan to begin cooking (only 10 minutes for a gas grill). Remove the cooking rack and build the fire on the grate or fire base.

FIRE BASE:

If your grill doesn't have several metal ribs or grates to hold the charcoal up off the bottom, cover the bottom of the grill with a 1½" layer of small rocks, gravel, sea shells, or clay-based kitty litter. After 6 to 8 uses, rinse the ashes out of the rocks or shells or replace the kitty litter. This fire base also speeds up fire starting and prevents premature burn-out of the grill.

1. **LIQUID CHARCOAL LIGHTER FLUID:** (No substitution!)* There are three ways to arrange the charcoal:

    A. Pile the dry charcoal into a **pyramid** and soak it with lighter fluid.

    B. Remove both ends from a large metal can (a gallon or 46 oz. juice can), put the can upright on the bottom grate, fill with the needed amount of charcoal and soak with lighter fluid. This **chimney** method is faster and heats the coals more evenly.

    C. Put the charcoal into a cardboard (not styrofoam) egg carton, soak the charcoal with lighter fluid, close the lid and soak the outer carton.

    Let the lighter fluid soak in (one or two minutes) before igniting.

*If you've run out of charcoal lighter fluid, the **only** safe substitute is a candle cut into several 1" pieces. Light both ends of the candles, stash the little fellows in the charcoal, and allow 15 minutes longer for starting the fire this way.

CHARCOAL HEATING TIME:

The **heating time** is affected by both the outside temperature and the wind factor: cold outside temperature increases the time, and wind blowing around charcoal reduces it. Generally, the charcoal will need at least **30 minutes** to heat after the flames from the lighter fluid have died down (the chimney method may take less). If you are really in a hurry, create your own air flow with an electric or hand-held fan.

The **charcoal is ready** when all the briquettes are completely **covered in gray ash.** Tap the charcoal to knock off the ash and release the maximum heat. Arrange the charcoal for your method of cooking, "How Do You Grill What." Replace the cooking rack and allow a few minutes for the grill to reach the proper temperature.

And herein is the key to this kingdom! The rough places will be made plane **if** your coals are the proper temperature for the food you are going to cook. Simply determine what temperature you need and hold your hand over the coals at the height the food will be cooking. Count seconds (one thousand one, one thousand two, or one Mississippi, two Mississippi). If you must jerk your hand away after **2 seconds**, the coals are **hot**; 3 seconds, they are **medium hot**; 4, **medium**, 5, they are **medium slow**; and after 6 seconds, they are **slow**.

THE TIMING

The timing of the charcoal cooking is a good candidate for computerization because of the many variables: type of grill, amount of charcoal used, type and amount of food, air temperature, and wind factor. The times given in this section are approximations and are only meant to be a guide until you have enough experience with your grill to make your own timing chart or floppy disk.

COOKING TIMES

Cooking times are determined by the cooking temperature.

To **prolong** (slow down) the cooking time, **reduce** the heat by either:

1. **Closing** the vents on a **covered** grill (bottom vents on an open grill).
2. **Spreading** out the coals on a **brazier** or **open** grill.
3. **Turning down** the gas-flow knob on a gas grill.

To **shorten** (speed-up) the cooking time, **increase** the temperature by:

1. **Opening** the vents on a **covered** grill.

2. **Compacting** and/or **adding** more charcoal on a **brazier** or **open** grill.

3. **Turning up** the gas flow knob on a **gas** grill.

TIMING TIPS:

1. Have **all** meats at room temperature before grilling.

2. To speed up cooking time for poultry, place it in a foil-covered pan and bake in a 350° oven for 30 min. while your charcoal is heating.

3. Use a meat thermometer for larger cuts of meat (roasts, whole turkeys, chickens, hams).

4. To maintain an even cooking temp, anticipate the need for more charcoal and add it 15 minutes before the heat will be needed. For faster additions, keep a few briquettes warming off to the side and add them to the hot charcoal 5 to 10 minutes before more heat is needed.

THE FLAVORING

CHIPS:

Use aromatic, green wood chips or small sticks (hickory, mesquite, apple, walnut, oak, pecan). Soak them in water at least one hour before using. Add 2 to 4 sticks or ½ cup chips directly to the hot coals.

HERBS:

Fresh herbs and spices add interesting tastes to charcoaled foods. Toss unpeeled garlic buds, mint sprigs, ginger roots, whole cloves, oranges or lemon peels into the hot coals for the last 10 to 15 minutes. Soak basil, oregano, tarragon, thyme for 1 hour, drain, and add to coals when you put the foods on the grill.

SAUCES AND MARINADES:

Barbecue sauces and marinades are traditional for outdoor cooking. See SAUCES AND GRAVIES. Brush sauces on with a pastry brush or nylon paint brush. Sauces that contain sugar or tomatoes burn easily. Use them only on MEDIUM or LOW HEAT during the last 30 minutes of cooking.

THE COOKING METHODS:

GRILL-TYPE, MEAT, AND METHOD MATCH-UP

Your choice of methods and meats is dictated by the equipment you have. This chart will help you select a meat that will cook successfully on your particular grill. (Roasts, turkeys, and hams object strenuously to an open grill!)

METHOD	TYPE OF GRILL	TYPE OF FOOD	CHARCOAL ARRANGEMENT	CHARCOAL AMOUNT	FOOD PLACEMENT	LIDS & VENTS	TEMPS	COOKING SPEED
DIRECT	Any grill type	**Small or Thin** Cuts: Steaks, Hamburgers, Hot dogs, Chops, Fish, Shellfish, Kabobs	Spread in a layer 1 or 2 briquettes deep	Enough to cover an area slightly larger than food	Directly over hot charcoal	All open	HIGH	FAST The food cooks quickly
SEMI-DIRECT	Any grill except a round one with deep slanting sides	**Medium Size** Cuts: Chicken (pieces), Thick chops, Ribs, Kabobs	Arrange 5 or 6 piles 2" - 4" apart. Each pile needs 6-8 pieces	3 qts. (4 lbs.) will burn for 1 hour without adding more charcoal	Spaced evenly over hot coals	Lid closed with all vents open **half way.** Turn often if grill has no lid.	MEDIUM HIGH	MEDIUM
INDIRECT	Covered grill **only**	**Large, Whole** Cuts: Hams, Roasts, Chickens, Turkeys, Fish	Pyramid on one side of grill	3 qts. (4 lbs.) to start & 1 additional quart added each hour.	On opposite side of charcoal with a drip pan underneath the food	Lid closed with top vent open over food & bottom vent open under charcoal; other vents closed or slightly open if higher temp is needed.	MEDIUM LOW	SLOW Food cooks a prolonged time, usually several hours.

HOW DO YOU GRILL WHAT?

Once you have selected a meat and method compatible with your grill, use these secrets of success to determine the proper cooking temps. and times. REMEMBER: these are suggestions only — adjust them to suit your particular grill and preference.

SELECTION	OPEN GRILL	COVERED GRILL DIRECT METHOD	COVERED GRILL INDIRECT METHOD	TEMPERATURE OF COALS	PEARLS OF WISDOM	MEAT THERMOMETER
CHICKEN: Whole unstuffed			30 min. per lb.	MEDIUM	Indirect method is best for all chicken. Cook all poultry very well done.	185°
Halves	1½ hrs. (direct)	1 hr.	2 hrs.	MEDIUM (Open) LOW (Covered)		
Individual Pieces	30 min.	20 to 25 min.	1½ hrs.	MEDIUM	To speed up grill time, prebake 20 minuntes at 350° for open grilling.	
Cornish Hens			45 min. to 1 hr.	MEDIUM		180°
CHOPS: Lamb (1 inch)	20 to 25 min.	15 to 20 min.		MED. - HOT	Lamb chops are best cooked rare to MEDIUM. All chops should be 1" thick. Sear 1 min. on each side on HOT.	
Pork	22 to 25 min.	30 to 40 min.	1 to 1½ hr.	LOW		
DUCKLING: Whole			30 min. per lb.	MEDIUM		
FRANKFURTERS	15 min.	10 min.		MEDIUM		
HAMBURGERS: ¼ lb. patties	8 to 10 min. (R) 10 to 12 min. (M) 12 to 14 min. (W)	7 to 9 min. (R) 9 to 10 min. (M) 10 to 12 min. (W)	16 to 20 min. (R) 20 to 24 min. (M) 24 to 28 min. (W)	MED. — HOT		

SELECTION	OPEN GRILL	COVERED GRILL		TEMPERATURE OF COALS	PEARLS OF WISDOM	MEAT THERMOMETER
		DIRECT METHOD	INDIRECT METHOD			
HAM:						
1" fully cooked slices	10 to 15 min. on each side	8 to 10 min. each side		MEDIUM	Cook all pork well done.	
Whole fully cooked boneless			10 min. per lb.	LOW		140°
Whole fully cooked bone-in			10 min. per lb.	LOW		140°
Whole uncooked sugar cured			20 min. per lb.	LOW		170°
Whole fresh uncured			25-30 min. per lb.	LOW		180°
Whole smoked fully cooked			2 to 3 hours	LOW		125° - 130°
KABOBS						
See "The Steakout" and "Kabobing"						
RIBS:						
Spareribs	1 hour (Direct) 2½ hr. (Indirect)	45 min.	1 hour	LOW	Ribs may be precooked, then grilled on an open grill, direct heat, LOW	
Pre-cooked Country Style	15-20 min. (Direct) 2½-3 hrs. (Indirect)		2 hrs.	LOW		
Pre-boiled			30 to 45 min.	LOW		
ROASTS:						
Beef			14-18 min./lb. (R) 18-20 min./lb. (M) 22-25 min./lb. (W)	LOW TO MEDIUM	Use a meat thermometer	140° (R) 160° (M) 170° (W)
Pork			25 min. per lb.	MEDIUM	Cook well done	180°
Lamb		20-22 min. per lb.	3 hours	MEDIUM	Best rare to medium	140° (R) 160° (M)

SELECTION	OPEN GRILL	COVERED GRILL		TEMPERATURE OF COALS	PEARLS OF WISDOM	MEAT THERMOMETER
		DIRECT METHOD	INDIRECT METHOD			
SEAFOODS:						
Clams, mussels in shell	7 to 12 min. (until shells open)	5 to 10 min. (until shells open)		MEDIUM - HOT	See "Grilled Fish and Shell Fish. Turn once during cooking	
Fish - ½" fillets	2 to 3 min. on each side	1½ to 2 min. each side		MEDIUM		
Fish, whole, extra long (3-4 lb.) Fish, whole, large (1 lb.) Fish, whole, small (8-10 oz.)	10 min. per inch of thickness	10 min. per inch of thickness	45 min. - 1 hour	MEDIUM HOT (Open) MEDIUM (Covered)		
Fish 1" steaks	7 to 8 min. on each side	4 to 6 min. on each side		MEDIUM		
Lobster: tails (6 to 8 oz.) whole (1 to 2 lbs.)	12 min. 20 to 22 min.	10 min. 18 to 20 min.		MEDIUM — HOT MEDIUM — HOT	Do Not Overcook! See "Grilled Lobster"	
Oysters - in shell Oysters - shucked	7 to 12 min.	10 min. 2 to 3 min.		MEDIUM — HOT MEDIUM HOT	Shrimp, scallops, and shucked oysters are delicious grilled in a shallow pan in a marinade or basting sauce.	
Scallops	4 to 8 min.	3 to 7 min.		HOT	Grill quickly & serve immediately.	

SELECTION	OPEN GRILL	COVERED GRILL		TEMPERATURE OF COALS	PEARLS OF WISDOM	MEAT THERMOMETER
		DIRECT METHOD	INDIRECT METHOD			
Shrimp (peeled)	5 min.	3 to 4 min.		HOT	Small seafood must be either skewered or placed in a wire basket.	
(unpeeled)	5 min.	4 to 5 min. on each side		HOT		
King Crab Legs (shelled)	5 to 8 min.	2 to 5 min.		MEDIUM	Turn crab once	
(unshelled)	8 to 11 min.	5 to 8 min.		MEDIUM		
(freshly killed)		10 to 12 min.		HOT		
CLAMS		8 to 10 min.		HOT	Cook clams until shells pop open, turning once	
SAUSAGE (Pork, Smoked, Italian, Polish, Cajun)			45 min. - 1 hour	MEDIUM		
STEAKS	See "The Steakout"					
TURKEYS: whole unstuffed breast (4-5 lb.)			18-22 min. per lb. 1½ hours	LOW MEDIUM	Never cook **stuffed** anything (except fish) on the grill! Cook breast skin-side up.	185° - 190°
drumsticks		45 min. to 1 hour		MEDIUM		
wings		45 min. to 1 hour		MEDIUM		

THE STEAKOUT

Perfecting a steak or kabob is not a difficult art to master, but requires practice and a meaningful relationship with your grill.

GROUNDWORK:

Get the meat ready for cooking by either: (1) sprinkling both sides with garlic powder and pepper, (2) rubbing both sides with a clove of cut garlic, (3) coating both sides with Worcestershire, (4) basting with a marinade sauce before and during cooking, or (5) sprinkling both sides with seasoned meat tenderizer, Worcestershire, garlic powder and pepper. Slash the fat every 2 inches to prevent curling.

GRILLING:

The only safe way to grill a **thick** fillet (1" or more) to MEDIUM WELL or WELL DONE is to "butterfly" it first! Make a sideways cut almost through the fillet leaving only ½" still connected on one side. Open the fillet like a book and then grill it for a moist tender steak every time.

Sear the steak quickly on both sides by moving the rack to the position closest to the coals, opening the lid and all vents to make a very hot fire. Cook 1 to 3 minutes on each side, watching closely to prevent flame-up and burning. Then, return the rack to a higher position, following the timing chart below. Close the lid on a covered grill. If further heat reduction is necessary, partially close the vents (bottom vents on open grill).

After searing, turn the steak once half way through the time indicated on the chart (usually when a few red drops appear on top).

THE TIMING:

STEAKS OR KABOBS						
Direct Method						
	COVERED (Low Temp)			UNCOVERED (Hot Temp)		
THICKNESS	RARE	MEDIUM	WELL	RARE	MEDIUM	WELL
	MINUTES			MINUTES		
1"	7-10	10-15	13-22	7	10	13
1½"	10	15	20-30	13	17	22
2"	21	30	45	17	21	35

Rare — (brown on the outside and bright red with freely running juices inside); feels **soft** when touched.

Medium — (brown on the outside and hot pink inside; not quite as juicy as rare); feels firmer

Well-Done — (no pink; not juicy); feels very firm.

KABOBING

1. Select three or more foods that have complimentary tastes but offer a variety of colors and textures.

2. Prepare all foods for grilling **before** you start the fire. Everything should be approximately the same size for even cooking.

3. Select a Sauce or Marinade (SAUCES AND GRAVIES). **All** kabob meats are best if marinated before cooking. The less tender cuts (round, chuck, or even lean stew) **must** be marinated 3 to 4 hours or overnight. Remember, marinated meats require less cooking time!

4. Alternate the foods on the skewer and grill according to the Steak chart or the Seafood section of "How Do You Grill What?"

5. For easier skewering, thread corn pieces through the soft center of the cob from end to end.

6. For all fruit kabobs, use melted butter or a sweet and sour sauce in place of barbecue or marinades. Small or fast-cooking fruits such as bananas or orange sections can be cooked on a separate skewer and combined with the meat kabobs just before serving.

7. Turn kabobs often (at least 4 times) and baste with a sauce or marinade at each turn.

KABOBS

MEATS		VEGGIES & FRUITS	
Choose 1	**Groundwork**	**Choose at least 2**	**Groundwork**
Sirloin steak, tip roast, eye of round, round steak	Cut into ¾" to 1" cubes	Bell pepper	Cut into 1½" pieces
		Onions, cut	Peel; cut into wedges
Chuck, stew	Cut into ¾" to 1" cubes and marinate 3 to 4 hours	Onions, small, whole	Peel; boil 6 minutes
		Corn on cob, fresh	Cut into 1½" pieces; boil 5 min.
Ham, cooked	Cut into 1" to 1½" cubes	Corn on cob, frozen	Thaw; cut into 1½" pieces
Lamb	Cut into ¾" to 1" cubes	Potatoes, small, red	Wash; boil 6 minutes
		Potatoes, sweet, fresh	Cut into 1" to 1½" chunks, boil 6 minutes
Chicken, boneless	Cut into ¾" to 1" cubes		
		Mushrooms, large	Wash
Fish: Bass, catfish, grouper, snapper, halibut, sole, salmon	Cut into 1" cubes	Tomatoes, cherry	Wash
		Tomatoes, large, green	Wash, cut into wedges
Shrimp	Peel	Zucchini, fresh	Cut into 1" rounds
Lobster	Peel, cut into 1" pieces	Apple, fresh	Cut into wedges
		Apricot halves, canned	
		Banana, fresh	Peel; cut into 1" pieces
Clams, large	Remove from shells	Cherries, canned or fresh	
Oysters	Remove from shells	Crabapples, spiced, canned	
Scallops	Remove from shells	Grapefruit sections, canned or fresh	
		Lemon, limes, fresh	Cut into ¼" wedges or rounds
		Orange sections, fresh	Wash, cut into sections
		Peach halves canned or fresh	Peel
		Plums, canned or fresh	Wash with cold water
		Pineapple, canned or fresh	Cut into 1" pieces Peel and cut into 1" pieces.

BURGERS

Hamburgers are classics on the grill. They can be cooked on any type of grill, by any method, with basting sauce or "Additions," or a cappella depending on your taste preference and time frame. More about burgers in The Patty Wagon (LUNCH).

DIRECTIONS:

1. Select the grilling method from "How Do You Grill What?" and prepare the grill and fire as directed.

2. While the fire is starting, pat the meat into ½ to ¾-inch thick patties for Rare or Medium or ¼ inch for Well-Done burgers.

3. Season both sides of the patties to taste with salt, pepper, and garlic powder.

4. Select and prepare the basting sauce if using one.

5. Lightly grease the grill, arrange the patties according to the method selected, and grill the prescribed time, turning and basting often.

SAUCES:

A. Any commercially prepared barbecue sauce, oil-based salad dressing (Italian, herb). Universal Barbecue Sauce and Marinade (SAUCES AND GRAVIES).

FRANKFURTERS

A truly American delight when cooked on a grill! They, like the hamburger are extremely versatile and adapt easily to your lifestyle and equipment. They are equally at home on an OPEN or COVERED grill, DIRECT or INDIRECT mthod, basted or plain. More about Hot Dogs in Phabulous Phrankphurters (LUNCH).

DIRECTIONS:

1. Select the grilling method from "How Do You Grill What?"

2. Prepare the grill and fire as directed.

3. Select a basting sauce if desired.

4. Arrange the franks on the grill according to the method selected and grill the prescribed length of time, turning frequently with tongs and basting periodically if using sauces:

SAUCES:

A. Any commercially prepared barbecue sauce, oil-based salad dressing, Universal Barbecue Sauce (SAUCES AND GRAVIES).

SAUSAGE - SMOKED, ITALIAN, POLISH, CAJUN

1. Prepare the sauce.

2. Prepare the grill (COVERED or UNCOVERED) and the fire for the INDIRECT method.

3. Coat the sausage on all sides with the sauce and place them on the grill on the end away from the heat.

4. Cook 45 minutes to 1 hour, basting and turning frequently with tongs.

SAUCES:

A. Universal Sauce (SAUCES AND GRAVIES).

CHICKEN

Grilled chicken halves or quarters are economical and delicious on the grill. Although they are not quite as versatile as burgers and "dogs," they do adapt to almost any type of equipment except an habachi or a tiny portable whose grill surface is very close to the fire base.

For a special taste treat marinate chicken 1 to 2 hours or overnight.

DIRECTIONS:

1. Wash the chicken under cold water and pat dry with paper towels.

2. Prepare the Special Sauce, AND White Barbecue Sauce (SAUCES AND GRAVIES).

3. Marinate the chicken for at least 30 minutes in the Special Sauce.

4. While the chicken is marinating, select the grilling method from "How Do You Grill What?".

5. Prepare the grill and fire as directed for your method choice.

6. When the fire is ready, arrange the chicken, skin-side down, directly over the hot coals and cook 3 to 4 minutes to sear the skin.

7. Turn, rearrange the chicken, and grill according to the selected grilling method, basting and turning frequently.

8. Coat the chicken thoroughly on both sides with the White Barbecue Sauce during the last few minutes of the cooking time.

9. Serve with lots of extra White Barbecue Sauce.

SAUCES: Replace the Special Sauce with:

A. Universal Barbecue Sauce (SAUCES AND GRAVIES)

B. White-Wine Worcestershire

TURKEY OR HEN

1 whole turkey, hen, turkey breast, 2 drumsticks, or 4 wings
2 Tablespoons vegetable oil
½ teaspoon salt
½ teaspoon pepper

DIRECTIONS:

1. Prepare the grill and fire for COVERED INDIRECT COOKING.

2. Remove the giblets if using a whole bird, rinse the bird thoroughly under cold water, and pat the outside dry with a paper towel.

3. Coat the skin completely with oil and sprinkle liberally with salt and pepper.

4. Tuck the ends of the drumsticks (for whole bird) into the band of skin left near the tail for that purpose. If using wings, remove the last ½ inch of the tips and discard.

5. Place the turkey on the grill, breast-side up, and grill COVERED, INDIRECT, over MEDIUM heat as indicated in "How Do You Grill What?".

SAUCES:

A. Any commercially prepared oil-based salad dressing, Universal Barbecue or Special Sauce (SAUCES AND GRAVIES).

CHOPS (Pork or Lamb)

Chops on the grill are best if they are 1 to 1½ inches thick. **Pork** chops may be grilled either on an OPEN or CLOSED grill, DIRECT or INDIRECT method; **lamb** on either an OPEN or CLOSED grill, DIRECT method.

DIRECTIONS:

1. Select the grill method from "How Do You Grill What?".

2. Prepare the grill and fire as directed.

3. Select and prepare a basting or marinating sauce.

4. Slash the fat in several places to keep the chops from curling during cooking.

5. Season the chops with salt and pepper if desired.

6. Lightly grease the grill and arrange the chops according to the selected grilling method.

7. Grill the designated time, basting frequently.

SAUCES:

Lamb:

A. **NIFTY QUICKIE:**
Bottled French dressing makes an excellent instant marinade for lamb.

B. **QUICK & EASY LAMB MARINADE:**
1 cup lemon juice
⅔ cup olive or vegetable oil
¼ teaspoon pepper
2 Tablespoons rosemary
½ teaspoon salt

1. Combine all the ingredients in a jar, tighten the lid, and shake vigorously to mix.

Pork:

A. Any commercially prepared barbecue sauce or oil-based salad dressing, Universal Barbecue, or Special Sauce (SAUCES AND GRAVIES).

RIBS

Three types of pork ribs are available: spareribs, loin back ribs, or country-style ribs. The country-style ribs are shorter boned and more meaty than the spareribs. All ribs are best cooked slowly over LOW heat and flavored with hickory or other wood chips.

If desired, ribs may be pre-boiled until almost tender to remove the excess fat, and then grilled a relatively short length of time to brown and flavor them. This is the best method to use for country-style or when using an OPEN grill.

DIRECTIONS:

1. Select the grilling method for ribs from "How Do You Grill What?".

2. Prepare the grill and fire as directed.

3. Select and prepare the basting sauce.

METHOD I: (Preferred for COVERED cooking)

1. Salt and pepper both sides of the ribs.

2. Brush on both sides with the basting sauce.

3. Arrange the ribs on the grill as directed for the method you chose (COVERED, INDIRECT is the recommended method).

4. Grill the prescribed length of time, turning and basting about every 15 minutes until they are done.

NOTE: For crisper ribs when using the INDIRECT method, place the ribs directly over the heat for the last 10 to 15 minutes, being very careful not to burn them.

METHOD II: (Preferred for country-style ribs or cooking on an OPEN grill)

1. Bring 1 Tablespoon salt, the ribs, and enough water to cover the ribs to a boil in a large Dutch oven or saucepan.

2. Reduce the heat to MEDIUM LOW, cover, and cook 45 minutes until the ribs are almost tender.

3. (A) **Country-style** — arrange the pre-cooked ribs on the grill, either COVERED or UNCOVERED, directly over LOW heat and grill 45 minutes, turning and basting evenly 10 to 15 minutes.

   (B) **Spareribs** — arrange the pre-cooked ribs on the grill, COVERED or UNCOVERED, and cook over LOW heat for 15 to 20 minutes turning and basting every 5 minutes.

SAUCES:

A. Any commercially prepared barbecue sauce, oil-based salad dressing, Terriyaki sauce, Universal, or White Barbecue Sauce (White for the last 20 to 30 minutes of cooking time only).

B. For a special treat, marinate the ribs in Special Sauce (SAUCES AND GRAVIES) for 30 minutes, and use the remaining sauce for basting. For the last 20 to 30 minutes of grilling, baste them with the White Barbecue Sauce.

GRILLED FISH AND SHELLFISH

Fish and shellfish are delicacies when cooked on a grill. You may choose almost any type, large or small, skin or shells on or off, whole or cut into steaks or fillets.

Lightly coat the cooking rack with vegetable spray or oil, and handle fish gently — usually turning only once.

Use a wire mesh basket when grilling small to medium fillets or shrimp to keep the little rascals from plopping through the grids and into the heat. A piece of wire mesh (NOT Zink or Galvanized) placed under them makes a good substitute.

Cook fish until it is just **barely** done — it continues to cook briefly when removed from the heat and flakes easily with a fork when done.

Never marinate fish over an hour (it will fall apart during grilling). Pierce the skin in several places so the marinade will penetrate into the fish.

Roast oysters in the shell directly on the hot coals for 8 to 10 minutes.

BASIC GRILLED FISH
(2 Servings)

WHOLE	FILLETS	STEAKS
2 (1 lb.) fish or 1 (3 to 4 lb.) fish	4 large (1" thick) or 2 extra large (over ¾" thick) fillets	2 (1" thick) steaks
Bass Catfish Crappie Snapper Sole Whitefish	Bass Catfish Crappie Snapper Sole Whitefish	Halibut Salmon Swordfish Tuna

DIRECTIONS:

1. Wash the fish under cold water (inside and out if using whole fish) and pat dry with paper towels.

2. Sprinkle with salt and pepper.

3. Coat them thoroughly with the sauce OR place them in a shallow pan and marinate while preparing the grill.

4. Grill according to "How Do You Grill What?".

SAUCES:

A. Any commercially prepared oil-based salad dressing, Terriyaki sauce, or Lemon-Butter Sauce (SAUCES AND GRAVIES).

GRILLED LOBSTER

2 (6 to 8 oz.) rock lobster tails OR
2 (1 to 2 lb.) whole lobsters
¼ cup (½ stick) butter (melted)
2 teaspoons lemon juice
salt and pepper

1. Prepare the grill and fire for DIRECT method, "How Do You Grill What?"

2. If using whole, live lobsters, harden your heart and plunge them into boiling water for 2 minutes (or they'll get the heck out of Dodge when you put them on the hot grill!).

3. Cut the undershell of the tail (or tail section if using whole ones) lengthwise with sharp scissors or a knife.

4. Bend the tail backwards until the shell "cracks" to prevent its curling during cooking.

5. Heat the butter and lemon juice in a small saucepan and melt over MEDIUM LOW heat.

6. Place the lobster, shell-side down, directly over MEDIUM HOT heat.

7. Baste the underbelly liberally with the lemon butter.

8. Grill, either COVERED or UNCOVERED, 5 to 6 minutes for tails or 8 to 10 minutes for whole ones (½ the recommended cooking time, "How Do You Cook What?").

9. Baste again, turn them (meat-side down), and continue to cook for the remaining 5 to 10 minutes until the shells turn **bright red.**

Serve with salt and pepper, the remaining lemon butter, or melted butter and lemon wedges. Discard your dignity and use a bib, nutcrackers, and lots of napkins for a fun meal!

ACCOMPANIMENTS

These side dishes add balance or color to your meal.

AMBROSIA

Makes: 4 servings
Groundwork: 4 minutes
Need: medium mixing
bowl

**2 (11 oz.) cans mandarin oranges
(drained)
1 (8 oz.) can crushed pineapple
(drained)
¼ cup grated coconut
12 red or green maraschino cherries
(cut in half)**

1. Drain the fruit, cut the cherries in half and combine all ingredients in a medium mixing bowl.

2. Chill before serving.

OPTIONS:

A. Add one or more:

  1. 2 Tablespoons cherry or orange juice

  2. 1 sliced banana

B. Amazing Ambrosia Salad

  1. Replace the crushed pineapple with tidbits and add ½ cup sour cream and ½ cup miniature marshmallows

Ambrosia can be made a day or two ahead and refrigerated. Don't add the optional banana until just before serving.

WINTER FRUIT BOWL

Makes: 4 servings
Groundwork: 2 minutes
Refrigerate 30 minutes
Need: large glass bowl

**1 (16 oz.) can chunky mixed fruit
(drained)
1 (11 oz.) can mandarin oranges (drained)
1 (16 oz.) can grapefruit slices (drained)**

1. Drain the fruits, toss gently in a large glass bowl, and serve chilled.

HOT CURRIED FRUIT

Makes: 2 servings
Groundwork: 3 minutes
Bake: 30 minutes
Oven Temp: 350⁰
Need: 1 quart casserole

Serve with Lasagna
(page 112) and hot
French Bread (page
257-259), or Pork Roast
(page 154), Yeast Rolls
(page 264) and a
green veggie.

2 Tablespoons butter
$\frac{1}{4}$ teaspoon curry powder
1 Tablespoon sugar
1 (16 oz.) can chunky mixed fruit
  (drained)

1. Preheat the oven to 350⁰.

2. Melt the butter, sugar, and curry
   powder in the baking dish in the
   oven while it preheats and stir to
   blend.

3. Drain the fruit, add to the melted
   butter mixture, and stir well to coat
   the fruit completely.

4. Bake 30 minutes until hot and
   bubbling.

BAKED APPLES

Makes: 1 serving
Groundwork: 4 minutes
Bake: 45 minutes
Oven Temp: 375⁰
Need: small baking dish

Great with pork dishes
(pages 154-158).

1 large baking apple
1 slice fresh lemon OR
1 teaspoon lemon juice
1 Tablespoon brown or white sugar
$\frac{1}{8}$ teaspoon cinnamon
pinch ground cloves
1 teaspoon butter
water

1. Preheat the oven to 375°.

2. Wash and core the apple.

3. Fill the center hole with the sugar
   and spices, and lay the lemon slice
   over the top (or add lemon juice to
   the top).

4. Stand the apple upright in the
   baking dish, top with butter, and
   cover the bottom with $\frac{1}{4}$ inch
   water.

5. Bake uncovered 45 minutes.

GLAZED GRAPEFRUIT

Makes: 2 servings
Groundwork: 3 minutes
Broil: 3 to 4 minutes
Need: medium baking
  dish

1 grapefruit
2 marsaschino cherries
2 Tablespoons brown sugar, honey, or
  maple syrup

1. Preheat the oven to BROIL.

2. Cut the grapefruit in half across the middle, remove all seeds and, with the tip of a sharp knife, loosen the fruit from the membranes on all three sides of each section.

3. Sprinkle each half with 1 Tablespoon of sugar and place them in the baking dish.

4. Broil 2 to 3 minutes until they are light brown.

5. Top each with one cherry.

OPTIONS:

   A. Sprinkle brown sugar with $\frac{1}{8}$ teaspoon cinnamon and a pinch of nutmeg.

   B. Sprinkle with $\frac{1}{4}$ cup choped pecans 1 minute before the end of the broiling time.

BAKED PEACH HALVES

Makes: 5 halves
Groundwork: 3 minutes
Bake: 10 to 12 minutes
Oven Temp: 350°
Need: small baking
dish

Serve with ham, pork,
or chicken.

**1 (15 oz.) can peach halves (save the
syrup)**
15 to 20 whole cloves
syrup from peach can
¼ cup brown sugar
½ teaspoon cinnamon
5 teaspoons butter

1. Preheat the oven to 350°.

2. Lightly grease the baking dish.

3. Place the peaches, cut-side down,
   in the baking dish and push 3 or 4
   cloves into the rounded side of
   each.

4. Discard ½ of the juice from the
   peach can.

5. Add the brown sugar and cinnamon
   to the remaining syrup and stir to
   mix.

6. Pour the syrup over the peaches
   and top each with 1 teaspoon of
   butter.

7. Bake 10 to 12 minutes until hot.

OPTIONS:

   A. Fill the center of each half with 1
      Tablespoon of mincement before
      baking.

CHAMPAGNE MELONS

Makes: 10 to 14
  servings
Groundwork: 10
  minutes
Need: large mixing
  bowl

Notch or scollop the
top edge of the
watermelon for added
interest.

This is excellent as a
salad dessert, or party
centerpiece. Provide
small skewers when
this is not served as
part of a meal.

---

1 medium ripe watermelon
1 ripe honeydew or casaba melon
1 ripe cantaloupe
1 (25 oz.) bottle of champagne
(chilled)

1. Place the watermelon on a flat surface with the flat-side down so it is stable and will not roll.

2. Cut a lengthwise slice from the top deep enough to expose the red pulp.

3. Scoop the pulp into a mixing bowl with a spoon or melon baller.

4. Remove the seeds and cut the pulp into bite-size pieces (if you did not use a melon baller.)

5. Cut the cantaloupe and honeydew in half and repeat steps 3 and 4.

6. Drain any juice from the watermelon and fill with the melon chunks (or balls).

7. Just before serving, fill the shell with champagne and serve immediately.

OPTIONS:

A. Add fresh, hulled strawberries, fresh peach slices, or seedless grapes.

B. Replace the champagne with sparkling lemon-lime beverage.

MACARONI AND CHEESE

Makes: 2 servings
Groundwork: 6 minutes
Cook: 30 min. - LOW
Need: medium
   saucepan with lid

CAUTION: Cheeses
with reduced fat
(LIGHT) will not melt
evenly and should not
be used where
smoothness counts.

1 Tablespoon butter
1 teaspoon flour
½ teaspoon salt
dash pepper
1½ cups milk
½ cup (2 oz.) shredded Cheddar
   cheese
¼ cup (4 oz.) uncooked elbow
   macaroni or shells

1. Melt the butter in a medium saucepan on MEDIUM.

2. Add the flour, salt, and pepper, and stir until the flour is smooth.

3. Slowly add the milk, stirring constantly until the mixture is smooth.

4. Add the cheese and stir just until the cheese has melted.

5. Increase to MEDIUM HIGH, add the macaroni, stirring constantly, until it begins to bubble.

6. Immediately reduce to LOW, cover, and cook 30 minutes, stirring occasionally to keep if from sticking, until the liquid is absorbed and the macaroni is tender.

CHEESE GRITS CASSEROLE

Makes: 2 servings
Groundwork: 10 minutes
Bake: 25 minutes
Oven Temp: 350°
Need: small mixing bowl
1 quart casserole

For a lazy morning, mix ahead and refrigerate overnight. Return to room temp. and bake.

2 Tablespoons milk
1 egg
½ teaspoon salt
4 drops Tabasco (optional)
⅛ teaspoon garlic powder
⅔ rounded cup instant grits
1 cup boiling water
½ cup shredded Cheddar cheese
4½ teaspoons butter

1. Preheat the oven to 350°.

2. Grease the casserole.

3. Beat the milk, egg, and spices in a small mixing bowl.

4. Combine the grits and boiling water in the casserole, stirring until the grits are thoroughly moist and the water is absorbed.

5. Add the cheese and butter to the hot grits and stir until the cheese begins to melt.

6. Stir in the egg mixture.

7. Bake, uncovered, at 350° for 25 minutes until the liquid is absorbed but the grits are not dry.

OPTION:

    A. SAUSAGE GRITS:

        1. Pan fry ½ pound of bulk sausage or 6 links in a medium skillet until brown, and drain well.

        2. Spread the sausage in the bottom of the greased casserole before adding the cheese-grits mixture.

CORNBREAD DRESSING
(Stuffing for a 10 pound Turkey)

Makes: 5 servings
Groundwork:
  Cornbread - 30
  minutes
  Dressing - 10 minutes
Bake: 35 to 40 minutes
Oven Temp: 375°
Need: medium
  saucepan
large mixing bowl
2 quart baking dish

**2 (6.5 oz.) pkg cornbread mix
(5½ cups crumbled cornbread)**

**2½ cups herb-flavored croutons OR
¼ inch bread cubes
3 to 5 cups turkey stock ***
**¼ cup instant minced onions
⅓ cup instant celery flakes
3 Tablespoons parsley flakes
½ teaspoon pepper
½ teaspoon salt
1 Tablespoon poultry seasoning**

*Dressing is better when rich drippings from roasting the turkey are used, but stock from the giblets or bouillon can also be used. Melt ½ cup [1 stick] butter in the stock or bouillon before adding to the dressing.

Very fresh bread cubes desintegrate in dressing; use bread that is several days old, or allow it to air-dry overnight.

Two packages of cornbread mix makes a little more than 5½ cups.

Fresh onions, preferably green, including the tops (½ cup), and celery, including the leaves (1 cup) are also best if you have the time to chop them.

1. Preheat the oven to 375⁰.

2. Prepare the cornbread as directed on the package, or make your own (THE BREAD BASKET).

3. Bring the turkey stock, instant onion, celery, and parsley to a boil in a medium saucepan on MEDIUM HIGH and boil 1 minute until they are softened (or 10 minutes if using fresh).

4. Crumble the cornbread into a large mixing bowl, mix in the croutons (or tear the bread into ¼ inch cubes).

5. Add the stock mixture and seasonings to the breads and mix thoroughly.

6. Grease the baking pan, add the dressing and cook, uncovered, 35 to 40 minutes until it is golden brown.

OR To Stuff the Bird:

Spoon the dressing loosely into the turkey **just** before cooking (it spoils quickly) and bake any left over in a small baking pan.

NOTE: Increase or decrease the liquid for more or less moist dressing.

SAUCES AND GRAVIES

ELEGANT AU JUS
(Clear, unthickened gravy)

Groundwork: 1 minute
Cook: 1 to 2 minutes

Replace a small
amount of the water
with red wine for a
gourmet touch.

Au Jus technically means the pan drippings obtained from roasting, broiling, or pan broiling beef or pork and may be served with no embellishments whatsoever. However, since the amount of drippings varies greatly depending upon the cut of meat and method of cooking, it may be necessary (or desirable) to add some additional liquid. This is a very inexact procedure and is to be done according to your taste, but a good RULE OF THUMB is to add ½ **the amount** of hot water as you have drippings:

1. Remove the cooked meat from the pan.

2. Add the liquid to the pan, stirring and scraping the drippings from the bottom and sides to mix thoroughly.

3. Return the pan to the heat (oven, if roasting or broiling) and cook 1 to 2 minutes, stirring frequently.

GIBLET GRAVY

Makes: 2 cups
Groundwork:
Giblets - 1½ hours
Egg - 15 minutes
Gravy - 7 to 8 minutes
Cook: 5 minutes - LOW
1 minute - MEDIUM
3 to 4 min. - LOW
Need: medium
  saucepan

Hint: 3 chicken
bouillon cubes and 1
Tablespoon butter
dissolved in 2 cups
boiling water may be
substituted for the
stock.

giblets (cooked & chopped)
1 hard-cooked egg
¼ cup (½ stick) butter
¼ cup flour
2 cups turkey or chicken stock
salt and pepper

1. Cook giblets as directed in Roast
   Turkey (DINNER), cut them into
   medium-size pieces, and remove as
   much meat as possible from the
   neck.

2. Cook the egg, peel, and cut into
   pieces.

3. Melt the butter in a medium
   saucepan on LOW, add the flour,
   salt and pepper and cook, stirring
   constantly, until the mixture is a very
   light brown.

4. Remove the pan from the heat and
   gradually stir in the liquid.

5. Return the pan to the heat, bring the
   gravy to a boil on MEDIUM and
   cook 1 minute, stirring constantly.

6. Add the giblets, egg, and additional
   salt and pepper if needed.

7. Reduce the heat to LOW, cover, and
   cook an additional 3 to 4 minutes
   stirring occasionally until the giblets
   are hot.

PAN GRAVY

Makes: 1 cup
Groundwork: 3 minutes
Cook: 6 to 8 minutes
  MEDIUM

(Made from the fat and pan drippings left when roasting, broiling, or frying beef, pork, or chicken)

2 Tablespoons fat (from pan drippings)
2 Tablespoons flour
salt and pepper (if desired)
1 cup liquid (water, pan juices (with fat removed), meat stock, or broth made from bouillon cubes and water)

1. Remove the meat from the pan.

2. Pour the drippings into a heat-proof container leaving the rich, brown crumbles in the bottom of the pan.

The secret of good gravy is accurate measurements.

Using warm liquids and stirring with a wire whisk guarantees smooth sauces and gravies.

Paprika added to gravy makes a richer color.

1 bouillon cube added to the liquid improves the flavor. (1 cube & 1 cup water makes a substitute meat stock)

3. Skim the needed amount of fat off the top (being sure to measure accurately!) and return it to the pan. If the meat was roasted or broiled in the oven, use a small saucepan for making the gravy.

4. Heat the fat on **Medium**, add the flour and seasonings, and cook until the flour is a light brown, stirring **constantly.**

5. **Remove the pan from the heat** and gradually stir in the liquid.

6. Return the pan to the heat, (still stirring and scraping up the rich crumbles in the bottom), bring to a boil and cook 1 minute or until the gravy reaches the desired thickness.

OPTION:

A. Saw Mill Gravy: Use drippings from **FRIED** meat or poultry and replace the liquid with milk.

KETTLE GRAVY
(Made from the simmering liquid of roasts, stew, or chicken)

Makes: 1¼ cups
Groundwork: 8 minutes
Need: large mixing
  bowl
jar with lid

For easier mixing and smoother gravy, put the water into the jar first then add the flour, or mix in a small mixing bowl with a wire whisk (if you don't have a jar with a lid).

For each cup of medium gravy:

1 cup meat broth
¼ cup cold water
2 Tablespoons flour
salt and pepper

1. Remove the cooked meat from the broth.

2. Remove the excess fat from the top of the broth and pour the broth into a large mixing bowl.

3. Measure the needed amount back into the Dutch oven or saucepan.

4. Combine the needed amounts of water and flour in a jar with a lid and shake until it is thoroughly mixed.

5. Gradually add the flour mixture to the hot broth, stirring constantly.

6. Bring the gravy to a boil on MEDIUM HIGH, still stirring constantly, add the necessary salt and pepper, and boil 1 minute.

OPTIONS:

A. For CREAM GRAVY replace the water with milk.

B. Replace the flour with 1 Tablespoon corn starch.

Easy Marinating:
Pour the marinade into a **heavy** plastic bag. Add the food and seal the bag tightly. Turn or shake several times to thoroughly coat the food. Put the bag in a shallow casserole or pan and refrigerate. Turn the bag periodically to distribute the marinade evenly. Marinate **at least 45 minutes** or as long as **24 hours.**

Makes: ¾ cup
Groundwork: 1 minute
Cook: 2-minutes - MED. HIGH
Need: small saucepan

Micro Note:
Speed things up and eliminate clean-up by placing ingredients in a small jar and microwaving on HIGH (uncovered) for 2 to 2½ minutes or until the butter melts and the mixture begins to bubble. Store any unused sauce, covered, right in the jar!

Makes: 1½ cups
Groundwork: 1 minute
Need: 8 oz. jar with lid

ALL PURPOSE SAUCES AND MARINADES

INSTANT MARINADE - BASTING SAUCE:

Marinades are a tenderizer for meats and cause them to cook more quickly than unmarinated ones.

Any oil-based, bottled salad dressing (Italian, herb, etc.) makes an excellent marinade.

UNIVERSAL BARBECUE SAUCE AND MARINADE:

(Great on Almost Everything)

¼ cup (½ stick) butter
2 Tablespoons Worcestershire
½ teaspoon coarse-ground black pepper
¼ cup lemon juice
2 Tablespoons soy sauce
¼ teaspoon garlic powder

1. Combine all the ingredients in a small saucepan on MEDIUM HIGH.

2. Heat to the boiling point, but do not boil.

3. Stir to mix and allow it to cool slightly before using.

SPECIAL SAUCE:
(Good on chicken or pork)

½ cup red pepper sauce (not Tabasco!)
1 cup vinegar

1. Combine the pepper sauce and vinegar in a jar and shake well.

WHITE BARBECUE SAUCE:
(Good on chicken, pork chops, and ribs)

½ cup mayonaise
1 teaspoon to 1½ Tablespoons pepper
3 Tablespoons vinegar

1. Put all the ingredients in a jar, tighten the lid, and shake vigorously to mix.

2. Refrigerate indefinitely.

NOTE: One (1) teaspoon pepper makes a **very** mild sauce. Adjust the amount of pepper to the heroism of your taste buds.

Makes: ⅔ cup
Groundwork: 1 minute
Need: 8 oz. jar with lid

Serve this sauce as an **accompaniment** to the cooked meat. It may also be used as a basting sauce, but only during the last 15 to 20 minutes of the cooking time because it has a tendency to burn.

LEMON BUTTER

¼ cup (½ stick) butter
2 Tablespoons lemon juice
1 Tablespoon parsley flakes

1. Melt the butter in a small saucepan on MEDIUM LOW.

2. Add the lemon juice and parsley flakes and mix well.

OPTIONS: (Add your choice!)

A. **Spicy:** ⅛ to ¼ teaspoon garlic powder, or dill weed

B. **Wine:** 2 Tablespoons white wine Worcestershire

C. **Dill:** ⅛ teaspoon dill weed

D. **Amandine:** 2 Tablespoons sliced almonds (browned lightly in the melted butter)

Makes: ⅓ cup
Groundwork: 2 minutes
Cook: 2 minutes - MED. LOW
Need: small saucepan

Serve on seafood, steaks or vegetables.

Butterball Garnish: Use room temperature butter to mix with the lemon and parsley, roll into teaspoon-sized balls and chill. Great on hot seafood and steaks.

BLENDER HOLLANDAISE SAUCE

Makes: ⅔ cup
Groundwork: 3 minutes
Need: small saucepan
blender

Bearnaise: Add ⅛ teaspoon tarragon and ½ teaspoon parsley flakes to the Hollandaise sauce.

3 MINUTE MICROWAVE HOLLANDAISE
1. Melt ¼ cup butter in a glass bowl on HIGH.
2. Add 2 Tablespoons milk, 2 teaspoons lemon juice, 2 egg yolks. ⅛ teaspoon salt, and blend well with a wire whisk.
3. Cook on HIGH 2 to 3 minutes, stirring every 30 seconds until thickened.

Makes: 2¼ cups
Groundwork: 2 minutes
Cook: 5 minutes -
  MEDIUM
Need: medium
  saucepan

Serve with ham, roast pork, turkey, or Cornish hens.

½ cup (1 stick) butter
3 eggs (yolks only)
1 Tablespoon lemon juice
⅛ teaspoon salt
⅛ teaspoon pepper

1. Melt the butter in a small saucepan on MEDIUM.

2. Separate the eggs, putting the yolks into the blender.

3. Add the lemon juice, salt, and pepper and blend just until mixed.

4. With the blender on low, slowly pour in the melted butter in a small, thin stream.

5. Serve immediately or keep warm in the top of a double boiler over hot water.

ROYAL CHERRY SAUCE

¼ cup sugar
2 Tablespoons cornstarch
1 (16 oz) can dark pitted cherries
  (drained with liquid reserved)
¼ cup red wine

1. Combine the sugar and cornstarch in a medium saucepan.

2. Drain the liquid from the cherries into the saucepan and heat on MEDIUM until the sugar dissolves and the sauce begins to thicken.

3. Add the cherries and wine and continue cooking, stirring frequently until the sauce is thickened and the cherries are hot.

SEAFOOD COCKTAIL SAUCE

Makes: ⅔ cup
Groundwork: 2 minutes
Refrigerate: 10 minutes
Need: small mixing bowl

This sauce can be refrigerated for up to 2 weeks in an airtight container and will improve with age.

Serve on shrimp, crab or fish.

½ cup chili sauce or catsup
1 Tablespoon lemon juice
2 teaspoons Worcestershire
1 to 2 Tablespoons prepared horseradish

1. Combine all ingredients in a small mixing bowl, and chill 10 minutes.

OPTIONS:

A. Add any or all to the sauce:
¼ teaspoon instant celery flakes
¼ teaspoon parsley flakes
5 to 6 drops Tabasco
⅛ teaspoon coarse-ground black pepper

SHRIMP SAUCE:

Makes: 1½ cups
Groundwork: 5 minutes
Need: small saucepan or mixing bowl

Use as a baking sauce or a topper for any hot, cooked fish.

1 (10¾ oz.) can cream of shrimp soup
1 (4½ oz.) can shrimp (drained)
2 Tablespoons lemon juice OR
¼ cup white wine
⅛ teaspoon salt
¼ teaspoon pepper
¼ teaspoon paprika

1. Combine all the ingredients in a small saucepan on MEDIUM and heat until very hot (but not boiling) for topping, **or** just **mix** for use as a baking sauce.

MUSTARD DILL SAUCE

Makes: ⅔ cup
Groundwork: 2 minutes
Need: blender

Serve with seafood or chicken.

¼ cup Dijon mustard
2 Tablespoons vinegar
1 Tablespoon dill weed
¼ cup vegetable oil

1. Combine all ingredients in a blender and blend on HIGH until well mixed.

2. Cover and refrigerate until serving time.

HORSERADISH SAUCE

Makes: 1 cup
Groundwork: 2 minutes
Need: small mixing
  bowl

Serve with roast beef,
steaks, or Spiced Eye
of Round (DINNER).

½ cup mayonaise
½ cup sour cream
1 to 2 Tablespoons prepared
horseradish

1. Combine all ingredients in a small mixing bowl.

2. Cover and refrigerate until serving time.

SOUPER SAUCES

Marquery:

Makes: 1¾ cups
Groundwork: 3 minutes
Cook: 4 min. - MED. LOW
Need: small saucepan

Serve on steaks, roasts,
chops, chicken or fish.

1 (10¾ oz.) can golden mushroom
soup
½ cup white wine
½ cup sour cream (optional)

1. Combine in a small saucepan on MEDIUM LOW and stir frequently until hot.

Cheese:

Serve on potatoes,
rice, pasta,
vegetables, fish, or
omelettes.

1 (10¾ oz.) can Cheddar cheese soup
⅛ teaspoon Worcestershire
dash of Tabasco or cayenne pepper
dash of paprika
⅓ cup milk
2 green seeded and diced green chili
peppers (optional)

1. Combine in a small saucepan on MEDIUM LOW and stir frequently until hot.

Au Gratin:

Another quick cheese
sauce:

½ lb. Velveeta cheese
  (cubed)
¼ cup milk

1. Combine in a small
  saucepan on LOW
  until hot and smooth.

1 (10¾ oz.) can cream of chicken soup
1 cup (4 oz. pkg) shredded Cheddar
cheese
¼ cup white wine (optional)

1. Combine in small saucepan on MEDIUM LOW, and stir often until hot.

CLASSIC WHITE SAUCE

Makes: 1 cup
Groundwork: 3 minutes
Cook: 5 min. - MED. LOW
Need: small saucepan

	BUTTER	FLOUR	SALT	MILK	USE FOR
THIN	1 T	1 T	½ t	1 c	creamed soup
MEDIUM	2 T	2 T	½ t	1 c	"creamed" foods, gravy or sauces
THICK	3 T	3 T	½ t	1 c	souffles and croquettes

1. Melt the butter in small saucepan on MEDIUM LOW.

2. Add the flour to the melted butter and stir until smooth.

3. Slowly add the milk stirring constantly until smooth.

4. Continue cooking stirring frequently until the sauce is hot and thickened.

OPTIONS:

A. Add 1 cup shredded Cheddar cheese and 1 Tablespoon chopped pimientos to 1 cup of medium white sauce, and heat on LOW until the cheese is melted.

Remember!
T = Tablespoon
t = teaspoon
c = cup

Stirring sauces with a wire whisk rather than a spoon makes a smooth sauce.

SUPER SIMPLE DESSERT SAUCE

1 (4-serving size) pkg. instant pudding (any flavor)
3 cups milk

1. Combine the pudding and milk in a jar and shake well.

2. Refrigerate until ready to serve.

Makes: 3 cups
Groundwork: 2 minutes
Need: 1 pint glass jar

Serve over: Gelatin, Fresh Fruit, Ice Cream, Cake Slices

Try lemon pudding sauce over hot gingerbread.

THE BREAD BASKET
Home-made Taste with Packaged Ease

HOW TO WARM YOUR BUNS

1. Preheat the oven to 350°.

2. Wrap the buns in foil, fold the edges over twice to seal, and place directly on the oven rack.

3. Bake 10 to 13 minutes (15 minutes if refrigerated). (In a time crunch, put them in the oven while it preheats and turn them over several times.)

BEST BETS FOR HOT BUTTERED BREADS
FRENCH, ITALIAN, SOURDOUGH

Cut the bread, straight across or diagonally, into ½ to 1 inch slices, spread with butter (seasoned or sprinkle with garlic powder), layer on a cookie sheet and BROIL or BAKE (325°) until light brown.

FOR WHOLE OR PARTIAL LOAVES

Reassemble the buttered slices into a loaf, wrap in foil, seal tightly, and bake (375°) 15 minutes until hot.

257

TASTY TEXAS TOAST

Preheat a skillet or griddle on MEDIUM HIGH, butter both sides of thick-sliced Barbecue Bread and cook both sides until golden brown and crisp.

TOASTER BUNS

Split each bun in half crossways and flatten each half with a rolling pin enough to fit the toaster slot loosely. Toast until light brown on both sides. (These buns are an easy answer to buns that have been hanging around the neighborhood for awhile. They're great for breakfast or sprinkled with garlic powder as a partner with hot soup or stew.)

RESURRECTION

To rejuvenate stale or dried out breads, or to reheat biscuits or rolls, sprinkle with a little water and pop into a 350° oven 1 to 2 minutes or until as soft or as warm as desired. Hopelessly stale (but not moldy) bread makes great croutons and bread crumbs.

BAKER'S SECRETS FOR BROWN AND SERVES
FRENCH, ITALIAN, SOURDOUGH
(Or Any Breads, Rolls, or Crusts That Are NOT COVERED During Baking)

For These Finished CRUST COLORS:	Before Baking, Brush The Top With A COATING:	And Sprinkle Any Of The Coatings With TERRIFIC TOPPER:
Very Dark Brown	1 egg yolk & 1 teaspoon cream (beaten together)	Garlic or Onion Powder, Herbs, Italian Seasoning, Parmesan Cheese, Poppy or Sesame seeds
Dark Brown	1 egg yolk	
Golden Brown	1 to 2 Tablespoons butter	
Medium Tan	1 whole egg	
Light Tan	1 whole egg & 1 Tablespoon water (beaten together)	
Shiny, Clear Glaze	1 egg white	
Shiny, Golden Glaze	Milk	

SEASONED BUTTERS

Makes: ½ cup (butters one long loaf)
Need: small mixing bowl

For extra ease, just double or triple the amounts and refrigerate in a clearly labeled airtight container. The next loaf will be a quick fix.

When you don't have time to mix a seasoned butter, simply spread the bread with butter, sprinkle with garlic or onion powder, and pop into the oven.

1. Combine the butter and seasonings in a small bowl until well blended.

2. Spread on bread, vegetables, or use for basting meats, fish, or poultry. Any that contain oil must be brushed on with a pastry brush or small paint brush.

GARLIC

½ cup (1 stick) butter (room temp.)
½ to 1 teaspoon garlic powder

OPTIONS: (foil-wrapped loaves only)

A. Spoon 1 cup (4 oz. pkg.) shredded Cheddar or Mozzarella cheese between the slices.

ITALIAN

¼ cup (½ stick) butter (room temp.)
¼ cup Italian dressing
¾ teaspoon oregano or Italian seasoning

TOAST CUPS

Groundwork: 3 minutes
Bake: 10 minutes
Oven Temp: 375°
Need: muffin tin

These are extraordinary when filled with any cream-based dish. Try the Shrimp Newberg, or the Chicken Curry, SUPPER.

bread slices
1 Teaspoon of butter (room temp) per slice

1. Preheat the oven to 375°.

2. Trim the crusts from the bread.

3. Spread the butter on one side.

4. Press the bread, buttered-side down, gently into the muffin cups, folding or lapping the slices when needed.

5. Bake 10 minutes until crisp and light brown.

CROUTONS

Makes: 1½ to 2 cups
Groundwork: 5 minutes
Bake: 25 to 30 minutes
Oven Temp: 350°
Need: small baking
  pan

Double or triple this recipe and store the extras in an air tight container in the refrigerator or freezer. They keep indefinitely.

Give tired old bread a new life as croutons for salads, soups or casserole toppers!

---

2 slices bread
2 Tablespoons butter

1. Preheat the oven to 350°.

2. Melt the butter in the baking pan as the oven preheats.

3. Trim off the crusts (optional) and cut the bread into ½ inch cubes.

4. Add them to the melted butter and quickly toss with a spatula to coat all sides.

5. Spread evenly in the pan.

6. Bake 25 to 30 minutes until crisp and brown.

OPTIONS:

A. Sprinkle the hot croutons immediately with one choice of seasonings:
   1. ½ teaspon garlic, onion, or celery salt
   2. 2 teaspoons Parmesan cheese
   3. ¼ teaspoon garlic powder, oregano, thyme, basil or Italian seasoning
   4. 1 teaspoon poppy or sesame seeds

JAZZED-UP CRESCENT ROLLS

Makes: 4 rolls
Groundwork: 10
  minutes
Bake: 10-12 minutes
Oven Temp: 375°
Need: small mixing
  bowl
cookie sheet

Any of these make a great accompaniment for chili, soups, or stews.

1 (4 roll) pkg. refrigerated crescent rolls
1 choice of Jazzed-Up Spreads (listed below)
1 egg (optional)

1. Preheat the oven to 375°.

2. Prepare the jazzed-up spread of your choice.

3. Unroll the dough and separate it into 4 triangles.

4. Cover each triangle evenly with one choice of the spreads.

5. Starting at the wide end of each triangle, roll the dough loosely, place each roll on an ungreased baking sheet with the point down, and bend the ends toward each other to form a crescent.

6. Beat the egg in a small mixing bowl and brush it on each roll (optional).

7. Bake 10 to 12 minutes until golden brown.

JAZZED-UP SPREADS: (for 4 rolls)

CHEESY CRISPS:

2 Tablespoons butter (room temp.)
¼ cup cheese flavored crackers (crushed)

1. Spread each triangle with butter and sprinkle evenly with crushed crackers.

BACON CHEESE:

¼ cup shredded Cheddar cheese
2 strips bacon (cooked and crumbled)

1. Sprinkle each triangle evenly with cheese and crumbled bacon.

CINNAMON:

4 teaspoons butter (room temp.)
1 teaspoon cinnamon
1 Tablespoon sugar
¼ cup chopped pecans (optional)

1. Combine the butter, cinnamon, and sugar in a small mixing bowl until smooth.

2. Spread evenly on the triangles and sprinkle with pecans.

DEVILED HAM & CHEESE:

1 (2 oz.) can deviled ham
2 Tablespoons Parmesan Cheese

1. Sprinkle each triangle with deviled ham and sprinkle evenly with cheese.

HERB BUTTER:

2 Tablespoons any herb butter

1. Spread evenly on the triangles.

ONION:

4 teaspoons butter (room temp.)
2 teaspoons dry onion soup mix (mix well before measuring)
2 teaspoons parsley flakes

1. Combine in a small mixing bowl.

2. Spread evenly on the triangles.

SWISS SESAME:

2 slices Swiss cheese
1 Tablespoon sesame seeds

1. Cut the cheese into triangles the same size as the roll dough, place the cheese on top of the dough, and sprinkle evenly with sesame seeds.

CAMOUFLAGED REFRIGERATOR BISCUITS

Makes: 5 biscuits
Groundwork: 5 minutes
Bake: 10 minutes
Oven Temp: 450°
Need: baking pan
waxed paper

Flakey biscuits are richest with shortening in the dough that helps separate them into layers after cooking.
"Buttermilk" biscuits are tender with a texture more similar to breads.

Flakey biscuits can be separated into 2 thin rounds before coating or sprinkling. For added interest, pierce the top of each round twice with the prongs of a fork.

Other biscuit options are included in BREAKFAST.

DANISHES:
Omit the Coaters and Toppers, flatten each slightly and make a depression in the center of each with the back of a spoon. Fill with 1 teaspoon jam, jelly, or preserves, and sprinkle lightly with powdered sugar.

TASTE TEMPTERS:

1 (5 count) pkg. refrigerator biscuits
2 to 3 Tablespoons butter
1 choice of Coaters or Toppers (listed below)

1. Preheat the oven to 450°.

2. Melt the butter in a medium baking pan in the oven while it preheats.

3. While the butter is melting, separate the biscuits and prepare the Coaters on a piece of waxed paper.

4. Dip both sides of each biscuit in the melted butter and then dip **one side** into the Coater or sprinkle the top with a Topper.

5. Discard any excess butter and place the biscuits ½ inch apart in the baking pan.

6. Bake 10 minutes until golden brown.

COATERS:

A. ½ cup finely crushed rice crispies or cheese crackers.

B. ¼ cup Parmesan cheese and 2 teaspoons parsley flakes (stir the cheese & parsley together)

TOPPERS:

A. Bacon bits

B. Poppy, caraway, celery or sesame seeds

C. Shredded cheese (Cheddar, Parmesan, Swiss, Mozzarella, Colby or Monterrey Jack)

D. Any herbs or spices (do not use any herb-flavored salt)

QUICKY REFRIGERATOR YEAST ROLLS

Makes: 12 rolls
Groundwork: 5 minutes
Bake: 15 minutes
Oven Temp: 400°
Need: medium mixing
  bowl
muffin tin

Store the dough in an air-tight container in the refrigerator for up to one week and use as needed.

1 (¼ oz.) pkg. yeast
¾ cup warm water
1 egg
1 Tablespoon sugar
2 cups biscuit mix
1 Tablespoon poppy seeds (optional)

1. Preheat the oven to 400°.

2. Grease the desired number of muffin cups.

3. Sprinkle the yeast over the warm water in a medium mixing bowl and ignore it for 2 to 3 minutes until the yeast has completely dissolved.

4. Add the egg and sugar and stir until the egg is well mixed.

5. Add the biscuit mix and poppy seeds and mix well.

6. Fill each muffin cup ⅔ full.

7. Bake 15 minutes until crisp and brown.

BEER BISCUITS

Makes: 6
Groundwork: 5 minutes
Bake: 12 to 15 minutes
Oven Temp: 350°
Need: medium mixing
  bowl
cookie sheet

Honey Butter and Strawberry Butter are in BREAKFAST.

⅓ cup beer (room temp.)
2¼ teaspoons sugar
1 cup biscuit mix

1. Preheat the oven to 350°.

2. Combine all the ingredients in a medium mixing bowl and stir only until the biscuit mix is not lumpy.

3. Grease a cookie sheet.

4. Drop heaping Tablespoon-size mounds on the cookie sheet.

5. Bake 12 to 15 minutes until brown.

BREW BREAD

Makes: 18 (½") slices
Groundwork: 3 minutes
Bake: 45 minutes
Oven Temp: 350°
Need: medium mixing
  bowl
9" x 5" loaf pan

For speedy cooking,
fill 12 greased muffin
cups ⅔ full and bake
25 minutes.

---

3 cups self-rising flour
3 Tablespoons sugar
1 (12 oz.) can of beer (room temp.)

1. Preheat the oven to 350°.

2. Grease the loaf pan.

3. Combine all the ingredients in a medium mixing bowl just until well blended.

4. Spoon the batter into the loaf pan.

5. Bake 45 minutes until the bread is brown and sounds hollow when thumped in the center.

OPTIONS:

A. Glaze with one of the Baker's Secrets.

B. Add **one** choice to the batter:

    1. ½ teaspoon dill weed

    2. 1 Tablespoon instant minced onions or parsley flakes

    3. 2 teaspoons poppy or caraway seeds

C. **Cheese Bread**

    1. Replace the sugar with ¼ teaspoon cayenne pepper and add 2 cups (8 oz. pkg.) shredded Cheddar cheese.

BANANA BREAD

Makes: 9 (1") slices
Groundwork: 5 minutes
Bake: 60 minutes
Oven Temp: 325°
Need: medium mixing
  bowl
9" x 5" inch loaf pan

Banana Bread is a
great culinary solution
for over-ripe bananas!

½ cup (1 stick) butter (room temp.)
¾ cup sugar
3 very ripe bananas
2 eggs
2 cups self-rising flour
½ cup chopped pecans or walnuts (optional)

1. Preheat the oven to 325°.

2. Grease the loaf pan.

3. Mix the butter and sugar in a medium mixing bowl.

4. Peel and slice the bananas into the butter mixture and mash the bananas finely.

5. Add the eggs and mix thoroughly.

6. Stir in the flour and pecans until well mixed.

7. Pour the batter into the loaf pan.

8. Bake 60 minutes until golden brown and the sides have pulled away from the pan.

OPTIONS:

A. Ice the top with ¼ inch layer of chocolate icing or melted chocolate chips.

CORNBREAD

Makes: 6 wedges
Groundwork: 5 minutes
Bake: 25 minutes
Oven Temp: 425°
Need: 8 inch skillet
(cast iron is best)
medium mixing bowl

The cornbread pan must be hot enough to make the batter sizzle when it's poured in to keep the cornbread from sticking.

SOUR CREAM CORNBREAD
½ cup vegetable oil
1 cup self-rising cornmeal
2 eggs
1 Tablespoon instant minced onion
1 (8 oz.) can cream corn
1 (8 oz.) carton sour cream

Follow the directions for cornbread (opposite) and bake on 425° for 35 to 40 minutes.

2 Tablespoons vegetable oil, shortening or bacon drippings
2¼ cups self-rising corn-meal mix
1¾ cups milk
1 egg

1. Preheat the oven to 425°.

2. Heat the oil (shortening, or drippings) in a 8-inch skillet in the oven while it preheats.

3. Combine the corn-meal mix, milk, and egg in a medium mixing bowl and mix well.

4. Swirl the hot oil carefully in the skillet to coat the sides, and pour the remaining oil into the corn-meal mixture, mixing well.

5. Pour the corn-meal mixture into the hot skillet.

6. Bake 25 minutes until brown and crusty.

OPTIONS:

Add your choice to the batter:

A. 1 cup shredded Cheddar cheese

B. 3 chopped jalapeño peppers

C. 1 Tablespoon instant minced onions

D. 4 strips crisp, crumbled bacon

HUSH PUPPIES

Makes: 8 puppies
Groundwork: 5 minutes
Cook: 2 min. - MED.
  HIGH (375°)
Need: small mixing
  bowl
medium saucepan OR
  deep fat fryer

If you are also cooking fish, drop the pups and french fries right in the hot fish grease.

The case of Mix vs. Mix:
Corn-**meal** mix contains both cornmeal and flour, salt and one or more levening agents.
Corn**bread** mix contains all of these things plus shortening.

---

vegetable oil
1¼ cups corn-meal mix
1 egg
⅓ cup milk
¼ teaspoon pepper

1. Heat to 375° or a full boil, on MEDIUM HIGH, enough vegetable oil to fill a medium saucepan or deep fat fryer at least 4 inches deep.

2. Mix the corn-meal mix, egg, milk and pepper together in a small mixing bowl. The batter should be stiff, but a little more milk may be needed, depending on the size of the egg.

3. Carefully form into ping-pong size balls OR drop the batter by rounded Tablespoons into the hot grease. (Do not crowd - cook only a few at a time.)

4. Fry these until they float to the top and are golden brown.

5. Drain the hush puppies on paper towels.

OPTIONS:

  A. Add one or all of the following:

  1½ teaspoons instant minced onions and/or parsley flakes
  ⅛ teaspoon garlic powder
  dash cayenne pepper

  B. Replace the corn-meal mix with ½ (6 oz. pkg.) cornbread mix.

THE DESSERT CART
THE COOKIE JAR, THE CANDY DISH, THE CAKE TIN, THE PIE PAN, THE SUNDAE, AND THE PARFAIT GLASS

THE COOKIE JAR

Here's the way the cookie crumbles:

A. If you're short on cookie sheets, line one with several layers of foil. Then simply lift off the top layer when each batch of cookies is done, or turn a baking pan upside down and use the bottom part for baking cookies.

B. Bake only one pan of cookies at a time leaving 2 inches of air space on all 4 sides of the cookie sheet so the heat will circulate evenly.

C. Do not over-bake cookies.

D. Remove the cookies immediately from the pan and cool on a wire rack.

CHOCOLATE CREAM BARS

Makes: 15 squares
Groundwork: 10 minutes
Bake: 40 to 50 minutes
Oven Temp: 350°
Need: medium mixing
   bowl
   8" x 8" baking pan.

Remember: If using a
glass baking dish,
reduce the oven temp
to 325°.

**1 (16 oz.) pkg. refrigerator chocolate or
   chocolate chip cookie dough (very
   cold)**
½ (8 oz.) pkg. cream cheese (room temp)
1 egg
¼ cup sugar

1. Freeze or chill the cookie dough well.

2. Allow the cream cheese to reach
    room temperature.

3. Preheat the oven to 350°.

4. Grease the baking pan.

5. Combine the cream cheese, egg and
    sugar in a medium mixing bowl and
    mix until smooth.

6. Slice ½ the package of cookie
    dough into ¼ inch rounds and place
    in the pan, mashing together to
    entirely cover the bottom. (Return the
    remaining dough to the freezer).

7. Spread the cream cheese mixture
    evenly over the cookies.

8. Slice the remaining dough and
    arrange it over the cheese mixture.

9. Bake 40 to 50 minutes.

10. Cool completely and cut into 2 inch
    squares.

SPICED OATMEAL DROPS

Makes: 50 to 60
  cookies
Groundwork: 5 minutes
Bake: 12 to 14 minutes
Oven Temp: 350°
Need: large mixing
  bowl
cookie sheet

1 (18¼ oz.) pkg. spice cake mix
2 cups uncooked oats
2 eggs
¾ cup oil
½ cup milk
¼ cup brown sugar
2 cups raisins
1 cup pecans or walnuts (chopped)

1. Preheat the oven to 350°.

2. Lightly grease the cookie sheet.

3. Combine all ingredients in a large mixing bowl and stir until it is completely blended.

4. Drop rounded teaspoon-size mounds on the greased cookie sheet.

5. Bake 12 to 14 minutes until light brown.

GIRDLE BUSTERS

Makes: 48 to 50
  cookies
Groundwork: 5 minutes
Bake: 10 to 12 minutes
Oven Temp: 350°
Need: large mixing
  bowl
small mixing bowl
cookie sheet

When using a white or yellow cake mix, add ¼ teaspoon almond, rum or coconut flavoring.

1 (18½ oz.) pkg. cake mix (any flavor)
2 cups whipped topping (thawed)
1 egg
½ cup powdered sugar

1. Preheat the oven to 350°.

2. Lightly grease a cookie sheet.

3. Combine the cake mix, whipped topping and egg in a large mixing bowl and stir until the mixture is well blended.

4. Pour the powdered sugar into a small mixing bowl.

5. Spoon 1 inch balls of dough (a few at a time) into the powdered sugar and coat completely.

6. Place the cookies 2 inches apart on the cookie sheet.

7. Bake 10 to 12 minutes until the edges are very light brown.

CHINESE TEA BALLS

Makes: 70 tea balls
Groundwork: 10
   minutes
Bake: 12 to 15 minutes
Oven Temp: 300°
Need: medium mixing
   bowl
cookie sheet
small bowl

1 cup (2 sticks) butter (room temp.)
2 cups flour
¼ teaspoon salt
1 teaspoon vanilla
1 egg yolk
5 Tablespoons sugar
1 cup finely chopped pecans
½ cup powdered sugar

1. Preheat the oven to 300°.

2. Combine the butter, flour, and salt in a medium mixing bowl and stir until smooth.

3. Separate the egg and discard the white.

4. Add the vanilla, egg yolk, and sugar and stir until well mixed.

5. Stir in the nuts.

6. Form the dough into ½ inch balls (about 1 teaspoon each) and place them ½ inch apart on an **ungreased** cookie sheet.

7. Bake 12 to 15 minutes until very light brown.

8. Place the powdered sugar in a small bowl.

9. Drop the cookies (2 or 3 at a time) into the sugar and roll gently to coat.

PEANUT BUTTER COOKIES

Makes: 24 cookies
Groundwork: 12
  minutes
Bake: 10 minutes
Oven Temp: 375°
Need: medium mixing
  bowl
cookie sheet

½ **cup sugar**
½ **cup brown sugar**
½ **cup shortening or butter**
1 egg
½ **teaspoon vanilla**
½ **cup peanut butter (smooth or
  chunky)**
1½ cups flour
pinch salt
½ **teaspoon soda**

1. Preheat the oven to 375°.

2. Combine the sugars and shortening in a medium mixing bowl and mix until smooth.

3. Add the egg and vanilla and beat until it is fluffy.

4. Add the peanut butter and mix well.

5. Add the flour, salt, and soda and stir thoroughly.

6. Shape Tablespoon-sized amounts of dough into small balls and place them 2 inches apart on **ungreased** cookie sheet.

7. Flatten the balls with the back of a fork twice to form criss-cross pattern.

8. Bake 10 minutes until light brown.

OPTION:

A. Add ½ to ¾ cup chocolate chips to the batter.

SUGAR DROP COOKIES

Makes: 24 (2") cookies
Groundwork: 12
  minutes
Bake: 8 to 10 minutes
Oven Temp: 350°
Need: medium mixing
  bowl
cookie sheet
wire whisk

Just for fun, sprinkle
with colored crystals or
any cookie decora-
tions between steps
7 and 8.

1 egg
⅓ cup vegetable oil
1 teaspoon vanilla
½ teaspoon grated lemon rind
  (optional)
⅓ (heaping) cup sugar
1 cup flour
1 teaspoon baking powder
¼ teaspoon salt
¼ cup sugar

1. Preheat the oven to 350°.

2. Beat the egg with a wire whisk in a medium mixing bowl until well blended.

3. Add the vegetable oil, vanilla, and lemon rind and stir to mix thoroughly.

4. Stir in the sugar and blend until the mixture thickens.

5. Add the flour, baking powder, and salt and stir to mix.

6. Lightly grease a cookie sheet.

7. Drop teaspoon-sized mounds of dough about 2 inches apart on the cookie sheet.

8. Pour the ¼ cup of sugar on a small piece of waxed paper.

9. Grease the bottom of a glass, dip it into the sugar, and flatten each cookie (dipping the glass in the sugar after flattening each one).

10. Bake 8 to 10 minutes until the cookies are lightly browned around the edges.

11. Loosen the hot cookies with a spatula and allow to cool on the pan.

CLASSIC TOLLHOUSE COOKIES

Makes: 50 (2") cookies
Groundwork: 8 minutes
Bake: 8 to 10 minutes
Oven Temp: 375°
Need: large mixing
  bowl
cookie sheet

½ cup (1 stick) butter (room temp.)
6 Tablespoons sugar
6 Tablespoons brown sugar
½ teaspoon vanilla
1 cup plus 1 Tablespoon flour
½ teaspoon salt
½ teaspoon baking soda
1 egg
1 (6 oz.) pkg. (1 cup) semi-sweet
  chocolate chips
¼ cup chopped pecans or walnuts
  (optional)

1. Preheat the oven to 375°.

2. Combine the butter, sugar, brown sugar, and vanilla in a large mixing bowl and beat until the mixture is creamy.

3. Add the egg and beat until it is well blended.

4. Add the flour, soda, and salt and mix well.

5. Add the chocolate chips and nuts and mix.

6. Place teaspoon-sized mounds of dough on an **ungreased** cookie sheet.

7. Bake 8 to 10 minutes until the cookies are light brown.

OPTIONS:

Makes: 24 (2") squares
Bake: 12 to 15 minutes
Need: 9" x 13" baking
pan

A. Pan Cookie

  1. Lightly grease a 9 x 13 inch baking pan.

  2. Spread the dough evenly in the pan.

  3. Bake 12 to 15 minutes until the cookie is light brown.

  4. Cool before cutting into 2" squares.

THE CANDY DISH

GRANDDADDY LONGLEGS

Makes: 50 pieces
Groundwork: 5 minutes
Need: medium
  saucepan
waxed paper

These freeze well.

TARANTULAS substitute
milk chocolate chips
for the butterscotch.

---

2 (6 oz.) pkgs. butterscotch chips
1 (6½ oz.) can salted peanuts
1 (5 oz.) can Chow Mein noodles

1. Melt the butterscotch chips in a
   medium saucepan on LOW stirring
   frequently until completely melted.

2. Add the peanuts and noodles and
   stir gently to coat completely.

3. On a long strip of waxed paper, drop
   teaspoon-size mounds of the mixture.

4. Cool completely before removing.

FABULOUS FAST FUDGE

Makes: 1¾ lb.
Cook: 5 minutes - LOW
Refrigerate: 2 to 3
  hours
Need: large saucepan
8" x 8" baking dish

1 (12 oz.) pkg. (2 cups) semi-sweet
  chocolate chips
1 (14 oz.) can condensed milk
dash salt
1 teaspoon vanilla
1 cup chopped pecans or walnuts
  (optional)
1 Tablespoon butter (for greasing dish)

1. Combine the chips, milk, and salt in
   a large saucepan.

2. Cook on LOW until the chocolate
   melts and the mixture is smooth,
   stirring frequently.

3. Butter the bottom and sides of the
   baking dish while the chocolate melts.

4. Remove from the heat and stir in the
   vanilla and nuts.

5. Spread evenly in the baking dish.

6. Refrigerate 2-3 hours or until firm.

CREAMY FUDGE

Makes: 2½ pounds
Groundwork: 3 minutes
Heat to boiling: 8 to 10
  min.
Boil: 5 minutes
Cook Temp: MEDIUM
Refrigerate: 2 hours
Need: large saucepan
8" x 8" baking dish

1 Tablespoon butter (for greasing dish)
1 (7½ oz.) jar marshmallow cream
1½ cups sugar
⅔ cup evaporated milk
¼ cup (½ stick) butter (room temp.)
¼ teaspoon salt
½ teaspoon vanilla
2 (6 oz.) pkgs. (2 cups) semi-sweet
  chocolate chips
½ to 1 cup chopped pecans or
  walnuts (optional)

1. Using the 1 Tablespoon of butter, grease the bottom and sides of the baking dish thoroughly.

2. Combine the marshmallow cream, sugar, milk, butter, and salt in a large saucepan.

3. Bring to a **full boil** on MEDIUM, **stirring constantly.**

4. Boil **5 minutes**, again stirring constantly. Remove from the heat.

5. Add the chocolate chips and stir until they are melted and the mixture is smooth.

6. Mix in the vanilla and nuts.

7. Pour into the baking dish and refrigerate 2 hours or until the fudge is firm.

OPTIONS:

A. To make an even richer fudge, use a 13 oz. jar of marshmallow cream and increase the nuts to 1½ cups.

ROCKY ROAD

Makes: 100 pieces
Groundwork: 10
  minutes
Refrigerate: 1 hour
Need: medium
  saucepan
9" x 13" baking pan

These little vagabonds
love the freezer.

2 Tablespoons butter
1 (12 oz.) pkg. semi-sweet chocolate
  chips
1 (14 oz.) can condensed milk
1½ teaspoons vanilla
1 (10½ oz.) pkg. miniature
  marshmallows
2 (4 oz.) pkgs. chopped almonds

1. Line a 9 x 13 inch baking pan with
    waxed paper.

2. Melt the butter in a medium
    saucepan on MEDIUM LOW.

3. Add the chocolate chips to the
    melted butter, stirring often until they
    are completely melted.

4. Add the condensed milk and stir
    until blended.

5. Remove from the heat, add the
    vanilla, marshmallows and almonds
    and stir gently to mix completely.

6. Spoon the mixture evenly into the
    baking pan, cover, and refrigerate 1
    hour before cutting into 1 inch
    cubes.

THE CAKE TIN

Grandma never had it so easy. What took her half a day can now be done in just a few minutes with packaged mixes and icings. With a little added creativity, even Grandma will be impressed!

IMPORTANT INFO!!

Cake Pans: Most cakes **must** be baked in pans that are greased and dusted with flour. Shortening works best but butter or oil can be used. Vegetable spray can also be used if it is sprayed heavily (unless the directions state otherwise). One tablespoon of each will grease and flour 2 cake pans or 1 medium baking pan.

1. Using a plastic sandwich bag or waxed paper, cover the bottom and sides with shortening.

2. Add the flour and shake it around to completely cover the bottom and sides.

3. Gently tap the sides to release the excess flour and pour it into the second pan.

4. Repeat the process and discard any excess flour.

Make any plain cake mix extra moist by adding an additional ½ cup of vegetable oil or melted shortening.

PINK ANGELS

Makes: 8 servings
Groundwork: 5 minutes
Need: large mixing
  bowl
plate

PARTY ANGELS for a
whopping (24 servings)
cake use:
1 (20 oz.) round angel
food cake, 2 (10 oz.)
pkgs. strawberries, and
1 (12 oz.) carton of
whipped topping.

---

1 (10¾ to 13 oz.) angel food cake
1 (10 oz.) pkg. frozen, sweetened,
  sliced strawberries (thawed)
1 (8 oz.) carton whipped topping
  (thawed)

1. Slice the cake sideways into three
   equal layers and center the bottom
   layer on a plate.

2. Combine the strawberries (including
   the juice) and whipped topping in a
   large mixing bowl until well mixed.

3. Spread ¼ of the mixture evenly on
   the bottom layer.

4. Stack the second layer on top,
   spread it with another ¼ of the
   mixture and top with the third layer.

5. Spread the entire cake (top and
   sides) with the remaining mixture.

6. Refrigerate any leftovers.

OPTIONS:

Replace the strawberries with:

A. **Fallen Angels**
   1 (4 serving size) pkg. instant
     chocolate pudding
   2 teaspoons instant coffee
     granules

B. **Herald Angels**
   1 pint ice cream or sherbet
     (slightly softened)
   1 (4 oz.) carton whipped
     topping (thawed)

   1. Spread the ice cream or
      sherbet between the layers.

   2. Spread the whipped topping
      over the sides and top of the
      cake.

   3. Freeze; remove from the freezer
      15 minutes before serving.

PZAZZED POUND CAKE

Groundwork: 5 to 6
  minutes
Broil: 2 to 4 minutes
Need: cookie sheet

Pound cake
Butter
Pzazzer

1. Preheat the oven on BROIL.

2. Cut the cake into ½ inch slices.

3. Lightly butter and toast both sides before pzazzing.

PZAZZERS:

I. Simple Scoopers:

Top with 1 scoop of your favorite ice cream.

Need: small saucepan

II. Lucious Layers:

Layer on top of each slice in the order listed:

A. Sliced bananas, strawberries, or hot cherry pie filling (with 1 Tablespoon brandy added), hot fudge sauce.

B. Vanilla ice cream, chopped peanuts, hot caramel sauce.

C. Crushed pineapple (drained), whipped topping, mandarin orange slices.

CAKE MIX MAGIC TRICKS

BLACK FOREST CAKE

Makes: 12 to 14
  servings
Groundwork: 5 minutes
Bake: 25 to 35 minutes
Oven Temp: 350°
Need: medium mixing
  bowl
3 (8") cake pans
REFRIGERATE

Any packaged cake
mix can be prepared
as directed on the
package and baked
in a tube or bundt
pan.

Cake:
1 (18¼ oz.) pkg. devils food cake mix
Additional ingredients as required on the box

Icing:
1 Tablespoon brandy or sherry (optional)
1 (21 oz.) can cherry pie filling
1 (8 oz.) carton frozen whipped topping (thawed)

1. Preheat the oven to 350°.

2. Bake the cake according to the directions on the package (except divide the batter equally into 3 cake pans and reduce the cooking time by 5 to 10 minutes); cool completely.

3. Pour the brandy into the pie filling and mix well.

4. Spread one layer with ⅓ of the topping and spoon on ⅓ of the pie filling; repeat with the second and third layers, stacking them as you go.

OPTIONS:

  A. **Spring Garden**
    Replace the devil's food cake with lemon cake and replace the cherry pie filling with blueberry pie filling.

COLOSSAL COCONUT CAKE

Makes: 12 servings
Groundwork: 5 minutes
Refrigerate: overnight
Bake: 35 to 40 minutes
Oven Temp: 350°
Need: 9" x 13" baking
  pan
2 medium mixing
  bowls
drinking straw or
  skewer

REFRIGERATE

The coconut may also
be toasted first.
Spread it out in a
large baking pan and
bake (350°) 10 minutes
or until lightly brown.

Cake:
1 (18¼ oz.) yellow or white cake mix
  with pudding
Additional ingredients as required on
  the box

Icing:
1 (14 oz.) can condensed milk
1 (12 oz.) carton frozen whipped
  topping (thawed)
1 (7 oz.) pkg. grated coconut

1. Preheat the oven to 350°.

2. Prepare and bake the cake in a **9 x 13 inch baking pan** according to the directions on the package. Cool the cake **without** removing it from the pan.

3. Combine the milk, whipped topping, and coconut in a medium mixing bowl.

4. Using a drinking straw or skewer, make holes in the cake every 1 to 2 inches.

5. Pour the coconut mixture evenly on top, cover, and refrigerate overnight.

THE DEVIL'S DELIGHT

Makes: 24 slices
Groundwork: 8 minutes
Bake: 50-60 minutes
Oven Temp: 350°
Need: large mixing
  bowl
mixer
Bundt cake pan

4 eggs
1 cup sour cream
½ cup vegetable oil
½ cup water
1 (18¼ oz.) pkg. devil's food cake with
    pudding
1 (12 oz.) pkg. chocolate chips
powdered sugar

1. Preheat the oven to 350°.

2. Grease and flour the cake pan.

3. Combine the eggs, sour cream, oil and water in a mixing bowl and beat with a mixer until smooth.

4. Add the cake mix and blend until completely mixed.

5. Stir in the chocolate chips.

6. Bake 1 hour.

7. Cool and dust with powdered sugar.

DREAM CAKE

Makes: 12 to 14
  servings
Groundwork: 10
  minutes
Bake: 30 minutes
Oven Temp: 350°
Cool: 15 minutes
Need: large mixing
  bowl
electric or rotary mixer
3 (8") cake pans

CAUTION
Ignore the ingredients
and baking times on
the box for this one!
Use a mix that does
not have pudding
added.

1 (18¼ oz.) pkg. plain cake mix (yellow, white, or devil's food)
1 envelope (2.4 oz.) powdered whipped topping mix
4 eggs
1 cup cold water

1. Preheat the oven to 350°.

2. Grease and flour the pans.

3. Combine the cake mix, powdered topping mix, eggs, and water in a large mixing bowl.

4. Blend until the dry ingredients are moistened, and then beat on MEDIUM for **4 minutes**.

5. Pour the batter into the pans and bake 30 minutes until light brown.

6. Cool 15 minutes before removing from the pan and ice with your choice of icings.

INSTANT ICINGS

Ices: 1 (9"x13") sheet, 1
  (9") 2 layer cake, or
  24 cupcakes
Groundwork: 5 minutes
Need: medium mixing
  bowl

PINEAPPLE

1 (8 oz.) can crushed pineapple (drained)
1 (8 oz.) carton whipped topping (thawed)
1 (4-serving size) instant vanilla pudding

Garnish the pineapple
frosting with mandarin
orange slices.

1. Drain the pineapple well and combine with the whipped topping and pudding in a medium mixing bowl.

For Easy Cake Decorating:
Spoon ½ cup of any soft, spreadable icing into one corner of a plastic sandwich bag and twist the open edges together to close the bag. Snip a pencil-point bit from the point of the filled corner and gently squeeze the bag to enhance the cake or send your "love" a message! And remember — a little practice makes perfect.

BUTTER CREAM

½ cup (1 stick) butter (room temp.)
1 teaspoon vanilla
1 (16 oz.) box powdered sugar
1 to 2 Tablespoons milk

1. Combine the butter and vanilla in a medium mixing bowl and stir until the butter is smooth and soft.

2. Add half of the sugar and mix.

3. Add the remaining sugar and 1 Tablespoon of milk and mix well.

4. Add the remaining milk, 1 teaspoon at a time, until the icing is soft enough to spread.

OPTIONS:

A. Chocolate: Add ½ cup cocoa

B. Eggnog: Replace the milk with 2 Tablespoons bourbon.

C. Lemon, Lime, Orange: Omit the vanilla and replace the milk with lemon, lime, or orange juice (1 teaspoon of dried citrus peel can also be added).

D. Mocha: Add 1 Tablespoon instant coffee granules

CREAM CHEESE

½ cup (1 stick) butter (room temp.)
1 (8 oz.) pkg. cream cheese (room temp.)
1 (16 oz.) box powdered sugar
1 teaspoon vanilla

1. Combine the butter and cream cheese in a medium mixing bowl and stir until smooth.

2. Add the powdered sugar and vanilla, and stir until well mixed.

THE PIE PAN

Simple Simon would love these wares! One tenth the time with twice the taste!

PIE CRUSTS

GRAHAM CRACKER

Makes: 1 (9") pie shell
Groundwork: 5 minutes
Bake: 8 to 10 minutes
Oven Temp: 375°
Need: medium
  saucepan
9" pie plate

When using purchased graham cracker crust, save the plastic inside protector — invert it over the pie and recrimp the edges for an instant pie protector.

½ cup (1 stick) butter
24 (2½ inch) graham cracker squares
½ cup sugar (optional)

1. Preheat the oven to 375°.

2. Melt the butter in the pie plate in the oven while it preheats.

3. Crush the graham crackers finely and add them to the melted butter.

4. Add the sugar and stir well.

5. Press the mixture firmly into the pie plate with the back of a spoon.

6. Bake 8 to 10 minutes.

OPTIONS:

    A. Replace the graham crackers with vanilla wafers and omit the sugar.

    B. Replace the graham crackers with 18 chocolate cream-filled cookies and omit the sugar.

CREAM CHEESE CRUST
(for baked pies only)

Makes: 1 (9") pie shell
Groundwork: 5 minutes
Need: small mixing
  bowl
9" pie plate
waxed paper
rolling pin

Best for pecan or
chicken pie.

For festive occasions,
cut the crust to fit mini-
muffin tins, fill and
bake for individual
tartletts.

---

1 (3 oz.) pkg. cream cheese (room temp.)
½ cup (1 stick) butter (room temp.)
1 cup flour
¼ teaspoon salt

1. Combine the cream cheese and butter in a small mixing bowl and stir until the mixture is smooth.

2. Add the flour and salt, and stir until well mixed.

3. Form into a ball, place the ball on 18 inches of waxed paper. Top with another sheet of waxed paper and roll with a rolling pin until it is large enough to fit the pie plate.

4. Remove the top waxed paper, turn the pie plate upside down and center it on the crust.

5. Turn the plate, crust, and waxed paper over together and remove the waxed paper.

6. Press the crust evenly into the pan and trim off excess with a small sharp knife.

7. Add your choice of pie filling before baking.

OVEN FRIED APPLE PIES

Makes: 10 pies
Groundwork: 10
  minutes
Bake: 10 - 15 minutes
Oven Temp: 350°
Need: large baking
  pan
rolling pin
waxed paper or
  plastic wrap
small mixing bowl

6 Tablespoons (¾ stick) butter
1 (10 count) pkg. refrigerator biscuits
⅓ cup flour
1 (21 oz.) can apple pie filling
1 teaspoon cinnamon
½ teaspoon nutmeg

1. Preheat the oven to 350°.

2. Melt the butter in the baking pan in the oven while it preheats.

3. Dust 18 inches of waxed paper or plastic wrap with flour and roll each biscuit to ¼ inch thick.

4. Combine the pie filling, cinnamon, and nutmeg in a small mixing bowl.

5. Put 3 Tablespoons of the filling mixture in the center of each biscuit.

6. Moisten the edges of each biscuit with water (one at a time), fold each in half, and seal the cut edges by pressing firmly with the prongs of a fork.

7. Place the pies in the melted butter and turn them over once to coat.

8. Bake 10 to 15 minutes until golden brown.

CHERRY PIE

Makes: 6 to 8 servings
Groundwork: 5 minutes
Refrigerate: 2 hours
Need: large mixing
bowl

**To Bake An Unfilled
Pastry Pie Crust Shell:**

1. Preheat the oven to
400°.

2. Let a frozen crust thaw
15 minutes. Prick the
sides and bottom of
the crust every inch
to prevent bubbling.

3. Place another pie
plate of the same
size (with the bottom
greased) directly on
the crust OR fill the
crust with dried
beans or rice.

4. Bake 8 to 10 minutes
until the crust is
brown. Cool 2 to 3
minutes before
removing the extra
pie plate.

If not completely done
in the center after
removing the plate or
beans, return it to the
oven for 2 to 3 minutes.

Thrifty Note:
Cool the beans and
store them in a jar
labeled "pie crusts"
and reuse them for
years!

**1 pie crust (graham cracker, chocolate
or baked pastry)
1 (14 oz.) can condensed milk
⅓ cup lemon juice
1 (15 oz.) can pitted cherries (drained)
1 cup chopped pecans (optional)
1 (8 oz.) carton whipped topping
(thawed)**

1. If using a baked pastry pie crust,
bake according to the directions on
the package.

2. Mix the milk and lemon juice in a
large mixing bowl.

3. Drain the cherries.

4. Mix the cherries and pecans with
the milk mixture.

5. Gently fold in the whipped topping.

6. Garnish with pecan halves
(optional).

7. Refrigerate 2 hours.

OPTIONS:

Replace the cherries with:

1. Blueberry: 1 (15 oz.) can
blueberries (drained)
Garnish: 1 Tablespoon berries

2. Mandarin: 2 (11 oz.) cans
mandarin oranges (drained)
Garnish: orange slices and a
maraschino cherry in the center

3. Miranda: 1 (8 oz.) can crushed
pineapple (drained)
1 (8 oz.) can sliced peaches
(drained)
Garnish: maraschino cherries

4. Strawberry: 1 (10 oz.) pkg. frozen
strawberries (thawed and
drained).
Garnish: fresh berries

SIMPLE COCONUT PIE

Makes: 6 to 8 servings
Groundwork: 5 minutes
Bake: 35 to 40 minutes
Oven Temp: 350°
Need: medium
  saucepan

Bake pies on cookie
sheets to avoid oven
clean-up.

2 Tablespoons butter
1 cup sugar
1 heaping Tablespoon flour
2 eggs
1 cup milk
1 cup grated coconut
1 (9") pastry pie crust (unbaked)

1. Preheat the oven to 350°.

2. Melt the buttter in a medium saucepan on MEDIUM, remove from the heat.

3. Add the sugar and flour, and stir until smooth.

4. Add the eggs and milk and beat with a wire whisk until the eggs are completely blended.

5. Add the coconut and stir to combine.

6. Pour the mixture into the unbaked pie shell.

7. Bake 35 to 40 minutes until the center is firm.

MILE HIGH LIME PIE

Makes: 6 to 8 servings
Groundwork: 2 minutes
Freeze: 1 hour
Need: large mixing
  bowl

1 (12 oz.) can frozen limeade (thawed)
1 (14 oz.) can condensed milk
1 (12 oz.) carton whipped topping
  (thawed)
2 to 4 drops green food coloring
1 (10 oz.) pkg. frozen strawberries
  (optional)
1 chocolate pie crust

For a change try using
lemonade and a
graham cracker crust.

1. Combine the limeade and con-
    densed milk in a large mixing bowl.

2. Add the whipped topping and food
    coloring and mix until well blended.

3. Pour into the crust.

4. Freeze and serve frozen.

5. Top with the thawed, drained
    strawberries just before serving.

PECAN PIE

Makes: 6 to 8 servings
Groundwork: 4 minutes
Bake: 40 minutes
Oven Temp: 350°
Need: medium mixing
  bowl

1 (9") pastry pie crust shell (unbaked)
1 cup chopped pecans
¼ cup (½ stick) butter (room temp.)
1 cup dark brown sugar
½ cup sugar
3 eggs
1 teaspoon vanilla
½ teaspoon salt

Delicious in the cream
cheese crust.

1. Preheat the oven to 350°.

2. Spread the pecans evenly in the
    bottom of the unbaked shell.

3. Combine the butter and both sugars
    in a medium bowl until smooth.

4. Add the eggs, vanilla, and salt and
    mix until well blended.

5. Pour the mixture slowly into the pie
    crust shell.

6. Bake 40 minutes until the center is firm.

GEORGIA CRACKER PIE

Makes: 6 to 8 servings
Groundwork: 11
  minutes
Bake: 20 to 25 minutes
Oven Temp: 350°
Need: electric or
  rotary beater
9 inch pie plate
large mixing bowl

REFRIGERATE

Believe it or not! This tastes exactly like a homemade pecan pie and has a top and bottom crust. Garnish with whipped topping.

Hollandaise Sauce (SAUCES AND GRAVIES) is a simple solution for the unused egg yolks or they may be covered with cold water and refrigerated for 2 days.

½ cup plus 1 Tablespoon saltine cracker crumbs
3 egg whites
1 cup sugar
1 teaspoon vanilla
1 teaspoon baking powder
1 cup chopped pecans

1. Preheat the oven to 350°.

2. Grease a 9 inch pie plate.

3. Crush the crackers into crumbs.

4. Separate the eggs, putting the whites into a large mixing bowl. (Either save the yolks for another recipe or discard.)

5. Beat with an electric or rotary beater until the egg whites are stiff, gradually adding the sugar, vanilla, and baking powder.

6. Fold in the cracker crumbs and nuts.

7. Spoon the mixture into the pie plate and bake 20 to 25 minutes.

8. Allow the pie to cool and top with the whipped topping.

OPTIONS:

   A. Top each slice with a dollop of whipped topping.

   B. Replace the pecans with walnuts or shelled, unsalted peanuts.

LEMON ICE BOX PIE

Makes: 6 to 8 servings
Groundwork: 10
  minutes
Bake: 5 minutes
Oven Temp: 350°
Refrigerate: 1 to 1½
  hours
Need: medium mixing
  bowl
small mixing bowl
mixer

Tips for separating
eggs and yolk storage
are in The Egg Basket
(BREAKFAST).

Simple Puddin 'n' Pie:
Simply fill a chocolate
or graham cracker
crust with 1 (6-serving
size) box any flavor
instant pudding
(prepared as directed
on the package) and
chill until firm.

Bake: 15 minutes

6 Tablespoons lemon juice
1 (14 oz.) can condensed milk
dash salt
2 eggs (separated)
2 Tablespoons sugar
1 (9 inch) graham cracker crust

1. Preheat the oven to 350°.

2. Combine the lemon juice,
    condensed milk, and salt in a
    medium mixing bowl and mix well.

3. Separate the eggs, putting the
    whites in a small bowl. (Either save
    the yolks for other uses or discard.)

4. Beat the egg whites very stiff with a
    rotary or electric mixer.

5. Add the sugar to the egg whites
    and continue beating for 45 seconds.

6. Gently fold the egg whites into the
    milk mixture.

7. Pour the mixture into the crust.

8. Bake 5 minutes. Refrigerate 1-1½
    hours before serving.

OPTIONS:

Lemon Meringue Pie

1. Combine the lemon juice,
    condensed milk, and salt in a
    medium mixing bowl.

2. Separate the eggs, putting the
    whites into a small mixing bowl and
    adding **only** the yolks to the
    condensed milk mixture, stirring well.

3. Increase the sugar to 4 Tablespoons,
    add to the egg whites, and beat
    with a mixer until stiff peaks form.

4. Pour the condensed milk mixture into
    crust and top with beaten egg whites.

5. Bake 15 minutes until light brown.

THE CLASSICS

Time honored favorites that will never let you down!

BANANA PUDDING

Makes: 6 servings
Groundwork: 5 minutes
Refrigerate: 10 minutes
Need: 1 quart
  casserole
small mixing bowl

15 to 20 vanilla wafers
1 (4-serving size) pkg. instant vanilla or banana pudding
2 cups milk
1 or 2 bananas (peeled and sliced)

1. Line the bottom and sides of a casserole with vanilla wafers.

2. Prepare the pudding in a small mixing bowl as directed on the package.

3. Peel and slice the banana(s) into the mixture and stir gently to distribute them evenly.

4. Pour immediately into the wafer-lined bowl and top with 5 or 6 more wafers.

5. Refrigerate 10 minutes until the pudding is firm.

COSMOPOLITAN CREAM

Makes: 1 serving
Groundwork: 2 minutes

*Chocolate Curls:
Make these from either a plain chocolate bar or a block of cooking chocolate. Simply peel off the strips with a vegetable peeler — they will curl as they peel off.

¾ cup vanilla ice cream
1½ oz. liqueur
1 topping

LIQUEUR	TOPPING
Creme de Menthe	Mint sprig or chocolate curls*
Cream de Cocoa	Chocolate curls or coconut
Amaretto	Toasted Almonds
Cherry Brandy	Marachino cherry
Galliano	Orange slice or Twist
Drambuie	Nothing - does not need one!

Scoop the ice cream into a small bowl or wine glass, add the liqueur and compatible topping, and serve immediately — the liqueur melts the ice cream!

CHOCOLATE FONDUE

Makes: 2 cups
Groundwork: 1 minute
Cook: 5 minutes
Need: medium double
boiler or saucepan,
chafing dish or
fondue pot

A saucepan may be
used in place of a
double boiler, but you
must **stir constantly** on
LOW.

To improvise a double
boiler, fit a metal bowl
or small saucepan
snugly inside a larger
pan. Be sure it does
not slide down and
touch the water.

1 (12 oz.) pkg. semi-sweet chocolate chips
¼ cup whipping cream (or ¼ cup milk
   and 1 Tablespoon butter)
2 to 4 Tablespoons water
2 teaspoons vanilla
pinch of salt
4 Tablespoons brandy (optional)

1. Combine all the ingredients in the top
   of a double boiler on MEDIUM with 1 to
   2 inches of water in the bottom section.

2. Heat, stirring frequently, until the
   chocolate melts.

3. Serve in a fondue pot or chafing
   dish with your choice of dippers:
   Apple wedges, banana chunks,
   dried fruit, mandarin orange
   sections, maraschino cherries (with
   stems), marshmallows, pineapple
   chunks, poundcake (cut in 1 inch
   cubes), or strawberries.

CHOCOLATE STRAWBERRIES

Makes: 1 pint
Groundwork: 5 minutes
Refrigerate: 10 minutes
Need: double boiler
wire rack

WARNING:
The chocolate will not
stick to wet
strawberries!

These can be made
one day ahead and
kept refrigerated until
serving time.

1 pint fresh strawberries
1 (12 oz.) pkg. semi-sweet chocolate chips
1 Tablespoon vegetable oil

1. Wash the strawberries under cold
   water, drain well, and **dry with
   paper towels.**

2. Melt the chocolate with the oil in a
   double boiler with 1 inch of water in
   the bottom section on MEDIUM.

3. Lightly grease a wire rack.

4. Hold each berry by its green hull
   and dip each into the melted
   chocolate coating it only ⅔ of its
   length and cool them in a single
   layer on the wire rack.

5. Refrigerate 10 minutes.

MISSISSIPPI MUD

Makes: 32 (2") squares
Groundwork: Brownie:
  5 minutes
Topping: 6 minutes
Bake: 28 to 31 minutes
  (see pkg.)
Oven Temp: 350°
Need: 9" x 13" baking
  pan
medium mixing bowl
medium saucepan

Brownie:
**1 (19 to 25 oz.) pkg. chocolate or
fudge brownie mix**
**Additional ingredients as required on
the box**

Topping:
4 cups miniature marshmallows
**1 (16 oz.) container chocolate fudge
icing**
½ to 1 cup chopped pecans

1. Preheat the oven to 350°.

2. Prepare and bake the brownie mix as directed on the package.

3. Heat the icing and nuts in a medium saucepan on MEDIUM until warm and easy to spread. **(Do not overheat!!)**

4. Cover the entire top of the hot brownie with a single layer of marshmallows.

5. Turn the oven to OFF and return the brownie to the oven for 2 to 3 minutes until the marshmallows are melted.

6. Spread the warm icing and nuts evenly over the marshmallows and cool completely before cutting into 2 inch squares.

STRAWBERRIES ROMANOV

Makes: 4 servings
Groundwork: 2 minutes
Need: small mixing
  bowl

Two cups of fresh
peach slices make an
elegant change!

---

1 pint fresh strawberries
1 (8 oz.) carton sour cream
½ cup brown sugar
1 Tablespoon rum (optional)
½ teaspoon cinnamon (optional)

1. Wash the strawberries and remove the hulls.

2. Combine the sour cream, brown sugar, rum, and cinnamon in a small mixing bowl.

3. Arrange the strawberries in individual wine glasses or small bowls and top with the sauce.

OPTION:

  A. Replace the strawberries with 2 cups fresh raspberries.

PEACH MELBA

Makes: 2 servings
Groundwork: 2 minutes
Cook: 5 minutes -
  MEDIUM LOW
Need: small saucepan

For a Hollywood effect,
dip a sugar cube in
151 proof rum or
lemon extract, place
in top of the Peach
Melba, ignite, and
serve it flaming.

A 16 oz. can of peach
halves usually
contains 4 to 6 halves.

½ (12 oz.) jar raspberry preserves or jam
1 Tablespoon brandy
4 canned peach halves (drained)
½ pint vanilla ice cream

1. Combine the jelly and brandy in a small saucepan on MEDIUM LOW and heat until very hot but not boiling.

2. Drain the peaches and place 2 halves cut-side-up in small bowls.

3. Add one scoop of ice cream to the center of each peach half.

4. Top with the hot raspberry sauce and serve immediately.

STRUEDEL

Makes: 6 to 8 servings
Groundwork: 5 minutes
Bake: 45 minutes
Oven Temp: 350°
Need: 8" x 8" baking
pan

If the 9 oz. cake mix is not available, use ½ of an 18 oz. pkg.

---

1 (21 oz.) can pie filling (cherry, peach, apple or blueberry)
1 (8¼ oz.) can crushed pineapple (do not drain)
1 (9 oz.) box yellow cake mix
1 cup (2 sticks) butter
¾ cup chopped pecans

1. Preheat the oven to 350°.

2. Lightly grease an 8 x 8 inch baking pan.

3. Spread the pie filling, pineapple (and juice) evenly in the pan.

4. Sprinkle the dry cake mix on top making a layer ½ inch thick.

5. Cut the butter into 1 inch pieces, and place on top of the cake mix.

6. Top with the pecans.

7. Bake 45 minutes until brown and bubbly.

Top with whipped cream or vanilla ice cream.

UP TO DATES

Makes: 35 to 40
Groundwork: 10
  minutes
Need: small paper
  bag

These can be stuffed and refrigerated up to 3 days before coating in sugar.

---

1 (8 oz.) pkg. pitted whole dates
½ cup pecan halves (approximately)
1 (3 oz.) pkg. cream cheese
½ cup sugar

1. Stuff each date with ½ teaspoon cream cheese and 1 pecan half.

2. Pour the sugar in a small paper bag, drop in the stuffed dates, a few at a time, and shake.

3. Refrigerate, covered, until ready to serve.

THE PARFAIT GLASS

A fantastically easy dessert to serve in any **clear** container, from a parfait glass to a wine goblet. Good looks **do** count, so make sure that each layer shows on the outside of the glass. Parfaits can be prepared in advance and frozen or refrigerated until ready to serve. Remove them from the freezer 15 minutes before serving and add the suggested topping.

Layer in the order listed starting with the top of the list in the bottom of the glass and repeating the layers two to three times until it is full:

INDIVIDUAL FROZEN PARFAITS

BUTTER PECAN

½ cup butter pecan ice cream
¼ cup butterscotch topping
¼ cup pecans (chopped)

TOPPING:
Maraschino cherry

ESKIMO PIE

½ cup vanilla ice cream
1 (1 oz.) chocolate brownie (crumbled)
⅓ cup whipped topping

TOPPING:
Maraschino cherry, chopped pecans, or walnuts

NEOPOLITAN

¾ cup sherbet (use ¼ cup each two or more flavors)
¼ cup whipped topping

TOPPING:
Green or red maraschino cherry

PEACHES & CREAM

¼ cup sliced canned peaches (drained)
¼ cup vanilla ice cream

TOPPING:
Finely crushed graham cracker crumbs

PEPPERMINT PATTY

6 chocolate wafers (crushed)
½ cup vanilla ice cream
1 peppermint stick (crushed)

TOPPING:
Maraschino cherry

VERY BERRY

¼ cup ice cream
¼ cup fresh or frozen strawberries, blueberries or raspberries

TOPPING:
Fresh mint sprigs

PARTY PARFAITS
(4 servings)

CHOCOLATE-COVERED CHERRY

1 (21 oz.) can cherry pie filling
2 oz. rum
1 pint chocolate ice cream

TOPPING:
Whipped topping and a
maraschino cherry

1. Combine the pie filling and rum in a medium mixing bowl.

2. Make several layers with ice cream and pie filling and crown with the topping.

GELATIN PARFAITS

These American favorites are quick and simple. Prepare the gelatin as the package directs, chill until firm (about 2 hours) and cut into ½ inch cubes. Layer the cubes in the glasses with your selection of fruit, ice cream, sherbet, and/or whipped topping.

GELATIN	LAYER WITH	GARNISH
Orange	Mandarin orange slices and/or orange sherbet	Whipped topping & orange slices
Strawberry	Fresh or frozen strawberries and/or vanilla ice cream	Whipped topping & strawberries
Strawberry-Banana	Banana slices and/or vanilla pudding	Banana slices

GELATIN	REPLACE THE SAME AMOUNT OF WATER WITH	LAYER WITH	GARNISH
Lime	1 Tablespoon creme de menthe	Whipped topping	Mint sprigs
Cherry	½ cup dry red wine	Vanilla ice cream	Maraschino cherry
Raspberry	¼ cup sherry	Vanilla ice cream	Whipped topping & maraschino cherry
Lemon	½ cup peach juice	Sliced peaches & whipped topping	Sliced peaches

THE SUNDAE

This robust first cousin to the elegant parfait is too filling to serve after a full meal, but it is an easy and moderately priced way to entertain at a "Come for Dessert" party or a "Sunday Sundae Supper."

Arrange your choice of goodies in a mouth-watering array. Have available shallow bowls or dishes (oblong or round), and plenty of spoons. Then turn the crowd loose to create their own masterpieces.

Like the parfait, almost anything goes in this Gastric Goliath...from the old drugstore favorites of banana splits and hot fudges to whatever heights imagination can conjure. Here are a few suggestions to get you started on your pig-out:

ICE CREAMS	FRUITS (CANNED OR FRESH)	TOPPINGS	
		SAUCES	WHOLE BERRY PRESERVES
Old Standbys are: Vanilla Chocolate Strawberry (But any kind may be used!)	Banana, peeled & split lengthwise Peaches Strawberries Pineapple Orange slices (on sherbet)	Hot Fudge Peanut Butter* Chocolate Strawberry Butterscotch Pineapple Pistachio Blueberry Blackberry Creme de Menthe	Strawberry Pineapple Blackberry Blueberry Raspberry

TIP TOPPERS	
Chopped Pecans Chopped Peanuts Walnuts Pistachios Toasted Almonds Sunflower Seeds Cashew Nuts	Whipped Cream Canned or Frozen Whipped Topping Grated coconut Chocolate Chips Maraschino cherries Strawberries (fresh or frozen) Mandarin Orange Slices

*PEANUT BUTTER SAUCE

Combine ¼ cup milk, ¼ cup crunchy peanut butter, and ½ cup butterscotch sauce in a small mixing bowl until smooth.

MUNCHIES

(Appetizers or Hors D'oeuvres)
Crunchies, Dips, Spreads
And
Appetizer Trays

Hors d'oeuvre was originally a French term meaning "outside of work" and now refers to an appetizer that's easy to eat.

CRUNCHIES

Chips, crackers, pretzels, nuts. . . popular, instant hors d'oeuvres! Give their egos a boost by serving them in a zingy bowl or a napkin-lined basket.

AH SO

Makes: 2 cups
Groundwork: 3 minutes
Bake: 12 to 15 minutes
Oven Temp: 275°
Need: large baking
　pan

3 Tablespoons butter
⅛ teapsoon garlic powder
1 (3 oz.) can Chow Mein noodles
2 teaspoons soy sauce
¼ teaspoon salt
½ cup cashew nuts

1. Preheat the oven to 275°.

2. Melt the butter in a large baking pan while the oven preheats.

3. Add the soy, garlic, and salt, mixing well.

4. Add the noodles and nuts and stir to coat them completely.

5. Spread the mixture evenly in the baking pan.

6. Bake 12 to 15 minutes until they are crisp and light brown.

ARMADILLO EGGS

Makes: 50 (1") eggs
Groundwork: 8 to 10
  minutes
Bake: 20 to 25 minutes
Oven Temp: 350°
Need: large mixing
  bowl
cookie sheet

You can stop at the end of #4 and freeze them on the cookie sheet. Place in an airtight container and return them to the freezer. Bake without thawing – just add 5 to 10 minutes to the baking time.

1 pound "hot" ground pork sausage (room temp)
1 to 1½ cups shredded sharp Cheddar cheese
2½ cups biscuit mix
½ teaspoon Tabasco (optional)

1. Preheat the oven to 350°.

2. Combine all ingredients in a large mixing bowl and mix thoroughly, making sure that the sausage is completely separated.

3. Shape into small balls no larger than 1 inch.

4. Place them ½ inch apart on an ungreased cookie sheet.

5. Bake 20 to 25 minutes until lightly browned (they will continue to darken as they cool).

ANGLES ON HORSEBACK

Makes: 8
Groundwork: 4 minutes
Broil: 10 minutes
Need: broiler pan with
  rack

Yokohama Angels:
Brush with Teriyaki
Sauce before and
during broiling.

8 fresh shucked or canned oysters
4 slices bacon
toothpicks

1. Preheat the oven to BROIL.

2. Cut the bacon in half to make 2 short strips.

3. Wrap each oyster with 1 piece of bacon and fasten it with a toothpick.

4. Arrange them in a single layer on the rack of a broiler pan.

5. Broil 5 minutes, turn them over, and broil 5 additional minutes until the bacon is crisp.

CHEESE STRAWS

Makes: 12 to 14
Groundwork: 5 minutes
Bake: 10 minutes
Oven Temp: 450°
Need: medium mixing
  bowl
cookie sheet

**1 cup (4 oz. pkg.) shredded Cheddar
  cheese**
¼ cup (½ stick) butter (room temp.)
½ cup flour
¼ teaspoon salt
⅛ teaspoon cayenne pepper

1. Preheat the oven to 450°.

2. Combine the cheese and butter in a medium mixing bowl and stir to combine completely.

3. Add the flour, salt and cayenne pepper and stir until thoroughly mixed.

4. Form the dough into small (1 inch) balls.

5. Place the balls 2 inches apart on an ungreased cookie sheet.

6. Bake 10 minutes until very light brown.

Party Straws:
Before baking, flatten each to ½ inch thick and press 1 pecan half into each.

FIRE CRACKERS

Makes: 48
Groundwork: 3 minutes
Broil: 2 to 3 minutes
Need: cookie sheet

**1 (8 oz.) pkg. Monterey Jack cheese
  with jalapeño peppers**
48 Triscuit crackers

1. Preheat the oven to BROIL.

2. Slice the cheese ⅛ inch thick.

3. Place the crackers in a single layer on the cookie sheet.

4. Top each cracker with 1 slice of cheese.

5. Broil until the cheese is melted and bubbling and the crackers are just beginning to brown.

Serve hot from the oven with a cold drink ready. These little guys are HOT!

FEISTY FINGERS

Makes: 32 fingers
Groundwork: 10
minutes
Bake: 45 minutes
Oven Temp: 250°
Need: small mixing
bowl
cookie sheet

8 slices of Pepperidge Farm or Earth Grain Bread (white or wheat)
½ cup (1 stick) butter (room temperature)
2½ teaspoons lemon pepper seasonings

1. Preheat the oven to 250°.

2. Mix the butter and seasoning in a small mixing bowl.

3. Spread the butter mixture evenly over the bread.

4. Stack the buttered bread slices one on top of the other 4 slices high.

5. Cut off and discard the crusts and slice the stacks into ½-inch wide fingers.

6. Place the fingers in a single layer on the cookie sheet.

7. Bake 45 minutes until they are crisp and brown.

OPTIONS:

   A. Add one of the following:
   ⅛ teaspoon garlic powder
   ⅛ teaspoon onion powder
   1 pinch red or cayenne pepper
   ⅛ teaspoon Italian seasoning
   ⅛ teaspoon chili powder

GARLIC HAM ROLLS

Makes: 12 rolls or 48
  pieces
Groundwork: 10
  minutes
Refrigerate: 20 to 30
  minutes
Need: small mixing
  bowl

1 (8 oz.) pkg. cream cheese (room
  temp.)
2 Tablespoons mayonnaise
½ teaspoon salt
¼ teaspoon garlic powder
1 cup finely chopped nuts (pecans or
  walnuts)
12 slices boiled ham

1. Combine the cheese and
   mayonnaise in a small mixing bowl
   and stir until smooth.

Don't forget about
Individual Party Pizzas
(SUPPER).

2. Add the garlic, salt, and nuts and
   mix well.

3. Spread an even layer of the cheese
   mixture on each ham slice.

4. Roll the slice tightly, cover, and
   refrigerate until they are firm.

5. Either serve "as-is" or cut each roll
   into 4 slices and serve on crackers.

HOT DIGGITY DOGS

Makes: 80 (½") pieces
Groundwork: 5 minutes
Cook: 1 hour - LOW
Need: medium
  saucepan

1 (10 to 12 oz.) jar jelly (grape, plum, or
  currant)
¼ cup prepared mustard
1 teaspoon Worcestershire
4 drops Tabasco
1 (16 oz.) pkg. hot dogs

1. In a medium saucepan on MEDIUM,
   combine the jelly, mustard, Tabasco,
   and Worcestershire and bring to a
   boil, stirring constantly.

Serve hot with
toothpicks.

Don't forget to try the
Saucy Meatballs in
SUPPER.

2. Cut the hot dogs into ½ inch pieces
   and add to the jelly mixture.

3. Reduce to LOW, cover, and cook 1
   hour, stirring frequently.

MARINATED MUSHROOMS

Makes: 1 cup
Groundwork: 2 minutes
Refrigerate: 24 hours
Need: 1 pint airtight
  container (a clean
  jar is great)
toothpicks
small serving bowl

These improve with
age and are best if
made 4 to 5 days
before serving.

**2 (4½ oz.) cans whole button
  mushrooms
1 (8 oz.) bottle Zesty Italian salad
  dressing**

1. Drain the mushrooms and place in a
   1 pint container.

2. Add the dressing, cover, and
   refrigerate.

3. Drain and serve.

ELEGANT OPTIONS:

  A. Several hours before serving,
     add:

     2 (7 oz.) cans drained shrimp
     1 (14 oz.) can drained and
        quartered artichoke hearts

NUT CRACKERS

Makes: 35 to 40
Groundwork: 4 minutes
Bake: 15 to 20 minutes
Oven Temp: 350°
Need: medium mixing
  bowl
cookie sheet

**1 cup (4 oz. pkg.) shredded sharp
  Cheddar cheese
½ cup (1 stick) butter (room temp.)
½ cup self-rising flour
⅛ teaspoon cayenne pepper
¾ cups rice crispies
¼ cup finely chopped pecans**

1. Preheat the oven to 350°.

2. Combine the cheese and butter in a
   medium mixing bowl until well mixed.

3. Add the flour and cayenne pepper
   and mix well.

4. Add the rice crispies and pecans
   and stir gently to mix well.

5. Drop Tablespoon-sized mounds
   2 inches apart on an ungreased
   cookie sheet.

6. Bake 15 to 20 minutes until very light
   brown.

NUTS AND BOLTS

Makes: 8 cups
Groundwork: 5 minutes
Bake: 30 minutes
Oven Temp: 300°
Need: large baking
pan

½ cup (1 stick) butter
4 Tablespoons Worchestershire
1 teaspoon salt
⅛ teaspoon garlic powder
2 cups bite-sized rice cereal
2 cups bite-sized corn cereal
2 cups bite-sized wheat cereal
1½ cups pretzel sticks
½ cup peanuts or pecans

1. Preheat the oven to 300°.

2. Melt the butter in a large baking
   dish or pan while the oven is
   preheating.

3. Add the Worcestershire, salt, and
   garlic and mix well.

4. Mix the cereals, pretzels, and nuts in
   the baking pan.

5. Stir well to coat, and spread the
   mixture evenly in the pan.

6. Bake for 30 minutes, stirring every 10
   minutes.

SHAKE-A-SNACK

Makes: 9 cups
Groundwork: 3 minutes
Need: 1 medium
paper or plastic bag

3 cups oyster crackers
3 cups bite-sized square cheese
crackers
3 cups pretzels (bite-size or sticks)
1 (1 oz.) pkg. ranch salad dressing mix
½ teaspoon dill weed
¼ cup vegetable oil

In the unlikely event
that any are left over,
store them in an
airtight container.

1. Combine everything except the oil
   in a paper or plastic bag.

2. Close the bag tightly and shake
   away!

3. Pour in the oil, close, and shake
   again.

PECANS

TOASTED:

Makes: 2 cups
Groundwork: 3 minutes
Bake: 40 minutes
Oven Temp: 250°
Need: medium baking
  dish

3 Tablespoons butter
¼ cup Worcestershire
½ teaspoon Tabasco
¼ to ½ teaspoon salt
¼ teaspoon garlic powder
pinch cayenne pepper (optional)
2 cups pecan halves

1. Preheat the oven to 250°.

2. Combine the butter, Worcestershire, and Tabasco in a medium baking dish and melt in the oven while it preheats.

For a Kinder, Gentler pecan, omit the Tabasco and cayenne pepper.

3. Stir in the garlic, salt, and cayenne pepper.

4. Add the pecans, stir to coat evenly, and spread them in a single layer.

5. Bake 40 minutes, stirring occasionally, until the liquid is absorbed and the nuts are crisp and brown.

6. Cool on paper towels.

GLAZED:

Makes: 1 cup
Groundwork: 1 minute
Cook: 7 minutes -
MEDIUM
Need: foil
medium skillet

1 cup pecan halves
pinch of salt
¼ cup sugar

1. Lightly grease a long piece of foil.

2. Combine all the ingredients in a medium skillet on MEDIUM.

Almonds can also be used for a gourmet touch.

3. Stir **constantly** until the sugar melts and the mixture has turned light golden brown.

4. Remove the nuts to the foil and quickly separate them into individual pieces using two forks.

Makes: 1 cup
Groundwork: 2 minutes
Cook: 3 minutes -
   MEDIUM
4 minutes - LOW
Need: foil
medium skillet

SPICED:

¼ **cup sugar**
2 Tablespoons water
¼ **teaspoon vanilla**
¼ **teaspoon cinnamon**
⅛ **teaspoon salt**
⅛ **teaspoon ground cloves**
1 cup pecan halves

1. Combine the first 6 ingredients in a medium skillet on MEDIUM.

2. Bring to a boil, reduce to LOW, cook 3 to 4 minutes, stirring constantly, until thickened; add pecans and stir to coat.

3. Remove the pecans to the foil and separate them gently.

SAUSAGE PINWHEELS

Makes: 40 pinwheels
Groundwork: 5 minutes
Refrigerate: 30 minutes
Bake: 20 to 25 minutes
Oven Temp: 350°
Need: plastic wrap
broiler pan
paper towels

1 (8 count) pkg. refrigerator crescent rolls
1 pound hot ground pork sausage

1. Place a piece of plastic wrap on the counter top.

2. Place the dough on the wrap and gently press the roll dough together at the perforations to form two rectangles.

3. Spread each rectangle with a thin layer of sausage.

4. Starting on the long edge, roll each rectangle tightly.

5. Wrap in the plastic wrap and refrigerate 30 to 45 minutes or until it's firm enough to cut.

You can stop at the
end of Step 5 and
freeze.

6. When ready to bake, preheat the oven to 350°.

7. Cut each roll into 20 slices, ¼ inch thick, and place them in a single layer on an ungreased broiler pan.

8. Bake 20 to 25 minutes until light brown.

9. Drain on paper towel.

311

WING DINGERS

Makes: 12 drumettes
Groundwork: 5 minutes
Bake: 45 to 50 minutes
Oven Temp: 400°
Need: small mixing
  bowl
broiler pan or baking
  pan with rack

Serve hot, spicy Wing
Dingers and Dipper
with cold, crisp carrots
and celery sticks.

The Chef's Spice is
HOT, so adjust the
amount used to the
heroism of your
tastebuds.

12 chicken drumettes
¼ cup vegetable oil
1½ Tablespoons vinegar
Chef's Spice (The Creole Cottage,
  page 201) to taste

1. Preheat the oven to 400°.

2. Combine the oil and vinegar in a small mixing bowl.

3. Dip each drumette into the oil mixture.

4. Sprinkle each with The Chef's Spice to taste.

5. Arrange in a single layer in the broiler pan rack, 1 inch apart.

6. Bake 45 to 50 minutes until tender and crisp, turning at least once.

DINGER DIPPERS:

   A. Ranch or Blue cheese dressing

   B. Horseradish or mustard dill sauce (SAUCES AND GRAVIES, pages 254 and 255)

   C. Hot mustard sauce:

       1 cup mayonnaise
       2 tablespoons hot mustard

DIPS

Ordinary dips become masterpieces when served in a creative container and dramatized with a splash of parsley or paprika. Top a cold dip with a lemon or lime twist or sprigs of dill or parsley.

CREATIVE CONTAINERS FOR DIPS	
WHAT TO USE	**HOW TO DO IT**
Grapefruit Half	Hollow it out.
Melon Half	Cut it in half and remove the seeds (and the meat of a watermelon).
Pineapple	Cut in half from top to bottom and scoop out the center.
Coconut	Saw in half and drain.
Green or Red Bell Pepper	Cut off the top or split it from top to bottom and remove the seeds.
Artichoke	Cut ½ inch off the top and hollow it out.
Purple or Green Cabbage	Cut off the top ¼; carefully remove the **inside** leaves, leaving a wall about ¾ inch thick.
Pumpkin (small)	Cut off the top and remove the seeds: fit a bowl inside to hold the dip.
Round or Oval (unsliced) Loaves of French, Italian, Rye, Pumpernickle Bread	Hollow it out with a knife and coat the inside with butter, or fit a bowl inside.

A Bowl may be fitted into any of these containers if you prefer, but is a MUST for hot dips.

VEGGIE DIPPERS

In addition to the traditional chips and crackers, fresh vegetables (crudites) make great dippers. Just rinse them in cold water and cut into sticks, strips, rings, or flowerettes. Arrange all the goodies attractively on a tray, platter, or plate around a bowl of your favorite dip. (Celery and carrots can be kept crisp by covering them in cold water and refrigerating.)

Broccoli	Cucumbers	Mushrooms
Carrots (peeled)	Green Onions	Yellow Squash
Celery	Green or Red Bell Peppers	Cherry Tomatoes (whole)
Cauliflower	Snow Pea Pods	Zucchini

313

CURRY DIP FOR VEGGIES

Makes: 2 cups
Groundwork: 2 minutes
Refrigerate: 1 hour
Need: medium mixing
  bowl

Quickie Dip for Veggies:
Try bottled salad dressings: Creamy Italian or Garlic, Green Goddess, or Ranch.

1 (8 oz.) carton sour cream
1 cup mayonnaise
½ teaspoon curry powder
2 finely sliced green onions (optional)

1. Mix all the ingredients in a medium mixing bowl.

2. Refrigerate at least 1 hour before serving to allow the curry powder to develop full flavor.

BONEY MARONEY

Makes: 2 cups
Groundwork: 3 minutes
Need: blender

Serve cold with chips, veggie dippers.

1 (8 oz.) bottle lo-cal blue cheese salad dressing
1 (8 oz.) carton cottage cheese

1. Combine the cottage cheese and salad dressing in the blender.

2. Blend on HIGH until smooth.

PRAIRIE FIRE

Makes: 3¼ cups
Groundwork: 5 minutes
Cook: 5 to 7 minutes - LOW
Need: medium saucepan

Serve hot with corn chips or crackers.

1 (1 lb.) Velveeta cheese
1 (10 oz.) can Rotel® tomatoes & green chilies (no substitutes)

1. Cut the cheese into 1 inch cubes.

2. Melt the cheese in a medium saucepan (or the top of a double boiler) on LOW, stirring constantly.

3. Add the tomatoes (do not drain) and continue cooking until bubbling hot.

OPTION:

A. Neat Meat Addition: 1 (15 oz.) can of chili without beans.

ARTICHOKE DIP

Makes: 2½ cups
Groundwork: 5 minutes
Bake: 20 to 25 minutes
Oven Temp: 350°
Need: 1 qt. casserole

Serve hot with corn chips or wheat crackers.

1 (14 oz.) can artichoke hearts (drained)
½ cup mayonnaise
½ cup Parmesan cheese
⅛ teaspoon garlic powder (optional)

1. Preheat the oven to 350°.

2. Drain the artichoke hearts; cut each one into 3 to 4 bite-sized pieces.

3. Combine the mayonnaise and cheese in a one quart casserole.

4. Add the artichoke pieces, and stir gently to combine.

5. Bake 20 to 25 minutes until hot and bubbling.

OPTIONS:

A. Spicy Additions:
   1 teaspoon Worcestershire
   ⅛ teaspoon garlic powder

B. **Elegant Additions:**
   1 (6 oz.) can crab meat (drained)
   ½ cup diced water chestnuts

SERENDIPITY

Makes: 1 cup
Groundwork: 3 min.
Cook: 5 minutes -
   MEDIUM
Need: small saucepan

Serve hot with bread sticks, corn chips, or French bread cubes and toothpicks.

1 (1¼ oz.) pkg. cheese sauce mix
¾ cup milk
1 (2 oz.) can deviled ham
3 drops Tabasco

1. Combine the cheese sauce and milk in a small saucepan on MEDIUM and cook 3 minutes until the sauce has thickened.

2. Add the deviled ham and Tabasco; mix well and continue cooking until hot.

SKINNY DIPPING

Makes: 2½ cups
Groundwork: 3 minutes
Refrigerate: 30 minutes
Need: blender

Serve cold with chips
or Veggie Dippers.

1 (8 oz.) carton cottage cheese
1 (10 oz.) pkg. frozen chopped spinach
  or broccoli
½ cup plain yogurt
1 envelope dry onion soup mix

1. Thaw and drain the spinach.

2. Combine the spinach and the
   cottage cheese in a blender
   container and process on MEDIUM
   until smooth.

3. Add the yogurt and soup mix and
   blend 30 seconds.

4. Refrigerate 30 minutes.

HOT SHRIMP DIP

Makes: 2¼ cups
Groundwork: 4 minutes
Cook: 5 minutes -
  MEDIUM
Need: small saucepan

Serve hot with chips or
Veggie Dippers.

Clam Diggers
(Spreads) also make a
great hot dip.

1 (4 oz.) can shrimp (drained)
¼ teaspoon Tabasco
1 (10¾ oz.) can cream of shrimp soup
1 cup (4 oz. pkg.) shredded Cheddar
  cheese
2 Tablespoons milk

1. Drain the shrimp, chop each in half,
   and set aside.

2. Combine all ingredients **except** the
   shrimp in a small saucepan and stir
   until well blended.

3. Cook on MEDIUM until the cheese
   has melted and the mixture is hot.

4. Add the shrimp and continue
   cooking 1 to 2 minutes until hot.

SMOKED OYSTER DIP

Makes: 3¼ cups
Groundwork: 8 minutes
Need: medium mixing
bowl

Serve cold with
crackers or Veggie
Dippers.

If time permits, make
this ahead of time. It
improves with age.

---

1 (8 oz.) pkg. cream cheese (room temp.)
1¼ cups mayonnaise
4 to 5 drops Tabasco
1 (4½ oz.) can chopped black olives
  (drained)
2 Tablespoons lemon juice
1 (3.6 oz.) can smoked oysters (drained)

1. Combine the cream cheese,
   mayonnaise, lemon juice, and
   Tabasco in a medium mixing bowl.

2. Drain and chop the oysters and olives.

3. Add the oysters and olives to the
   cream cheese mixture and stir
   gently until completely mixed.

LAYERED TACO NACHO DIP

Makes: a bunch!
Groundwork: 10
  minutes
Need: small mixing
  bowl
large, flat serving bowl

Serve with corn,
nacho, or tortilla chips.

---

1 cup sour cream
½ cup mayonnaise
1 (1¼ oz.) pkg. taco seasoning
1 medium bunch green onions (4 to 6
  onions)
2 medium ripe tomatoes
2 (3½ oz.) cans chopped or sliced
  black olives (drained)
2 cups (8 oz.) pkg. shredded Cheddar
  cheese
2 (7 oz.) cans of bean dip
1 (8 oz.) carton guacamole dip

1. Combine the sour cream,
   mayonnaise, and taco seasoning in
   a small mixing bowl with a wire whisk.

2. Finely dice the white and green
   parts of the onions; peel and dice
   the tomatoes; drain the black olives.

3. Layer the ingredients in this order
   spreading them evenly in a large
   flat serving bowl: bean dip,
   guacamole dip, sour cream mixture,
   green onions, tomatoes, olives, cheese.

317

SPREADS

Spreads are thicker than dip, and it's tough to try to gouge them out of a deep bowl with nothing but a cracker. Serve each spread with a spreader or small knife.

PARTY BRIE CHEESE WHEEL

Makes: 1 beautiful wheel
Groundwork: 5 to 10 minutes
Cook: 5 minutes - LOW
Need: platter
small saucepan

Serve with assorted crackers.

Remember:
The cheese rind is edible and the wheel is best served at room temperature.

For an instant gourmet wheel, just stir 1 Tablespoon of brandy into 1 (5 oz.) jar of walnuts-in-syrup and spoon it over an untopped wheel.

1 (12 to 14 oz.) wheel of Brie cheese
1 (or more) Toppers
1 glaze

1. Center the Brie wheel on an attractive plate.

2. Choose one or more toppers, prepare as directed, and arrange attractively on top of the wheel.

3. Melt one choice of glaze in a small saucepan on LOW until liquified (DO NOT BOIL).

4. Spoon a thin layer of the hot glaze over the Toppers on the Wheel.

TOPPERS: (Choose one or more)

Almonds - slice or sliver
Apple - peel and slice thinly
Grapes (seedless) - whole or slice
Kiwi - peel and slice
Macadamia nuts - chop
Peaches - (fresh or canned) - slice
Pecans - half or chop
Pineapple - (fresh or canned) - slice or dice
Raisins - (white or brown) - whole
Strawberries - remove hulls and slice

CATERER'S SECRET GLAZES (Choose one)

Light - apple jelly
Medium - mint jelly
Dark - raspberry or red currant jelly

ELEGANT CREAM CHEESE TOPPERS

Makes: 4 to 6 servings
Groundwork: 2 to 5
  minutes
Need: plate, platter or
  chopping block

Serve with assorted
crackers.

Most of these Toppers
can be found in the
gourmet section of the
supermarket.

Your friends won't
believe the A-1 Sauce
is not a gourmet
something straight
from Paris!

1 (8 oz.) pkg. cream cheese
1 Topper

1. Center the cream cheese on an
   attractive plate, platter or chopping
   block.

2. Top with your choice:

   A. ½ cup hot pepper jelly

   B. A-1 Sauce

   C. 1 (3⅔ oz.) can smoked oysters
       (drained)

   D. ½ cup chutney topped with ¼
       cup toasted sliced almonds

   E. 1 (6½ oz.,) can crab meat
           (drained)
       1 (9 oz.) bottle cocktail sauce
       ¼ teaspoon Tabasco
       (Mix the sauce and Tabasco
       and spoon over the crab meat.)

   F. 1 (6 oz.) jar shrimp cocktail
       ½ teaspoon Worcestershire
       ¼ teaspoon lemon juice
       3 drops Tabasco
       (Mix well.)

HELL'S BELLS

Makes: 1½ cups
Groundwork: 3 minutes
Need: small mixing
  bowl

Serve with crackers or
party breads.

1 (8 oz.) carton soft cream cheese
1 (4½ oz.) can deviled ham
⅓ cup pimiento-stuffed green olives
  (drained and chopped)

1. Combine the cheese and deviled
   ham in a small mixing bowl, stirring
   until smooth.

2. Drain and chop the olives and stir
   into the cheese mixture.

CLAM DIGGERS

Makes: 1½ cups
Groundwork: 5 minutes
Refrigerate OR
Cook: 3 minutes -
  MEDIUM LOW
Need: medium mixing
  bowl OR small
  saucepan

Serve with unflavored
crackers for **Cold
Spread; Bugles,
French bread cubes
and toothpicks for Hot
Dip.**.

**1 (6½ oz.) can minced clams (reserve
  juice)**
1 (8 oz.) pkg. cream cheese (room temp.)
1 teaspoon instant minced onion
1 teaspoon Worcestershire
2 teaspoons lemon juice
¼ teaspoon salt

1. Drain the clams, reserving the juice.

2. Blend the cream cheese and 1 to 2
   Tablespoons of the reserved juice in
   a medium mixing bowl until smooth.

3. Add all other ingredients, mixing well.

4. Cover, and refrigerate OR heat in a
   small saucepan on MEDIUM LOW
   until hot.

PINECONES

Makes: 1 (3") cone
Groundwork: 15
  minutes
Refrigerate: overnight
Need: medium mixing
  bowl
plastic wrap

Serve cold with
crackers or party
bread.

For a show-stopping
effect, start at one end
of the oval and lightly
press the almonds
onto the cheese sur-
face letting each new
row slightly overlap
the last until the mound
is completely covered.

---

5 slices of bacon
1 (8 oz.) pkg. cream cheese (room temp.)
½ cup mayonnaise
**1 Tablespoon green onions (finely
  chopped)**
½ teaspoon dill weed
⅛ teaspoon pepper
½ cup sliced almonds

1. Fry the bacon until crisp; drain and
   crumble.

2. While the bacon is frying, dice the
   onion and combine the ingredients
   (**except** the bacon and almonds) in
   a medium mixing bowl until well mixed.

3. Add the bacon and stir well.

4. Cover and refrigerate overnight.

5. Spread the almonds in a single
   layer on plastic wrap.

6. Form into an oval mound and roll it
   in the almonds.

GREAT BALLS OF FIRE

Makes: 2 (3") balls
Groundwork: 8 minutes
Need: large mixing
  bowl, small mixing
  bowl

Serve with party rye
bread or unflavored
crackers

If time permits, make
these several days
ahead, cover and
refrigerate — they
improve with age, OR
enjoy one now and
freeze the other for
later.

---

1 (4 oz.) jar chopped pimientos
1 (8 oz.) pkg. cream cheese (room
  temp)
1 (8 oz.) carton pimiento cheese
2 cups (8 oz. pkg.) shredded sharp
  Cheddar cheese
1 cup chopped pecans
½ teaspoon salt
⅛ teaspoon pepper
¼ to ½ teaspoon garlic powder
2 Tablespoons chili powder
2 Tablespoons paprika
2 Tablespoons cayenne pepper

1. Drain the pimientos and chop finely
   (or mash them with the back of a
   fork).

2. Combine the three cheeses in a
   large mixing bowl and mix well.

3. Add the pimientos, pecans, salt,
   pepper, and garlic powder; mix well,
   refrigerate until firm, and shape into
   2 balls.

4. Mix the chili powder, paprika
   and cayenne pepper in a small
   mixing bowl.

5. Roll each ball in the spices until
   completely covered, and refrigerate
   or freeze.

MIDDLE AGE SPREAD

Makes: 1 (4") ball
Groundwork: 8 minutes
Refrigerate: 2 hours
Need: medium mixing
  bowl
plastic wrap

Serve cold with
crackers.

For a quick chill, mix
in a **metal** mixing
bowl and freeze for 30
to 40 minutes (stirring
every 10 minutes until
it is firm but not frozen).

A popular party item
is Pineapple Spread in
sandwiches (LUNCH).

---

1 (6½ oz.) can tuna or boneless salmon
  (drained)
1 (8 oz.) pkg. cream cheese (room
  temp.)
1 Tablespoon prepared horseradish
1 Tablespoon lemon juice
¼ teaspoon liquid smoke
½ teaspoon instant minced onions
¼ teaspoon salt
½ cup chopped pecans
2 Tablespoons parsley flakes

1. Drain and flake the tuna (or salmon).

2. Combine the cream cheese,
   horseradish, lemon juice, liquid
   smoke, onion, and salt in a medium
   mixing bowl.

3. Add the tuna (or salmon) and stir to
   combine thoroughly.

4. Cover and refrigerate 2 hours or
   until it is firm enough to hold its
   shape.

5. Sprinkle the pecans and parsley on
   plastic wrap.

6. Shape the tuna (or salmon) mixture
   into a ball and roll in the pecan-
   parsley mixture.

APPETIZER TRAYS

Appetizer trays make a simple but spectacular addition to any party. Because trays need quite a variety of goodies to be attractive, save them for your larger gatherings. To add color and fill in the gaps, add cherry tomatoes, parsley, green and red bell pepper rings or gerkins.

THE ANTIPASTO TRAY

A tangy tray for gourmet appetites! It may also be served in place of a salad at a buffet dinner. Easy! Easy! Most of the morsels can be purchased at your local grocery or deli and used "as is." Simply drain all the liquids and arrange attractively on a tray or a platter.

SELECT SIX TO EIGHT OF YOUR FAVORITES:

Anchovy fillets
Sardines
Marinated Herring
Marinated Shrimp
Smoked Oysters
Boiled Ham
Salami
Pepperoni
Pastrami
Turkey

Marinated Pearl Onions
Marinated Mushrooms
Black or Green Olives
Marinated Artichoke
  Hearts
Pickled Eggs
  (slices/quarters)
Scallions*
Celery Hearts*
Broccoli*

Pickled Califlower
Whole cooked green
  beans*
Radishes*
Carrots (thin-sliced or
  fingerlings)*
Onion Slices
Pickled Okra
Pickled miniature corn
Sliced Tomatoes*

*These should be marinated overnight in one of the following:

Liquid from the marinated artichokes or mushrooms, Italian dressing (regular or lo-cal), or The Chef's Antipasto Marinade:

¾ cup olive oil
⅓ cup lemon juice
3 Tablespoons vinegar
3 Tablespoons water
2 Tablespoons parsley flakes

⅛ teaspoon garlic powder
¾ teaspoon sugar
¾ teaspoon salt
⅛ teaspoon pepper

THE VEGETABLE TRAY

For light refreshing lo-cal grazing, see Veggie Dippers (DIPS).

THE MEAT AND CHEESE TRAY

A **great** heavy hors d'oeuvre. . .but too much if you're also serving dinner. The secret is to arrange everything attractively on trays, platters, or chopping blocks, add the garnishes, and refrigerate until serving time.

CHOOSE TWO OR THREE FROM EACH GROUP:

Cheeses: Cheddar, Swiss, Hot Pepper. (Thinly sliced or cut into cubes.)

Meats: Ham, Turkey, Roast Beef, Pastrami, Pepperoni, Corned Beef. (Thinly sliced, either from your kitchen or the deli. Roll the slices cigar-fashion or cut them to fit the party bread or crackers.)

Crackers or Party-sized Breads: If using regular-sized bread, cut the slices in half. Serve separately in napkin-lined baskets.

Condiments: Compatible mustards, mayonnaise, Horseradish Sauce (SAUCES AND GRAVIES). Serve in small bowls, either on the tray or to the side. Don't forget a knife or a spoon for spreading.

THE SEAFOOD TRAY

Guaranteed to please even your hard-shelled, finicky friends.
Many large supermarkets have seafood shops that will cook purchased seafoods at no extra charge while you finish shopping. OH, what a relief it is!
Make your choices and include a sauce for dipping. Arrange attractively on a tray or large platter atop a bed of lettuce or surrounded by fresh parsley.

CHOOSE ONE OR MORE

Anchovies or Sardines: Drain well.

Clams: Steamed with shells removed or on the half-shell.

Herring: Creamed or in wine sauce (found in the deli, dairy, or gourmet section).

Lobster: (cooked) fresh or frozen, cut into bite-sized pieces.

Oysters: Fresh raw or roasted with shells removed or on the half-shell; canned smoked oysters; barbecued (DINNER).

Shrimp: Cold, boiled, peeled; (DINNER) marinated.

Smoked Fish: Salmon or whitefish cut into bite-sized pieces.

Sauces: Tartar sauce, Seafood Cocktail Sauce (SAUCES AND GRAVIES).

Garnish: Slices of lemon sprinkled with parsley, or lemon and lime wedges.

LIBATIONS
The Coffee House, The Tea Room, The Chocolate Shop, The Soda Fountain, Punches for Brunches and Lunches, Mocktails, The Wine Wizard and, The 2 Minute Bartender

THE COFFEE HOUSE

Over 2,500 years ago in Arabia, goat herders discovered their animals were frolicking around all night after feeding on the berries and leaves of the coffea tree. Anxious to share this exalting experience, the Arabians themselves began to eat the berries for lunch. This was so delightful, they tried fermenting them into wine, and later boiling them to a hot, black drink which they discovered sharpened their mental faculties. And, so these many years later, "Kaffia" is still the stimulating mainstay of great minds.

The art of making good coffee is as simple as following these rules:

1. **Always keep your coffee maker clean!** Wash it after each use with a mild detergent or several teaspoons of baking soda dissolved in warm water and rinse thoroughly with boiling or very hot water, and follow the manufacturer's cleaning directions if special ones came with your equipment.

2. **Always use the grind recommended** for your particular coffee maker. Follow the manufacturer's directions if you have them.

3. **Use fresh coffee.** Store it in an air-tight container in the refrigerator for maximum freshness.

4. Always **start with cold, fresh water.**

5. **Use the proper amount** of coffee for the desired strength. (See Below.)

6. **Fill the coffee maker completely,** or at least half full.

7. **Never boil coffee!**

8. **Don't make coffee too far ahead of serving time.**

9. **Never reuse coffee grounds!**

STANDARD PROPORTION

The strength of coffee is a matter of personal preference. Adjust the recommended amounts to suit your taste.

The strength does not depend on the length of brewing time, but on the amount of ground coffee used in brewing.

For MEDIUM strength coffee, use one (1) rounded Tablespoon of ground coffee for each ¾ cup (6 oz.) of water (and one extra for the pot if you prefer a richer, full-bodied brew).

NUMBER OF SERVINGS (6 oz. or ¾ cup)	AMOUNT OF WATER	AMOUNT OF COFFEE
12	72 oz. (9 cups)	¾ cup
18	108 oz. (½ gal. + 1 qt. + 1½ cups)	1⅛ cups
24	144 oz. (1 gal. + 2 cups)	1½ cups
30	180 oz. (1 gal. +1 qt. + 2½ cups)	1⅞ cups
50	300 oz. (2 gal. + 1 qt. + 1½ cups)	3⅛ cups

SPECIAL BREWS

Demitasse. Demitasse is a traditional strong, black after-dinner coffee and is always served in very small cups.

1. Any method may be used, but drip is customary.

2. Use 3 or 4 Tablespoons coffee for 8 oz. water and serve black.

Cafe au Lait

1. Follow the demitasse directions.

2. In a small saucepan on MEDIUM, heat the same amount of milk or half and half as you have coffee to **just below** the boiling point.

3. Pour equal amounts of hot milk and coffee into a cup simultaneously.

OPTIONS:

A. Add sugar, if desired.

B. Add 1 drop of Vanilla for an authentic touch.

QUICK COFFEE PERK-UPS

Prepare coffee by any method, and for each cup, take your choice of one of the following:

Swiss Mocha: 1 heaping Tablespoon instant hot chocolate mix.

Mocha Mint: to Swisse Mocha, add 1 drop of peppermint extract or a crushed, fresh mint sprig.

Orange Cappucchino: ¼ cup orange sherbet

Viennise: ¼ cup vanilla ice cream or whipped topping and pinch of Nutmeg.

Cafe Angelico: 2 Tablespoons orange juice, pinch of ground cloves, pinch of ground cinnamon, 1 teaspoon sugar

Amaretto: ¼ teaspoon almond extract (Top with 2 heaping Tablespoons of whipped topping.)

Makes: 1 serving

For the "Wearing of the Green," add a sprig of fresh mint to the Irish Coffee.

How to Make a Sugar Rim:
Put ¼ cup sugar in a saucer. Moisten rim of a mug with a water and dip the moistened rim in sugar.

Try Continental Coffees in a sugar rimmed mug.

CONTINENTAL COFFEES
(Dessert Coffees)

¾ cup hot, black coffee
2 Tablespoons whipped topping or vanilla ice cream
AND
Your choice of any one of the following:

A. Black Bayou: 1½ oz. Praline Liquer

B. Crazy Cajun: 1 oz. Praline Liquer and ½ oz. Brandy

C. Highland Fling: 1½ oz. scotch

D. Irish: 1½ oz. Irish Whiskey

E. Napoleon: 1½ oz. Brandy

F. Polynesian: Omit topping and add: 1½ oz. Kahlua OR 1 oz. Kahlua and ½ oz. Amaretto

G. Venetian: 1½ oz. Amaretto

INSTANT COFFEE MIXES

For the following instant mixes:

1. Combine all ingredients in a blender container.
2. Blend 15 seconds on HIGH until well blended.
3. Store in an airtight container.
4. Use 2 teaspoons of the mix with 6 oz. of boiling water.

CAFE AU LAIT

Makes: 1¼ cups mix (30 cups coffee)

For low-cal, use 12 packets of sugar substitute.

¼ cup instant coffee granules
½ cup sugar
½ cup powdered milk or coffee creamer

SWISS MOCHA

Makes: 1¼ cups mix (30 cups coffee)

¼ cup instant coffee granules
1 cup instant hot chocolate mix

ORANGE CAPPUCCINO

Makes: 2¼ cups mix (54 cups coffee)

For a low-cal mix, use 18 packets of sugar substitute in place of sugar.

½ cup instant coffee granules
¾ cup sugar
1 cup powdered milk or coffee creamer
½ teaspoon dried orange peel

THE TEA ROOM

Tea is an ancient drink and abounds with mystique and customs. Its origin is unknown but has been enjoyed in China since the 6th century and in Europe since the 1600's. Iced tea is a product of the 1904 St. Louis World's Fair.

Makes: 4 (8 oz.) servings (1 quart)

Refrigerate any unused tea in an airtight container. If tea becomes cloudy, add a little boiling water to clear it.

COLD-WATER ICED TEA

3 family size tea bags (or 9 small)
1 quart cold water

1. Remove tags from tea bags.

2. Place the bags in a large pitcher or glass jar and add the cold water.

3. Cover and refrigerate at least 4 hours.

4. Remove tea bags, stir, and serve over ice.

TEA TEASERS

Simply mix with strong, unsweetened tea and serve over ice!

LEMON FIZZ

Makes: 4 servings

For an extra punch, add vodka and a lemon twist.

3 cups tea
2 teaspoons lemon juice
16 oz. ginger ale

LEMON COOLER

Makes: 70 oz.

2 quarts tea
1 (6 oz.) can frozen lemonade
sugar (optional)

TROPICAL

Makes: 32 oz.

2 cups tea
1 (7 oz.) bottle club soda
2 Tablespoons lemon juice
1 cup orange juice
½ cup sugar

Makes: 72 oz.

FRENCH MINT

2 quarts tea
1 (6 oz.) can frozen orange juice
  (thawed)
1 cup sugar
¼ cup lemon juice
3 to 4 mint sprigs

INSTANT SPICED TEA MIX

Makes: 4¾ cups mix
(115 servings)
Need: large plastic
  bag

2 cups instant tea (unsweetened)
1 cup instant orange flavored
  breakfast drink
2 teaspoons cinnamon
1 cup sugar
¾ cup (8 oz. pkg.) lemonade mix
¾ teaspoon cloves (ground)
⅛ teaspoon nutmeg

For a low cal mix, use
24 packets of sugar
substitute in place of
the sugar and sugar-
free lemonade mix
and breakfast drink.

Store sealed in the
plastic bag.

1. Combine all the ingredients in a
   large plastic bag and shake to mix
   well.

2. To serve, use 2 teaspoons mix for 1
   cup hot water.

OPTION:

A. Add 1 teaspoon dried orange
   and/or lemon peel.

THE CHOCOLATE SHOP

The Aztecs thought the cocoa bean was a seed from Paradise and considered it so valuable they used it for money. Hernando Cortez enjoyed drinking chocolate with the Emperor Montezuma so much that he returned to Spain, bringing the ladies of the Court the world's first box of chocolates.

Makes: 28 servings
Groundwork: 2 minutes
Need: large plastic
  bag

Store sealed in the plastic bag.

Makes: 1 serving

INSTANT CHOCOLATE MIX

1 (4 quart) box instant non-fat dry milk
1 (3 oz.) jar non-dairy coffee creamer
1 (1 pound) can chocolate drink mix
¼ cup powdered sugar

1. Mix all ingredients together in a large plastic bag.
2. To serve use: ⅓ cup mix for 1 cup water (boiling water for hot chocolate; cold for chocolate milk.)

CONTINENTAL CHOCOLATES

6 oz. hot chocolate AND
your favorite of the following:

The Snuggler: 1½ oz. peppermint schnapps

The Cuddler: 1½ oz. Kahlua

That's Amore: 1½ oz. Amaretto, 2 Tablespoons whipped topping

New Orleans Charmer: 1½ oz. cherry liquer, miniature marshmallows

THE SODA FOUNTAIN

ICE CREAM SODA

1 cup ice cream
¼ cup milk

6 oz. club soda
Flavoring (see combos below)

1. In a tall glass, place the flavoring, milk, half of the club soda, the ice cream, and stir well.

2. Fill the glass with the remaining club soda, and garnish with whipped topping and a maraschino cherry.

3. Serve with a straw and an iced tea spoon for eating the ice cream.

SODA	FLAVORING	ICE CREAM
Vanilla	⅛ teaspoon vanilla extra 1 teaspoon sugar	Vanilla
Chocolate	3 Tablespoons chocolate syrup OR 3 heaping teaspoons chocolate milk mix (such as Nestle's Quik)	Chocolate or Vanilla
Mocha	Same as "Chocolate" PLUS ½ teaspoon instant coffee granules	Chocolate
Chocolate- covered Cherry	Same as "Chocolate" PLUS 1 Tablespoon cherry juice	Cherry or Vanilla
Tutti Fruitti:	¼ cup crushed bananas, strawberries, or peaches 1 teaspoon sugar (optional)	Vanilla, Banana, Strawberry, or Peach

MILK SHAKES

¼ cup milk   **Flavoring (see combos below)**
1 cup ice cream

1. Combine milk and ice cream in the blender container.

2. Add the flavoring of your choice.

3. Cover and blend on HIGH 15 to 30 seconds until smooth.

SHAKE	FLAVORING	ICE CREAM
Vanilla	¼ teaspoon vanilla 1 teaspoon sugar	Vanilla
Chocolate	3 Tablespoons chocolate syrup OR 3 heaping teaspoons chocolate milk mix (such as Nestle's Quik)	Chocolate or Vanilla
Mocha	½ teaspoon instant coffee	Chocolate or Vanilla
Tutti Fruitti:	¼ cup crushed bananas, peaches or strawberries 1 teaspoon sugar	Vanilla, Banana, Strawberry or Peach
Peanut Butter:	3 Tablespoons peanut butter	Vanilla, Banana or Chocolate
Orange	2 Tablespoons frozen orange juice concentrate	Vanilla
Banana	½ medium banana ⅛ teaspoon vanilla	Chocolate Vanilla

ICE CREAM FLOAT

1 cup vanilla ice cream
1 (6 oz.) bottle cola or root beer (chilled)

1. Spoon the ice cream into a tall glass.

2. Slowly pour in the soda.

Serve with a straw and iced tea spoon.

PUNCHES FOR BRUNCHES AND LUNCHES
AND
OTHER CROWDED OCCASIONS

1. Heat or chill the punch bowl by filling it with very hot or cold water and ice for 5 minutes before adding the punch. Glass or crystal bowls crack very easily. If you are serving a very hot liquid, place a silver spoon in the preheated bowl to absorb the heat and then add the punch very slowly.

2. Many punches can be mixed right in the punch bowl!

HOW TO MAKE AN ICE RING

Use a ring mold or any freezer-proof container. Either punch or water may be used, but an ice ring made of water will dilute the punch.

When using water, avoid a cloudy ice ring by allowing the water to stand for 15 minutes, stirring 4 or 5 times before freezing, or use distilled water.

1. Pour ¾ inch of liquid into the mold and freeze.

2. Arrange mint sprigs, orange or lemon slices, maraschino cherries, strawberries, grapes, or even fresh flowers on the ice (**attractive side down**).

3. Gently pour in enough liquid to cover and freeze.

4. Finish filling the mold with liquid and freeze.

5. To unmold, place the mold gently in warm (not hot) water briefly until loosened.

6. Invert the ring into a punch bowl before adding the punch.

HOW TO MAKE LEMON PETALS

1. Cut 6 or 8 V-shaped wedges ¹⁄₁₆ inch wide length-wise (from the top stem to the bottom of the lemon).

2. Remove the wedges.

3. Turn the lemon on its side and slice into thin slices across the middle for a flower-petal effect. Use in ice ring or punches.

Makes: 75 (4 oz. servings)
Need: 3 gallon container

Quick Thaw: Forget to thaw the juice? Just fill the sink with very hot water deep enough to cover the juice cans, drop them in while you mix everything else and add them last. If they are still not completely thawed, give them a lick with a potato masher.

Makes: 25 (4 oz.) servings
Need: small bowl party-sized electric percolater

PROHIBITION PUNCH

1 (2 oz.) pkg. citric acid (available in drugstores)
1 (12 oz.) can frozen orange juice (thawed)
1 (12 oz.) can frozen pineapple juice (thawed)
6 cups sugar
2 gallons cold water

1. Mix all ingredients in large container.

2. Chill well (8 to 12 hours).

3. Stir before serving.

HOT SPICED APPLE CIDER

¾ cup powdered sugar
½ cup very hot water
1 quart apple cider
6¾ cups cold water
¼ cup lemon juice
3 (6 oz.) cans frozen orange juice (thawed)
2 sticks whole cinnamon
15 whole cloves

1. Combine the sugar and hot water in a small bowl and stir until it is dissolved.

2. Pour the sugar mixture, cider, water, lemon juice and orange juice in the bottom of a party-sized electric coffee pot.

3. Put the cinnamon sticks and cloves in the top basket of the coffee pot and perk for a complete cycle.

4. Remove the basket with the spices and serve hot.

CINNAMON CIDER

Makes: 8 (4 oz.)
  servings
Need: large saucepan

1 quart apple cider
¼ cup red hot cinnamon candies

1. Heat together in a large saucepan on MEDIUM until the candy has dissolved and serve hot.

P.T.A. PUNCH

Makes: 44 (4 oz.)
  servings

½ gallon sherbet (orange, lime, or pineapple)
4 (28 oz.) bottles chilled ginger ale

1. Five minutes before serving, put the frozen sherbet in a punch bowl, pour the ginger ale over the sherbet, let it stand five minutes, and stir gently to mix.

OPTIONS:

    A. Replace the ginger ale with:
        1 (46 oz.) can pineapple juice
        1 (6 oz.) can frozen limeade (thawed)
        1½ cups cold water

        1. Mix all ingredients together before pouring over sherbet.

QUICK AND EASY PARTY PUNCH

Makes: 32 (4 oz.)
  servings
Need: one gallon jug

Garnish: Add an ice ring with strawberries, lemon slices, or mint sprigs.

1 (6 oz.) can frozen orange juice (thawed)
1 (6 oz.) can frozen lemonade (thawed)
2 small (.21 oz.) pkgs. strawberry powdered drink mix
1 (20 oz.) can pineapple juice
2 cups sugar
water

1. Combine all ingredients in a one gallon jug, add enough water to make one gallon, and serve cold.

WASSAIL

Makes: 32 (4 oz.)
   servings
Cook: 10 min. -
   MEDIUM HIGH
Need: large saucepan
   or stockpot

For a festive touch, wash 3 or 4 oranges, stick them full of whole cloves and bake at 350° for 30 min. Puncture them a time or two and float them in your punch bowl. Remember to reduce the amount of ground cloves in the wassail by half. Cinnamon sticks may be used as swizzle sticks.

1 gallon apple cider or juice
2 teaspoons allspice
6 cinnamon sticks
½ cup lemon juice
2 teaspoons ground cloves
2 teaspoons nutmeg
**2 teaspoons orange or lemon peel
   (optional)**

1. Combine all the ingredients in a large saucepan.

2. Heat on MEDIUM HIGH just to the boiling point, but do not boil.

3. Serve hot.

SPIRITED PUNCHES

SPEAKEASY PUNCH

1. Make Prohibition Punch.

2. Add 2 to 3 quarts of vodka.

CHAMPAGNE PUNCH

Makes: 30 (4 oz.
   servings)
Need: small mixing
   bowl

Other crowd-pleasers are in The 2 Minute Bartender: Fuzzy Navels, Mimosas, Pina Coladas, The Recipe

2 cups chilled lemon juice
2 cups powdered sugar
2 quarts chilled sauterne
1 quart chilled champagne

1. Mix the powdered sugar and lemon juice in a small bowl until the sugar dissolves.

2. Pour the mixture into a punch bowl.

3. Add sauterne and stir.

4. Add champagne and stir gently.

EASY EGG NOG

Makes: 10 (4 oz.)
  servings

Remember: The rum **can** be omitted.

1 quart purchased Egg Nog (chilled)
¾ cup bourbon
¼ cup rum
nutmeg

1. Mix the egg nog, bourbon, and rum in a punch bowl.

2. Sprinkle the top lightly with nutmeg.

INSTANT EGG NOG

Makes: 8 (4 oz.)
  servings
Refrigerate: 1 hour

For a Dickens of a holiday tradition, add 2 cups of rum to **HOT WASSAIL**.

1 quart milk
1 (4-serving size) instant vanilla
  pudding
⅓ cup sugar
1 cup bourbon
1 teaspoon vanilla
whipped topping
nutmeg

1. Combine all ingredients except the whipped topping, chill one hour.

2. Top with whipped topping and sprinkle with nutmeg.

PJ PUNCH

Makes: 20 (4 oz.)
  servings without
  vodka
26 (4 oz.) servings with
  vodka
Need: large block of
  ice

For a milder punch use crushed instead of block ice.

1 (12 oz.) can frozen grape juice
1 (12 oz.) can frozen orange juice
1 (46 oz.) can fruit punch drink
1 (10 oz.) jar maraschino cherries and
  juice
3 cups vodka (optional)

1. Combine all ingredients.

2. Place the block of ice in a punch bowl.

3. Pour the punch over the ice and serve.

SANGRIA

Makes: 16 (4 oz.)
servings

1 quart red wine
5 Tablespoons orange juice
1 cup brandy
1 cup water
3 Tablespoons lemon juice
2 Tablespoons powdered sugar
1 (12 oz.) bottle club soda
1 lemon
1 orange

1. Refrigerate all liquids until well chilled.

2. Rinse the lemon and orange and slice (peeling & all) into thin rings and remove the seeds.

3. Pour the water, sugar, orange juice, and lemon juice into a large pitcher or punch bowl, and stir until dissolved.

4. Add the wine, brandy, and club soda and stir gently.

5. Add orange and lemon slices (include at least one slice in each glass served).

YUCCA FLATS

Makes: 38 (4 oz.)
servings without
vodka
44 (4 oz.) servings with
vodka

Add the cherry juice
to make a pink punch!

1 (46 oz.) can chilled grapefruit juice
1 (46 oz.) can chilled orange juice
1 (46 oz.) can chilled pineapple juice
1 (10 oz.) jar maraschino cherries (drained)
4 cups vodka (optional)

1. Combine and serve.

MOCKTAILS

Other Mocktails are in the 2 Minute Bartender: Virgin Mary (Bloody Shame), and Bull Feathers.

CONNECTICUT SUNRISE

Makes: 1 (6 oz.) serving

Garnish: skewered pineapple chunk and a cherry.

3 oz. peach or apricot nectar
3 oz. club soda

1. Combine and serve over ice.

SAN FRANCISCO SPRITZER

Make: 2 (7 oz.) servings

Garnish: 1 small strawberry or 1 to 3 seedless grapes (dropped into the bottom of the glass)

1 cup chilled grape juice (white, red, or purple)
1 (6½ oz.) bottle chilled, sparkling water

1. Combine gently and garnish.

SEATTLE SUNSET

Makes: 4 (5 oz.) servings
Need: blender

Garnish: skewered strawberry

1¼ cups orange juice
1 (10 oz.) pkg. frozen strawberries (thawed) OR
1 pint fresh strawberries (hulls removed)
Sugar to taste (fresh only)

1. Place the orange juice and strawberries (and sugar, if needed) in the blender container and blend 15 to 30 seconds until slushy.

SHIRLEY TEMPLE

Makes: 1 (6 oz.) serving

Garnish: maraschino cherry and orange wedge.

6 oz. ginger ale
1 teaspoon maraschino cherry juice or grenadine

1. Combine and serve over ice.

WINE COOLERS

BAHAMA MAMA

Makes: 1 [or 8] (5 oz.)
serving[s]
Need: blender

2 oz. [2 cups] chilled chablis
2 oz. [2 cups] chilled 7-up
1 [1-inch long] piece ripe banana (1 large)
1 [8] large ripe strawberry (hull removed)
1 oz. [1 cup] Rum (optional)

1. Combine in a blender container and blend 30 seconds until the fruit is completely smooth.

HULA COOLER

Makes: 1 (4 oz.) serving

2 oz. chilled chablis
1 oz. chilled pineapple juice
1 oz. chilled 7-up

1. Combine and stir.

MONTANA MORNINGS

Makes: 8 (6 oz.) serving

1 (12 oz.) can frozen orange juice concentrate
3 orange juice cans of white wine (36 oz.)

Great with brunch!

1. Combine the orange juice concentrate and wine in a freezer-proof container and freeze 3 hours to overnight; spoon from the container into a glass.

NUCLEAR FREEZE

Makes: 2 (6 oz.)
   servings
Need: blender

1 (6 oz.) can frozen lemonade
4 oz. dry white wine (Sauterne/Chablis)
2 cups crushed ice

1. Pour undiluted frozen lemonade into the blender.

2. Fill the empty can with wine and pour into the blender.

3. Add crushed ice, and blend on HIGH until the ice is completely crushed and the mixture is slushy.

PEACHTREE COOLER

Makes: 1 (5 oz.) serving
Need: blender

4 Tablespoons vanilla ice cream
2 oz. peach schnapps
2 oz. chilled orange juice

1. Combine in a blender container and blend 15 seconds until smooth.

POTTED PILGRIM

Makes: 1 (5 oz.) serving

2 oz. chilled Rosé wine
1 oz. chilled cranberry juice
1 oz. chilled orange juice
1 oz. chilled ginger ale or 7-Up

1. Combine and stir.

MIMOSA (for one)
[or more]

Makes: 1 [or 8] (6 oz.)
   servings

Garnish: A sprig of
fresh mint and a
maraschino cherry
with a stem.

3 oz. [1 fifth] chilled extra-dry
   champagne
3 oz. [3¼ cups] chilled orange juice

1. Pour the orange juice into a glass [large pitcher], add the champagne, stir and garnish.

THE WINE WIZARD

No longer must you be a French nobleman to enjoy wines. Understanding the pomp and circumstance will remove the mystique and return the fun!

	HOW MUCH SERVES HOW MANY		
DINNER WINES AND CHAMPAGNE average **4 ounces per serving.** APPETIZER AND DESSERT WINES average **2½ ounces per serving.**			
BOTTLE SIZE	**OUNCES**	**4 OZ. SERVINGS**	**2½ OZ. SERVINGS**
Split (2/5 pt.)	6.4	2 (barely)	2 (ample)
Tenth (4/5 pt.)	12.8	3	5
Pint	16	4	6
Fifth (4/5 qt.)	25.4	6	10
Quart	32	8	12
Magnum	52	13	20
Half Gallon	64	16	25
Gallon	128	32	50

FOR A CROWD:

1. One standard bottle of wine or champagne (a fifth or 25 oz.) will serve 6 (4 oz.) drinks.

2. A case of wine or champagne has 12 fifths, making 100 servings of 4 oz. each.

3. One case of fifths will serve 25 to 30 wine or champagne lovers with three to four glasses per person.

THE ROOM TEMPERATURE FARCE

Red wines have been served at room temperature since the Dark Ages. Of course, back then the "room" was next door to the dungeon and rarely got above 65° even in a heat wave. Today's red wines deserve better than our usual 72°. Five minutes in the refrigerator will drop the temperature 2°, fifteen minutes, 4° and thirty minutes, 7°.

In a crunch, whites and rosés can be cooled to the correct temperature in thirty minutes (reds in five minutes) by placing the wine up to its neck in an ice bucket or wine cooler, filling the cooler first with ice, and then with cold water. Spin the wine bottle in the iced water as often as you think about it. . .and Shazamm!

THE WINE SEQUENCE

Taste buds are unforgiving creatures that must be pampered if you are serving more than one wine. Start with the lightest, driest, young white wines before trying the older, robust reds. If you reverse the order of serving, the little buds will quit on you every time!

Serving your choices in this sequence is a safe bet!	
WHITES:	Chablis, Chardonnay, Rieslings, Chenin Blanc
ROSÉ OR BLUSH:	Chenin Blanc, White Bordeaux, Cabernet, Zinfandel
REDS:	Gamay, Beaujolais, Pinot Noir, Zinfandel, Cabernet Sauvignon, Burgundy

WHICH TO SERVE WITH WHAT, WHEN, AND HOW

RED WINES improve with age. . .the **older the better!**
WHITE WINES can be enjoyed straight from the winery, and usually reach their peak within two years.

WHAT	WHICH	WHEN	HOW
Appetizer	Sherry Vermouth	Before dinner	Chilled - 1 hour or room temperature (55°-68°)
Dessert	Gewurztraminer Port, Sauterne, Maderia	After dinner with dessert, cheese, or fruit	Chilled - 1 hour (55°-68°)
Red	Claret, Cabernet Sauvignon, Zinfandel, Burgundy, Gamay, Chianti	Anytime or with beef, pork, game, or any hearty meal	Cool room temperature or slighty chilled - ½ hour (60°-70°)
Rosé or Blush	White Bordeaux White Cabernet White Zinfandel	Anytime with most foods	Chilled - 2½ hours (45°)
Sparkling	Champagne Sparkling Burgundy Cold Duck Sparkling Rosé	Anytime with or without food	Chilled - 3 hours (40°-50°)
White	Chablis, Rhine, Riesling, Fumé Blanc, Chardonnay, Chenin Blanc	Anytime or with fish, poultry, lamb or any light meal	Chilled - 1 to 2 hours (50°)

THE SERVING RITUAL

IN A RESTAURANT:

1. Make your selection from the wine list or ask the waiter or wine steward for suggestions.

2. The waiter will bring the bottle for your inspection. Make sure it is what you ordered — brand, type and vintage.

3. With your approval, the waiter opens the bottle, removes the cork, and smells it to make sure the wine has not been exposed to air and spoiled. The cork would smell very musty or acid.

4. The waiter puts the cork beside your plate for your inspection. If it is a **white wine**, a small amount is poured for your taste. With your approval, he will immediately pour the other glasses. If it is a **red wine**, he leaves the open bottle on the table or in a wine bucket to "breathe." This short exposure to air improves the taste and bouquet. The waiter returns shortly before the main course is served to pour the red wine. A small amount is poured for you to taste and approve before pouring any other glasses. If the wine has turned bad (off) the waiter must bring you another bottle and you get to start over.

5. Never, never return a wine simply because you do not like the taste. Only a genuinely spoiled wine may be returned for replacement unless your life insurance is paid in full.

AT HOME:

1. Open all **red** wines 15 to 30 minutes before serving to allow them to "breathe." (The older the wine, the less time needed.)

2. Pour a small amount in your glass to sample for taste or stray cork bits.

3. Then pour the wine for guests with **never** more than ⅔ of the glass filled (even less is better) to allow room for the fragrance to collect.

STORAGE

All wine bottled with corks must be stored on its side (never upright) — EXCEPT: Vermouth, Port, Sherry, and Maderia.

THE TWO-MINUTE BARTENDER

All drinks can be made in 2 minutes or less. All recipes have the correct size and style of glass for serving.

WARNING

Before you drink or serve alcoholic beverages, it's only fair that you know the facts!

1. 12 oz. beer = 5 oz. wine = 1½ oz. liquor. That sure shoots down the old theory that you cannot get drunk on beer or wine.

2. Many factors determine an individual's tolerance level: age, weight, overall state of physical and mental health, metabolism, medications, and recent food intake.

3. As a party host, you can be held legally responsible for any damages if an accident is caused by your inebriated guest. Be a real friend and call a cab or find a sober sole to drive your guest home.

4. If going out for a "night on the town," be sure to limit your consumption or have a "designated driver."

5. Excessive alcohol consumption on a daily basis over a prolonged period of time can lead to permanent liver damage and destruction of brain cells controlling memory, learning and behavior.

THE PARTY BARTENDER

1. Plan for 2 glasses per guest.

2. For pre-dinner drinks, plan on 1 to 2 drinks per person and 2 to 3 drinks for a cocktail party.

3. Each guest will average 1 pound of ice. Increase to 1¼ lb. in summer and decrease to ¾ lb. in winter. Allow for extra ice if you are using a wine cooler or beer chest.

BEVERAGE NEEDS			
Liquid	Quantity	No. of Servings	Serving Size
Beer	1 Keg (15½ gallons) 1 pony (7¾ gallons)	165 83	12 oz. 12 oz.
Cola	1 quart	5	6 oz.
Liquor	1 liter 1 quart ½ gallon	22 21 42	1½ oz. 1½ oz. 1½ oz.
Punch	1 gallon	42	3 oz.
Wine & Champagne	Ask the Wine Wizard		

MIXER NEEDS

Mixer needs vary regionally. Adjust the amounts to local preferences. Southerners usually prefer their bourbon with branch water.

A good rule of thumb is to allow 2 quarts of mixer for each quart of vodka or gin; 1 quart of mixer for each quart of bourbon, scotch, rum or rye.

GARNISH FANCIES

1. **Cartwheel:** Slice a lime, lemon, or orange into thin rings and float on the top of a drink. Insert a mint sprig in the center of the cartwheel, if desired.

2. **Fan:** Slice a cartwheel from the center through the outside peel. Slide the cut portion onto edge of glass, with or without mint.

3. **Spiral:** Cut cartwheel from the center through the outside peel. Twist into a spiral, place on a small wooden skewer with 1 cherry or strawberry in each of the 2 curves.

THE ETIQUETTE

Courtesy: Plan a non-alcoholic beverage to serve friends. Check out the Mocktails.

WAYS TO SERVE

MIXED:

Fill the glass with ice, pour in the liquors, fill the glass with mixer, stir and garnish.

MIST:

Same as **mixed** except use crushed ice.

WITH A SPLASH:

Same as **mixed** except use ½ the amount of ice and mixer.

ON THE ROCKS:

Put several ice cubes in a small glass, pour 1½ oz. liquor over the ice.

STRAIGHT UP: (straight)

Pour liquor(s) and mixers over cracked ice in a shaker and **shake well.** Strain into a glass, and garnish.

NEAT:

Do **not** use ice. Pour the liquor and mixer together and stir.

Makes: 6 (5 oz.) serving

Garnish: an orange slice and a maraschino cherry.

Quick Tip: Measure the bourbon and soda in an empty lemonade can to avoid clean-up (2 "fill-ups" equal 12 oz.)

WHISKEY SOURS-IN-A-BLENDER

1 (6 oz.) can frozen lemonade
12 oz. bourbon
12 oz. club soda

1. Pour the lemonade into the blender, add the bourbon, and blend until well mixed.

2. Add the club soda and stir with a **spoon! Do Not** turn the blender on or you will have a mega-mess!

3. Pour over crushed ice in a glass and garnish.

Makes: 1 [or 8] (7 oz.)
serving

Garnish: lemon or lime
wedges OR celery rib
cut 2" to 3" taller than
the glass.

Makes: 8 (6 oz.)
servings

Create a **Mama Mia**
with:
1 green pepper ring
and 1 raw onion ring
hung over 1 celery
rib. Skewer 1 green
stuffed olive, 1
pepperoni slice, and
1 pearl onion on a
wooden pick and
stick in the celery rib.

Garnish: Lemon
cartwheel

BLOODY MARY (for one)
[or more]

1½ oz. [1½ cups] vodka
5 oz. [5¾ cups] tomato, V-8, or Clamato
juice
⅛ to ¼ teaspoon [1 to 2 teaspoons]
Tabasco
½ teaspoon [4 teaspoons] lemon or
lime juice
¾ teaspoon [2 Tablespoons]
Worcestershire
⅛ teaspoon [1 teaspoon] celery salt
⅛ teaspoon [1 teaspoon] coarse-
ground black pepper

1. Pour all ingredients in a glass
    [pitcher], stir, serve over ice, and
    garnish.

VIRGIN MARY (BLOODY SHAME)

Make a Bloody Mary, omit the vodka
and garnish.

BULLDOZER

Replace the tomato juice with
Beefamota OR equal parts of tomato
juice and beef consommé.

BULL FEATHER

Make a Bulldozer, omit the vodka, and
garnish.

Makes: 1 (6 oz.) serving

Garnish: lemon wedge
or cartwheel

Makes: 1 [or 14] (6 oz.)
servings

Makes: 1 (5½ oz.)
serving

DOWN UNDER

2 oz. brandy
4 oz. ginger ale

1. Pour the brandy and ginger ale over ice cubes in a glass, stir and garnish.

FUZZY NAVEL (for one)
[or more]

2¼ oz. [1 qt.] peach schnapps
1½ oz. [2⅔ cups] vodka
2¼ oz. [1 qt.] orange juice

1. Pour all ingredients over ice [in a pitcher], stir and serve.

OPTIONS:

    A. **Woo-Woo:** Replace the orange juice with cranberry juice.

    B. **Georgia Belle:** Replace the vodka with 4 Tablespoons [1 pint] vanilla ice cream and blend until smooth.

GIN AND TONIC

1½ oz. gin
½ teaspoon lime juice OR
1 lime wedge
4 oz. tonic water

1. Fill the glass with ice cubes, pour the gin over the ice, and add the lime juice or wedge.

2. Fill with tonic water and stir.

OPTIONS:

    A. **Gin Ricky:** Replace tonic water with club soda.

    B. **Rum Ricky:** Replace the gin with white rum.

Makes: 6 (4 oz.)
servings
Need: blender

How To Frost A Glass:
A. Rinse the glass in cold water and shake off the excess. Put the glass in the freezer for 3 to 4 minutes.

B. Bury the glass in shaved ice for 3 to 4 minutes.

How to Make a Salt Rim: Pour 2 Tablespoons of salt and 1 teaspoon of sugar into a saucer. Rub the top edge of the glass with a wedge of lime or a few drops of lime juice. Dip moistened rim into the salt.

Makes: 2 (5 oz.)
servings
Need: blender

Makes: 1 (6½ oz.)
serving

Garnish: maraschino
cherry

FROZEN DAIQUIRI OR MARGARITA

1 (6 oz.) can frozen limeade
1 cup rum (Daiquiri) or tequila (Margarita)
2 cups crushed ice

1. Combine all the ingredients in a blender and blend on HIGH 1 minute until slushy.

2. Serve Daiquiries in frosted glasses and Margaritas in salt-rimmed glasses. Freeze leftovers and spoon directly into a glass.

OPTIONS:

   A. For either drink, use ¾ cup rum or tequila and ¼ cup of Triple Sec.

   B. Add to either drink, 1½ cups fresh or frozen fruit (strawberries, bananas, or peaches) and sugar to taste.

GRASSHOPPER IN A BLENDER

2 cups vanilla ice cream
1½ oz. green creme de menthe

1. Blend on HIGH for 1 minute or until foamy.

HARVEY WALLBANGER

1½ oz. vodka
1 oz. Galliano
4 oz. orange juice

1. Pour the vodka and orange juice over crushed ice in a glass and stir.

2. Float the galliano on top, without stirring, and garnish.

Makes: 1 (6 oz.) serving

Garnish: cinnamon
stick and nutmeg

Makes: 1 (3½ oz.)
   serving
Need: cocktail shaker
   or pitcher

Garnish: olive or
lemon twist. (A pearl
onion turns it into a
Gibson!)

Makes: 1 (4½ oz.)
   serving

HOT BUTTERED RUM

2 oz. rum
1 teaspoon sugar
1 teaspoon butter
½ cup boiling water

1. Place the sugar and butter in a mug, add the boiling water and rum, stir, and garnish.

2. Throw another log on the roaring fire and enjoy.

MARTINI

1½ oz. dry vermouth
2 oz. gin

1. Pour the vermouth and gin over ice cubes in cocktail shaker or pitcher, stir gently, strain into a glass and garnish.

OPTIONS:

A. **Vodka Martini:**
   1. Replace the gin with vodka.

B. For an extra dry martini, use ¼ oz. vermouth. For a super dry martini, just wave the bottle of vermouth over the glass and let two or three drops fall into the shaker.

MID-LIFE CRISIS

1½ oz. green creme de menthe
3 oz. club soda

1. Pour the creme de menthe and club soda over ice in a glass. Stir and suffer!

Makes: 1 [or 4] (7 oz.)
  serving

Garnish: Top with shredded coconut or spear a 1" pineapple chunk and a maraschino cherry on a toothpick and hook it on the edge of the glass.

Variation: For a pink Pina Colada, add 1 teaspoon Grenadine.

Makes: 2 (3 oz.)
  servings
Need: blender

Makes: 10 (6 oz.)
  servings
Need: 2 qt. container.

A great tailgater!

PIÑA COLADA (for one) [or more]

2 oz. [8 oz.] rum
2 oz. [8 oz.] cream of coconut
3 oz. [12 oz.] pineapple juice

1. Pour all liquids over ice cubes in a glass [pitcher], stir well and garnish.

THE CHEF'S CREAM OF COCONUT:

Cover 1½ cups of grated coconut with 2 cups of **boiling** water in blender container. Let it stand for 5 minutes and then blend 1 to 2 minutes. Strain and press to remove all liquid. Cover and refrigerate any unused amount.

RAGIN CAJUN

2 cups vanilla ice cream
1½ oz. praline liquor
1 oz. vodka

1. Blend on HIGH until frothy.

THE RECIPE

1 (2 quart size) pkg. lemonade mix
1 cup Amaretto
¼ cup bourbon
Water and ice

1. Combine lemonade mix, Amaretto, and bourbon in a 2 quart container.

2. Fill with water and ice cubes to make two quarts.

Makes: 1 (4½ to 5½ oz.)
 serving

Garnish: Orange fan
or a maraschino
cherry

Makes: 1 (5 oz.) serving

Garnish: a thin lemon
or lime slice and 1
maraschino cherry

Collins Mix:
A Collins Mix substitute
can be made by
mixing:
1 Tablespoon lemon
 juice
1 Tablespoon
 powdered sugar
3 oz. club soda

SCREWDRIVER

**1½ oz. vodka
3 to 4 oz. orange juice**

1. Put several ice cubes in a glass,
   pour the vodka over the ice, fill the
   glass with orange juice, and stir.

OPTIONS:

   A. **Phillips Screwdriver:**
     Replace the orange juice with
     grapefruit juice.

   B. **Orange Blossom:**
     Replace the vodka with gin in a
     screwdriver.

TOM COLLINS

**2 oz. gin
3 oz. Collins Mix**

1. Fill the glass with ice cubes, pour
   gin and Collins Mix over the ice,
   and garnish.

OPTIONS:

   A. Vodka, Rum, or Tequila Collins:
     Replace the gin with vodka, rum
     or tequila.

   B. John Collins: Replace the gin
     with bourbon.

   C. Sloe Gin Fizz: Replace the gin
     with sloe gin.

   D. Singapore Sling: Add ½ oz. of
     cherry brandy to Tom Collins.

NONESSENTIALS

THE WELL-DRESSED TABLE AND OTHER HO-HUM THINGS
SERVING AND SEATING
HOW TO HAVE A PARTY WITHOUT A NERVOUS BREAKDOWN
PROTOCOL FOR SPECIAL PARTIES

A little knowledge goes a long way in this department and will add finesse and a touch of class to your life.

THE WELL-DRESSED TABLE
AND
OTHER HO-HUM THINGS

Whether you are dining alone or entertaining the local celebrity, tables are "set" for a reason. No one cries over spilt milk if the glass is where it belongs. If you master the following boring details, you will be comfortable no matter WHO is coming to dinner.

CASUAL AND SEMI-FORMAL TABLE SETTINGS

Casual

SEMI-FORMAL
From Simple to Elegant

PLATES AND BOWLS

DINNER PLATES: Each person needs at least 24 inches of "space" and the dinner plate is placed in the middle of this space. . .one to two inches from the edge of the table.

BREAD AND BUTTER PLATE: Place one inch above the forks on the left of the dinner plate.

SALAD PLATE: Place on the left of the forks with the top of the salad plate even with the top of the forks.

APPETIZER PLATE, BOWL, OR SHELL: Place appetizer container on a small (liner) plate (such as a salad plate), and center both in the middle of the dinner plate. Remove the appetizer and liner plates before serving the next course.

FLATWARE (Silverware):

Never use more than four pieces of silverware on either side of the dinner plate. If more than four are needed, bring them when the course is served.

FORKS:

> **DINNER:** Place on the **left** of the dinner plate.

> **SALAD:** Place on the **left** of the dinner fork if salad is first course, or **between** the dinner fork and the dinner plate if salad is served with dinner.

> **SEAFOOD FORK:** Place on the extreme right of the knives.

> **APPETIZER FORK:** Place either on the appetizer plate, on the extreme left of the forks, or on the extreme right of the knives and spoons.

KNIVES: The cutting edge of all knives face the dinner plate.

> **DINNER:** Place on the **right** of the dinner plate.

> **BREAD AND BUTTER:** Place across the top of the bread and butter plate.

> **SALAD:** Place between the dinner plate and the bread and butter plate. Use salad knives only if The Chef is serving cheese with the salad or is too lazy to tear the salad greens into bite-size pieces.

SPOONS:

> **COFFEE OR TEA:** Place on the right of the knife. Coffee or teaspoons may also be brought on the saucer.

> **SOUP:** Place on the right of the coffee spoon.

> **DESSERT:** Place above the dinner plate, below the dessert fork, with the bowl pointing to the left, or it may be brought on the dessert plate.

GLASSWARE AND COFFEE CUPS

The water glass goes one inch above the tip of the dinner knife. Iced tea, wine, or coffee goes below and to the right of the water glass.

CLOTHS, MATS AND NAPKINS

TABLECLOTHS vs. MATS: Placemats are used where there is plenty of room and the table needs added interest. For a more formal, less-crowded look use a table cloth. It should overhang the table 8 to 12 inches. A white, cream, ecru or pastel cloth is the most elegant. Bright colors and patterns are for casual occasions.

Some experts recommend that the cloth overhang the table 15 to 20 inches. The Chef, however suggests 8 to 12 inches. It is really a matter of preference.

NAPKINS: The open side of the folded napkin faces the right or the plate if placed at the top. Napkins, folded or in rings, are placed either:

1. To the **left** of the forks (not **under** them)

2. In the center of the plate (most formal)

3. At the top of the plate.

4. Napkins may also be arranged in a wine glass, either unfolded and tucked in the glass, or pleated (like a fan).

NAPKIN FOLDS

CENTERPIECES

The centerpiece should be low enough to allow seated guests to see one another without needing physical therapy immediately after dinner.

1. Coordinate colors with dishes and table covering.

2. Reflect the party theme or season of the year, if desired.

3. Fresh-cut flowers are always a safe bet, but you are bound only by the limits of your imagination.

CANDLES

Use candles only if you intend to light them, and they should not be lighted before sundown except during a power failure. Keep the flame either above or below the eye level of the seated guest.

Don't **blow** your candles out. . .you'll blow wax to kingdom come! If you don't have a candle snuffer, use a piece of foil or the bottom of a glass **after** your last guest has left the table.

HOW TO SERVE (WHEN YOUR BUTLER HAS RUN OFF WITH THE UPSTAIRS MAID)

There are five types of table service: Family, English, Russian, Mixed and Buffet. Your menu, space, type of party, and lifestyle will dictate your choice.

STYLES OF SERVICE

FAMILY — Very Casual: All serving dishes are placed on the table for the guests to serve their own plates and then passed to the **left.**

BUFFET - CASUAL TO MODERATELY FORMAL: All food is arranged on a separate table or side-board for guests to serve themselves. (See Protocol for Special Parties.)

ENGLISH - Moderately Formal: The plates are stacked at the host or hostess' place at the table for serving the meat and vegetables before passing the plates to the guests.

MIXED - Moderately Formal: The soup, salad, and dessert courses are served at the table, English style.

RUSSIAN - Most Formal: All food is served on the plate in the kitchen and brought to the seated guest. Or, the food may be placed on platters in the kitchen and presented to the guests to serve their own plates (but only if you have a maid or resident waitress!).

WHEN DOES ONE SERVE WHAT?

WHAT	WHEN
Water and/or iced tea; all condiments: salt, pepper, sugar, cream, relishes. Cold appetizer or salad	Place on the table BEFORE guests are seated.
Wine	See The Wine Wizard
Soup; Coffee	Bring to the table AFTER guests are seated.
Dessert	AFTER the meal is completed and all dirty dishes have been removed from the table except the glasses, unused flatware, and centerpieces.
Ashtrays	AFTER dessert is completed.

HOW DOES ONE SERVE WHAT?

Everything but the drinks is served, passed, and/or removed from the **left** of each guest. All drinks are served and removed from the **right**.

A glass should not be lifted from the table for refilling.

SEATING

Usually, the ladies and gentlemen are seated alternately around the table, and the host/hostess and date or spouse at either end unless you are a knight of the "Round Table." In which case, Arthur would face Guinneviere.

Always sit down from the **left** side of the chair to avoid rear-end collision. And even in these days of women's lib, a man may help the lady on his **right** with her chair (and she'll love it even if she **is** Chairman of the Board).

Remember to seat a left-handed person at the South-paw end of the table to avoid elbow battles.

EATING

Do not begin to eat until your host has begun or signaled for you to proceed.

If in doubt which fork to use first, you'll be safe to use your flatware from the "outside" in toward the dinner plate.

HOW
TO HAVE A PARTY WITHOUT
A
NERVOUS BREAKDOWN

(A Magic Method for Effortless Entertaining)

Having a party does not **have** to be as complex as launching a Space Probe. Anything from a gala to a cookout will be much easier with some common sense and the following guidelines:

PLAN AHEAD

1. **Select your party type and size.** Keep it within your budget, space, and ability. (Only in the New Testament can the multitudes be fed with three loaves and five fishes.)

2. **Make a guest list.** Invite either a group you **know** is compatible, or an interesting mixture that will spice up the evening. Do **not** invite two sworn enemies. . .the bad vibes make everybody uncomfortable!

3. **Do as much ahead of time as you possibly can.** No one enjoys a frazzled host or hostess!

COUNT DOWN TO THE PERFECT PARTY

1 to 3 weeks ahead   **INVITE YOUR GUESTS.** Give date, place, time, type of party, and dress. (Black tie at a fish fry is tacky!)

5 Days Ahead   **SELECT THE MENU.** Whenever possible, plan foods that can be prepared a day ahead rather than at the last minute. For a super-easy party, try making one **spectacular** dish and buying everything else. Keep in mind your friends with dietary or religious restrictions. Stick with the tried and true. . .now is not the time to experiment with complicated new recipes.

UNEARTH THE NEEDED RECIPES and use them to:
1. MAKE A GROCERY LIST and
2. CALCULATE YOUR TIME TABLE:

A. **Decide what time you want to serve dinner.** If no drinks and appetizers are served, give your guests a little while to gear down and mingle before serving. Allow one hour between guests' arrival and dinner if you are serving drinks and appetizers.

B. **List** all of the **cooking times** and **temps** to avoid last-minute scratching through cookbooks. Keep the list handy for easy reference. **Calculate the time** to begin cooking each dish. If one dish takes an hour to cook and another three-quarters of an hour, start the longer one fifteen minutes before the other. Then, voila! Everything finishes at the same time!

4 Days Ahead   **GET OUT YOUR CHINA, GLASSES, SILVERWARE, LINENS.** Wash, polish, or launder everything and cover with plastic wrap to keep them clean. You do not want to do this job but once!

3 Days Ahead   **BEGIN HOUSE CLEANING.** The more you get done today, the easier tomorrow will be.

2 Days Ahead   **BUY YOUR GROCERIES** and make sure you buy everything you need — food, paper products, and incidentals.

1 Day Ahead   **(1) GET AS MUCH FOOD FIXED TODAY AS POSSIBLE.**
   A.   Casseroles: ready for oven.
   B.   Meat: marinate, cut, cook (if necessary). Don't add salt or meat tenderizer until just before cooking.
   C.   Salad ingredients: Chop, tear, cut or shred and refrigerate in separate plastic bags for easy last-minute tossing. Make salad dressing if you do your own.
   D.   Congealed salads, desserts, appetizers: prepare and refrigerate.
(2) IF USING A GRILL, GET EVERYTHING READY SO ALL THAT'S NEEDED IS TO STRIKE A MATCH.
(3) FINISH ANY LAST MINUTE HOUSE CLEANING.

D-DAY   (1) **IF YOUR MANSION IS HARD TO FIND, GIVE DIRECTIONS AND MARK THE SPOT** with bows, balloons, signs, or a yellow ribbon round your old oak tree.
(2) **SET THE TABLE and THE BAR** (if drinks are to be served).
(3) **FILL THE COFFEE POT, CHILL WHITE WINES, MAKE TEA.**
(4) **CLEAN THE KITCHEN, WASH AND PUT AWAY ALL UNNEEDED COOKING EQUIPMENT.**

(5) **DOUBLE CHECK THE WHOLE HOUSE** (and don't forget the bathroom. . . it needs tissue and clean hand towels.
(6) **PREHEAT THE OVEN** fifteen minutes before your first cooking time. **PLUG IN THE COFFEE POT AND TURN IT ON.**
(7) You are now entirely too late for a nervous breakdown, so you might as well **RELAX AND ENJOY YOUR PARTY.**

K-P

For ease in clean-up, wash (or load) all dishes or equipment as you finish with them. This rids you of a cluttered kitchen and a sink full of dirty dishes.

Parties generate trash and dirty dishes. Make some plan for handling these problems. . .either a special table for housing dirty dishes at a buffet and/or a large container in a convenient place for the disposables at a cookout.

For a seated dinner, leave everything except the perishables on the table from the last course until the last guest has left.

NEVER start washing dishes while your guests are still there unless you want to abruptly end the party and quite a few friendships at the same time.

P.U.

Kitchen odors can be killed by simmering a pot of water, cloves, cinnamon, allspice and half an apple.

Cigarette odors are destroyed with a bowl of water mixed with several tablespoons of baking soda, or a bowl of white vinegar left in the party room overnight.

PROTOCOL FOR SPECIAL PARTIES

THE BUFFET

From jeans to tux, the easiest way to entertain!

THE TWO TYPES OF BUFFETS

1. **THE COCKTAIL BUFFET** is a stand-up affair that does not require a chair or dinner plate. . . just a small cocktail plate and bite-size foods that need no silverware.

2. **THE DINNER BUFFET** is a "sit-down-do" with two types of seating arrangements:

   A. **Organized Seating:** After serving themselves from the food table, guests sit at either one large table or several small ones that have been pre-set with everything but the food and dinner plates.

   B. **Random Seating:** After serving themselves and getting silverware and napkins from the food table, guests find their own place to roost. Everyone should have access to a small table (end table, coffee table) or a tray unless your guests are professional jugglers. More guests can be invited to this type of buffet than to an organized seated dinner, but don't get carried away and invite more than you can seat somewhere! Wrapping a napkin around each set of silverware makes everything easier to handle.

THE BUFFET FOOD TABLE

Convenience is the key to the food table!

Obviously, plates first, then foods: beginning with main dishes, next vegetables or salads, then breads, relishes and for random seating only, sets of silverware wrapped in napkins. Be sure everything is in a logical order: if sandwiches are to be made, put the bread first then the meat, condiments, etc.

Make sure there is enough room on the food table for the guests to put a plate down beside a dish that takes two hands to serve (tossed salad, etc.).

Dessert and beverages may be served one of three ways:

1. With the rest of the food at the end of the buffet table.
2. On a separate table. This is easiest for both the guests and the traffic flow.
3. Brought to the guests on a tray. This is usually the best method for Random Seating.

THE FORMAL DINNER

This is to be attempted only by the very experienced host or hostess after the castle has been completely staffed with servants and chefs. A formal dinner is always elegant, but an elegant dinner need not be formal. Technically, a formal dinner is a ceremonious affair (like a state dinner) with an inflexible progression of defined courses. Your caterer will handle all of this for you.

FORMAL DINNER PROGRESSION

COURSE:	BEVERAGE
1. Oysters or Clams	
2. Soup	Sherry
3. Fish (optional)	White Wine
4. Meat & Accompaniments	Red Wine
5. Salad and Cheese	
6. Dessert	Champagne
7. Coffee	

For progression through a formal dinner, for each guest you will need:

7 plates
1 rimmed soup bowl
11 pieces sterling flat ware
1 set individual salt and peppr shakers
4 crystal glasses - 2 wines, 1 sherry, 1 champagne
1 servant for each 6 guests
AND a fat paycheck

Guest attire is as well defined as the courses. For gentlemen — black tie (tux or dinner jacket) or white tie (cut-away or tails). For ladies — long or tea-length gown.

TEMPEST IN A TEAPOT
(Much Ado About Nothing)

THE A.M. COFFEE AND THE P.M. TEA

The only difference between the two is the time of day and the confusing fact that in the past, coffee was not served at a Tea, but tea could be served at a Coffee. Customs vary with each region of the country and the size of the guest list.

THE A.M. COFFEE
9:30 to 11:30
The Small, Casual Coffee

This usually consists of a few close friends getting together just for the heck of it. Invitations are casual — fill-in-the-blank, handwritten, or telephoned. The food served is light and simple: sweet rolls, coffee cakes, small finger sandwiches with hot coffee, tea or chocolate. If the weather is hot, serve them cold. These are usually served from large trays placed on the coffee table for guests to serve themselves or be served.

THE LARGE, ELABORATE COFFEE

This is usually given for a reason: welcomes or departings, introductions, showers, rush parties. Invitations can be either professionally printed or written by hand.

The protocol and arrangements are identical to the Large Afternoon Tea.

The foods resemble a light brunch more than a tea party.

THE SMALL AFTERNOON TEA

This is a gathering of a few close friends, and is a ritual unto itself. Invitations are casual, either face to face, handwritten, or telephoned. The foods are dainty: breads and spreads, nuts and cookies, and small or thinly sliced cakes placed beside the tea tray or on a separate table.

The tea tray is set on a small, low table to make pouring easy, and the arrangement should be simple and convenient. You will need:

1. A large tray (without a cloth)

2. A teapot filled with strong, hot tea

3. A jug of boiling water (for diluting when needed)

4. A bowl of sugar cubes and a pair of tongs

5. A pitcher of milk (never cream)

6. A plate of lemon slices and a fork

7. Tea cups and saucers (in stacks of two)

8. Teaspoons

The **tea pouring ritual** is not as complex as a Japanese Tea Ceremony, but it **is** rigid.

1. The hostess or her pinch-hitting friend always "pours."

2. First, ask the guest "How do you like your tea?"

3. For a weak response, pour the teacup ⅔ full and dilute it with boiling water.

4. Now for the big scene! Ask, "one lump or two?" and then add the requested amount of sugar.

5. Add milk or lemon, if requested.

6. Place a spoon on the saucer behind the cup.

7. Place the cup and saucer on the tea plate (on top of the napkin) and give to the guest.

THE LARGE AFTERNOON TEA

This is the first cousin to a reception and is often in honor of a special occasion or person.

The invitation may be either written by hand, printed, or engraved. A large table is required and should be convenient and attractive. A table covering is optional, but a centerpiece is a must.

TABLE ARRANGEMENT

The coffee or tea pot, sugar, cream, milk and lemon are arranged on a large tray at either one or both ends of the table. The cups are on the right of the serving tray. Don't stack more than two high — they'll look like a line of drunken sailors. When one serving tray is used, plates and napkins are placed at the end of the table opposite the serving tray. . .when two serving trays are used, plates and napkins are placed at both ends of the table.

BEVERAGES

Two are usually served, one at each end of the table unless it is very casual, and then both can be served from the same tray at one end of the table. If you are serving punch that must be ladled into a cup, the server usually stands.

FOODS

Serve only foods that can be eaten without a fork: small sandwiches, cakes, nuts, cookies, mints.

How the food is arranged on the table is no consequence whatsoever. Hallelujah!

DISH DISPOSAL

Provide a convenient table for used plates and cups. Who wants dirty dishes on the doilies?

HIGH TEA
5::00 to 7::00 P.M.

Despite the mystique, High Tea is nothing but a half-breed . . . half tea and half cocktail-buffet. The time is a bit later than a tea and a tad earlier than a cocktail buffet. The food is more ample than on the tea table and is meant to tide one over until a later dinner. Usually a more hearty fare is served along with the traditional tea foods. Liquors may also be served in addition to tea.

High Tea takes place either in your living room on a tea table, in the dining room, or den according to your preference and the size of the guest list. If you are inviting 1,500 of your closest friends, consider the ballroom of a nearby hotel or your local club.

THE WINE AND CHEESE PARTY

With very little effort you can have an impressive but possibly expensive evening to delight even your most continental friends.

THE NECESSESSITIES

Obviously, several wines and cheeses
Baskets for crackers or bread
Corkscrew
Cheese slicer or planner
Cheese boards or attractive chopping blocks
Napkins
Small plates (optional)

THE WINES

1. Serve one or more **reds;** one or more **whites:** Roses' are optional.

2. Chill whites and roses' two or three hours.

3. Chill red one hour, remove from refrigerator and open 30 to 45 minutes before serving.

4. Check the wine sequence in The Wine Wizzard for serving or personal tasting.

5. Remember, one fifth (standard size) bottle of wine makes 6 servings of 4 ounces each. Allow three to four servings per person. (Two bottles for every three people.)

THE CHEESES

A mild cheese should be served with a light wine and a stronger cheese is best with a heartier red. Select 4 or more of different varieties including one hard, one semi-soft and 1 blue-veined. Plan a **total** of ½ pound of cheese per person.

GOOD COMBINATIONS

WITH WHITES:

Gouda, Edam, Monterrey Jack, Baby Swiss, Neufachatel, Brie.

WITH REDS:

Cheddar (mild, sharp or Smokey), Camembert, Port Wine, Port du Salut, Munster, Blue-veined (Roquefort Stilton, Gorgonzola, etc.) The crust is edible on Camembert and Brie.

HOW TO SERVE CHEESES

1. Cheeses are best served at room temperature. Remove hard cheeses and cheese balls from the refrigerator two to three hours before serving, and soft cheese one hour.

2. Serve at least one large cheese wheel with a cheese planer for guest to serve themselves.

3. Pre-cut other cheeses into thin slices, wedges, or cubes, or serve them in blocks on cutting boards and provide a cheese cutter for each. Keep cheeses wrapped in plastic until ready to serve so they will stay moist.

4. Have accompaniments close by: Crackers (not highly seasoned), crusty bread (French, Italian, Sour-dough) cut into chunks of two to three bites each, chilled fruit (seedless grapes, apple and pear wedges, unpeeled with the core cut out). Remember, slice the fruits **just** before serving so they won't turn dark. To lessen darkening, dip the slices in cold water with a small amount of either salt or lemon juice added.

THE ARRANGEMENTS

For a large crowd, have several tables available, each with two or more choices of wines and compatible cheeses, fruits, crackers, and clean glasses. Provide a tray for dirty glasses and remove it often. (If the butler is on holiday, plan several quick sessions at the sink!) For a small group, one table is usually all that is necessary.

The guests serve themselves and then find a comfortable place to perch or prop.

HOW TO PLAN AND
GUARANTEE A GREAT MEAL!

Are you ready for four simple steps to stardom?

1. **BALANCE** the meal with at least one from each group:

    A. A meat or dairy main dish

    B. Vegetable or fruit accompaniment

    C. Bread or starch side dish

    D. Desserts are up for grabs!

2. Add different **TEMPERATURE** and **TEXTURE TEASERS**. Mix soft with crunchy and hot with cold. These please the palate, enhance the quality, and free The Chef to fix the cold ones in advance.

3. Deliberately plan for **COLOR CONTRAST** using a variety of colors either in the foods or the garnishes. (No one appreciates a totally green meal.)

4. Never underestimate the importance of **EYE APPEAL**! If it looks great in the eye of the beholder, then it will taste even better! With only 30 seconds of artistic effort, ordinary can be extraordinary and you can advance from "just a cook" to a very knowledeable Chef with rave reviews!

THANKSGIVING GROANING BOARD
Turkey
Dressing
Giblet Gravy
Rice
Cranberry Sauce
Broccoli Casserole
Relish Tray
Sweet Potato Casserole
Yeast Rolls
Pumpkin Pie

EASTER
Ham
Potato Salad
Deviled Eggs
Fruit Salad
Jazzed Up Crescent Rolls
Fresh Asparagus
Strawberries Romanov
Cheese Brew Bread

TAIL GATE
Fried Chicken
Potato or Make Ahead Salad
Deviled Eggs, Stuffed Celery
Cheese Biscuits
Mississippi Mud

MONDAY NIGHT FOOTBALL
Super Sub
Baked Beans
Marinated Veggies
Cheese Straws
Rocky Road

CHRISTMAS FEAST
Turkey
Dressing
Giblet Gravy
Cranberry Sauce
Green Bean Casserole
Ambrosia
Pecan Pie
Coconut Cake

TEA
Chinese Tea Balls
Up-To-Dates
Chicken Salad Sandwiches
Cheese Straws
Chocolate Strawberries
Toasted Pecans

BUFFET DINNER
Wing Dingers
Brie Wheel
Oyster Dip
Chocolate Fondue
Meat and Cheese Tray
Vegetable Tray/Curry Dip

DINNER FOR THE BOSS
Spiced Eye of Round
Horseradish Sauce
Twice-Baked Potato
Broccoli Extraordinaire
Strawberry-Banana Salad
Quicky Refrigerator
   Yeast Rolls
Simple Coconut Pie

BLUE MONDAY
Chicken Hurry Curry
Broccoli/Lemon Butter
Jazzed-up Crescent Rolls
Cosmopolitan Cream

SEAFOOD SUPPER
Neptune's Newburg
Waldorf Salad
Asparagus Parmesan
Camouflaged Refrigerator
   Biscuits
Lemon Ice Box Pie

BRUNCH
Sausage Cheese Strata
Garlic Cheese Grits
Hot Curried Fruit
Purchased Croissants

INDEX

373

THE INSTANT CHEF

Please send _____ copies @ $18.95 per book .... $ _____
Add Postage and Handling @ $2.75 per book .... $ _____
Alabama Residents Add $.76 Tax per book $ _____
Enclosed is My Check _____ Money Order _____
☐ Visa   ☐ Mastercard   TOTAL $ _____
Card # _____ Exp. Date _____
Signature _____
Sorry No C.O.D.'s.
Make checks payable to:
Le Cou Rouge Publishers, Inc., P.O. box 537 – Decatur, AL 35602
Phone: (205) 350-7940   Fax: (205) 340-7212
PLEASE PRINT OR TYPE!
Name _____
Address _____ Apt. - _____
City _____ State _____ Zip _____

- -

THE INSTANT CHEF

Please send _____ copies @ $18.95 per book .... $ _____
Add Postage and Handling @ $2.75 per book .... $ _____
Alabama Residents Add $.76 Tax per book $ _____
Enclosed is My Check _____ Money Order _____
☐ Visa   ☐ Mastercard   TOTAL $ _____
Card # _____ Exp. Date _____
Signature _____
Sorry No C.O.D.'s.
Make checks payable to:
Le Cou Rouge Publishers, Inc., P.O. box 537 – Decatur, AL 35602
Phone: (205) 350-7940   Fax: (205) 340-7212
PLEASE PRINT OR TYPE!
Name _____
Address _____ Apt. - _____
City _____ State _____ Zip _____

- -

THE INSTANT CHEF

Please send _____ copies @ $18.95 per book .... $ _____
Add Postage and Handling @ $2.75 per book .... $ _____
Alabama Residents Add $.76 Tax per book $ _____
Enclosed is My Check _____ Money Order _____
☐ Visa   ☐ Mastercard   TOTAL $ _____
Card # _____ Exp. Date _____
Signature _____
Sorry No C.O.D.'s.
Make checks payable to:
Le Cou Rouge Publishers, Inc., P.O. box 537 – Decatur, AL 35602
Phone: (205) 350-7940   Fax: (205) 340-7212
PLEASE PRINT OR TYPE!
Name _____
Address _____ Apt. - _____
City _____ State _____ Zip _____

Would you like your favorite kitchen, gift, or book shop to carry THE INSTANT CHEF? If so, please add the name and address:

_____

_____

_____

_____

Would you like your favorite kitchen, gift, or book shop to carry THE INSTANT CHEF? If so, please add the name and address:

_____

_____

_____

_____

Would you like your favorite kitchen, gift, or book shop to carry THE INSTANT CHEF? If so, please add the name and address:

_____

_____

_____

_____